VIJAYANAGARA

ARCHAEOLOGICAL EXPLORATION, 1990-2000

PAPERS IN MEMORY OF CHANNABASAPPA S. PATIL

VIJAYANAGARA RESEARCH PROJECT MONOGRAPH SERIES

General Editors
JOHN M. FRITZ, University of Pennsylvania
GEORGE MICHELL, London
R. GOPAL, Karnataka Department of Archaeology and Museums

Jacket Illustration by Graham Reed:
Isometric view of the bridge at Vitthalapura

VIJAYANAGARA

ARCHAEOLOGICAL EXPLORATION, 1990-2000

PAPERS IN MEMORY OF CHANNABASAPPA S. PATIL

PART TWO

Edited by

JOHN M. FRITZ, ROBERT P. BRUBAKER and TERESA P. RACZEK

with the assistance of GEORGE MICHELL

MANOHAR
AMERICAN INSTITUTE OF INDIAN STUDIES
NEW DELHI
2006

First published 2006

© American Institute of Indian Studies, 2006

ISBN 81-7304-646-8

Published by
Ajay Kumar Jain for
Manohar Publishers & Distributors
4753/23 Ansari Road, Daryaganj
New Delhi 110002

Typeset by
A J Software Publishing Co. Pvt. Ltd.
New Delhi 110005

Printed at
Lordson Publishers Pvt. Ltd.
Delhi 110007

Distributed in South Asia by
FOUNDATION
BOOKS
4381/4 Ansari Road, Daryaganj
New Delhi 110002
and its branches at Mumbai, Hyderabad,
Bangalore, Chennai, Kolkata

CONTENTS PART TWO

PAPERS OF THE VIJAYANAGARA METROPOLITAN SURVEY

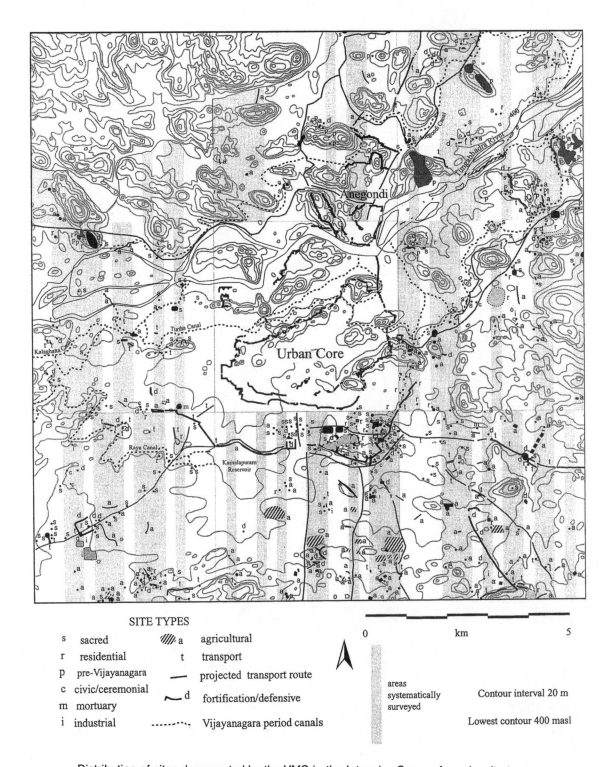

SITE TYPES

s   sacred   ▨ a   agricultural

r   residential   t   transport

p   pre-Vijayanagara   ──   projected transport route

c   civic/ceremonial

m   mortuary   ⌒ d   fortification/defensive

i   industrial   ·······⸱·   Vijayanagara period canals

0   km   5

areas systematically surveyed

Contour interval 20 m

Lowest contour 400 masl

Distribution of sites documented by the VMS in the Intensive Survey Area, by site type.

PRODUCTION AND LANDSCAPE IN THE VIJAYANAGARA METROPOLITAN REGION: CONTRIBUTIONS OF THE VIJAYANAGARA METROPOLITAN SURVEY

Kathleen D. Morrison and Carla M. Sinopoli

The Vijayanagara Metropolitan Survey (henceforth VMS) is a programme of systematic intensive surface survey in the hinterland of the imperial city of Vijayanagara. This project, the first systematic regional survey in India and the only one to investigate non-elite sites of the historic period, has identified a complex landscape of settlements, roads, temples and agricultural facilities. Although analysis and synthesis are still underway, the work of the VMS has already yielded important information on long-term land use and landscape dynamics in northern Karnataka and, more specifically, on the regional structure, organization, dynamics and contemporary impact of Vijayanagara period economic activities, political organization, religious practices and settlement. The project was designed to investigate the operation and structure of imperial economies as they are manifest in an urban and peri-urban archaeological landscape. Research was focused both on the organization of production of a range of goods – food, other agricultural produce, ceramics and metal goods – and on the ways in which agricultural and craft production changed through time. We paid specific attention to the ways in which constraints on and opportunities for production in complex societies structure the economic strategies of a range of producers (people of different statuses, castes, etc., or with variable access to significant resources such as water, arable land, metal ores and so on). One important form of economic change that can be examined in the context of an expanding empire is the intensification of production, a process we find

that was complex and that varied with the specific context of production.

The city of Vijayanagara was the capital of an empire that claimed hegemony over much of peninsular India between the fourteenth and sixteenth centuries. Although we once believed that Vijayanagara was established in an area that had never been politically central or densely occupied, our work has shown that the region actually saw several surges of population as well as associated dramatic changes in land use and settlement intensity. We now know that the survey area saw relatively intensive use by semi-sedentary pastoralists and dry farmers in the Neolithic (c. 3000-1000 BC), followed by a period of dense but unevenly clustered population in Iron Age (c. 1000-500 BC) and Early Historic (c. 500 BC-AD 500) towns, followed by a decline in settlement density in the Early Middle period (c. AD 500-1200). In this last period, settlement was widely dispersed across the region, and although there were many good sized towns, there were few truly urban places and none in the Vijayanagara Metropolitan Region. The intensive survey area itself had very limited occupation in the Early Middle period, as did the site of the city itself (in Block N, not part of our survey area).

However, the founding of the empire and the rapid expansion of the city of Vijayanagara in the early years of the fourteenth century prompted dramatic changes in the organization and scale of production of agriculture and craft goods. The initial period of urban growth led to a depopulation of neighbouring towns as the new imperial city swelled in size.

In the early sixteenth-century Vijayanagara again underwent a period of expansion manifest in terms of military conquest, construction of monumental architecture and population growth/in-migration. These two periods of rapid political, demographic and ecological change provide an excellent opportunity to investigate processes of economic change such as productive intensification. We find that each episode of intensification differs significantly from the other, and that both micro-spatial (local) concerns of topography, hydrology, rocks and soils intersect with broader issues of regional transportation and settlement and the location of markets. Together with these locational and organization concerns, the actual course or trajectory of intensification is critically dependent on prior conditions in any given place. That is, the process of intensification itself is powerfully historically contingent, a fact which suggests that studies of intensification – even those that aim at producing broad generalizations – need to be deeply rooted in particular localities and histories (Morrison 1995a and in press).

Building on eleven field seasons, we have been able to elucidate the structure of food and craft production, settlement, transportation, vegetation and fortification in the region immediately surrounding the city of Vijayanagara, the Vijayanagara Metropolitan Region. The following sections summarize some of our approaches and results; for more detailed information, see the VMS papers in this volume and the works cited in the Project Bibliography (pp. 599-606).

Regional Patterns of Production

In this project we were concerned to address two related problems: (1) the nature of imperial and urban economies, particularly as these relate the structure of local production with forms of political and social control; and (2) the intensification of production, both agricultural and non-agricultural, particularly as influenced by urban growth.

We began with a goal of elucidating the operation and structure of imperial economies as they relate to the organization of production and consumption within the polity. In particular, we documented the powerful impact of the supraregional military, political and other activities of the polity on non-elite producers and consumers at the imperial centre. The rapid expansion of the city of Vijayanagara and its subsequent periods of stasis and growth were, in large part, tied to the fortunes of the empire as a whole. Local agriculturalists and craftspeople both responded to this supraregional dynamic and also created their own nexus of local political and social organization. The increasing demands of the Vijayanagara elite for taxes in cash, the growth of urban markets and the participation of religious institutions in production changed the contexts of production and consumption radically through the period. Even in relatively distant areas, the pull of the city's urban markets and the demands of temples and political leaders for taxes and other obligatory payments helped structure agricultural production. In particular, many farmers focused on cash crops for urban markets; in irrigated areas these included rice, vegetables, coconuts, flowers and sugarcane. Numerous roads radiate out from the city to connect it with surrounding agricultural areas. Elite involvement in outlying areas is also well documented through the presence of temples and reservoirs, many of which were commissioned by local political leaders. Both temples and reservoirs vary a great deal in their architectural elaboration, size and ritual associations. Although this is not the context to discuss the complex interplay between local elites, the central government, temples and other corporate groups, we have been able to document, using both archaeological and textual remains, the dense relational networks between city, village and countryside, and to detect something of the "reach" of political and ritual power into areas far from the city (Morrison in preparation).

With the large-scale abandonment of the city in AD 1565 and the loss of much of the urban population, agricultural production was again radically restructured. However, this post-Vijayanagara agriculture was no "reversion" to the pattern of the Early Middle period. Instead, some of the most uncertain and high-maintenance facilities, runoff-fed reservoirs, were preferentially abandoned, as were areas of risky dry farming. The intricate network of canals constructed during the Vijayanagara period continued in use, as indeed it still is today. Even though these facilities required massive initial investments in labour, once they were built, they required only a moderate amount of maintenance and supported very reliable and intensive forms of production. Thus, the course of change associated with the fall of the city – here from more to less intensive agriculture if viewed in an overall regional context – actually involved the maintenance of certain high-intensity cropping practices and the abandonment of some extensive practices. On the other hand, other land-extensive practices such as pastoralism continued.

In contrast to the marked patterns of change in agricultural production, producers of low-status earthenware ceramics apparently varied their production strategies very little over the three hundred years of the city's occupation, producing large quantities of wheel-made vessels in small, perhaps family run workshops (Sinopoli 1998, 1999 and 2003b). Although we documented numerous villages or towns in the intensive phase of the survey, in neither this nor phase II survey did we identify any definite Vijayanagara-period ceramic workshops. Nevertheless, metric analyses by Sinopoli indicate a multitude of small production locales and we can expect that earthenwares were produced all across the study area.

Metal production did, however, change significantly through time. Textual sources make it clear that the volume of iron production in the sixteenth century was considerable, with iron and steel finished goods and ingots exported from South India to South-West Asia. XRF analysis by Gogte of metal objects, ores, bloom, slag and furnace elements from surface contexts indicate that Vijayanagara-era iron producers used local ores in a relatively efficient process of iron smelting (cf. Lycett, Morrison and Gogte in preparation). Surface indications make it clear that this activity was seasonal in nature and small in scale, and that it took place in contexts (usually in dry-farmed areas) as much as 1 km from the edges of a settlements; in a few cases, iron working took place away from any habitation

(Lycett 1995). In most cases, these small-scale iron smelting operations seem to have been positioned on or near the edge of the water-spread of a reservoir. In spite of the vast size of the city of Vijayanagara – estimates range up to 500,000, though this is probably overly generous – iron production in the region was organized into small productive units throughout the Vijayanagara period. This raises the likelihood that most of the city's metal needs were met by production elsewhere, most probably in the iron and steel producing regions of neighbouring Andhra Pradesh, where industrial-scale production dating back to the sixteenth century has been recorded. Thus, it seems that the Vijayanagara Metropolitan Region was integrated into international and subcontinent-scale exchange networks primarily as a consumer or iron goods, though small-scale smelting and smithing of Sandur ores was carried out in the area.

As an unexpected bonus, we were able to study iron working in the Early Historic period as well as in the Vijayanagara period, with our excavation of VMS-110 (Morrison and Johansen in preparation). Although we had expected the iron smelting here to be contemporaneous with the nearby Vijayanagara period reservoir (VMS-1004), in fact, it turned out to be associated with a specialized iron-production site dating to between 200 BC and AD 100. Here, local Sandur ores were collected from a seasonal stream channel, broken into small chunks and roasted before being fed into simple bowl-type furnaces for smelting (Lycett et al. in preparation). Tuyeres, also made of local materials, supplied air to the furnaces. Ore reduction, roasting and smelting all took place in discrete areas (Humayun and Gogte in preparation). The smelting activities produced a mountain of slag; some 1,500 years later this was modified into a reservoir embankment. There was clearly some permanent occupation associated with the Early Historic iron production site; however, the scale of production was quite large, dwarfing anything in the region associated with the Vijayanagara period (in spite of its vastly greater population), and thus it seems that most of the iron produced at VMS-110 must have been meant for consumption further afield. This is partially supported by XRF and chemical and morphological studies of slag and iron from other Early Historic settlements in the survey area. These indicate that other contemporaneous settlements used iron objects which were made from Sandur ores, and were technologically similar to those produced at VMS-110. Further, slags from other Early Historic settlements (all of which are located along the Tungabhadra River to the north of VMS-110) are all associated with smithing, not smelting, suggesting that they employed material brought in as bloom or ingots. It may be the case that although the scale of iron production in the Early Historic was much greater than that of the later Vijayanagara period, the regional networks through which raw materials and metals circulated were actually spatially smaller. More work remains to be done on this topic.

Beyond the production of foodstuffs, ceramics and metals, we were also able to document residues of the production of basalt pegs which were used for anchoring masonry walls to sheet-rock. Peg production was primarily expedient, using material mined from basalt dykes in the dominant granite formations. However, one small settlement in Block S, on the outskirts of the city where pegs were widely used (due to the density of structures; elsewhere walls were more rarely built up over granite boulders or sheet-rock), seems to have been a locus of peg production. Even though this settlement did not itself employ any pegs, there were pegs at all stages of manufacture across the settlement, as well as abundant remains of chipping debris. Other kinds of craft production indicators included lime kilns (for plaster) in which calcium carbonate or *kankar* nodules were processed. Finally, we documented a great many locales of granite quarrying and a few places in which sculptures and architectural elements such as columns were being created. In all cases, granite sculptures and architectural elements were made on the spot, adjacent to the quarrying locale (and see Sinopoli 2003b). Evidence from inside the city suggests that many columns were simply "roughed out" at the quarry and then finished (sculpted, dressed) in the process of construction.

Changes in Production: Intensification

A particular focus of our research on urban economies has been the process of productive intensification. Understandings of intensification underlie much of the debate about subsistence change and about the development of surplus production and of social complexity. Although discussions about the cause(s) of intensification abound, much less attention has been paid to the actual paths and process of intensification. We suggest that documenting the variability and locally inflected nature of such paths or trajectories is critically important for constructing more general models of change. This documentation, then, requires the reconstruction of structures of and changes in productive strategies. If we begin to develop an understanding of the course of intensification in different situations, we might, for example, be able to determine whether or not there is but a single route of intensification, measurable by a single parameter such as cropping frequency. Further, if we can begin to understand specific instances of change and the roles that, for example, elites played in different aspects of production, we might be a better position to evaluate the causal efficacy of elite demands in stimulating productive intensification, a topic much discussed in the literature. The special circumstances of Vijayanagara, with an excellent and accessible archaeological record, a record of vegetation and burning preserved in precolonial reservoir sediments, and a rich historical record provide the ideal opportunity for the study of intensification and of imperial economies.

In setting out to address issues of regional economy and productive intensification, we begin with the goal of documenting from survey data basic information on regional patterns of settlement, transportation and production. We have documented significant shifts in the location of settlements and their relation to agricultural facilities and other production locales, shifts that correspond with the hypothesized changes in productive organization and political economy in the fourteenth and sixteenth centuries. Briefly (see Morrison 1995a and in preparation), fourteenth-century Early Vijayanagara settlement was clustered in a few places, primarily associated with permanent water sources, either natural (the Tungabhadra River) or anthropogenic (river-fed canals and a river-fed reservoir). There were a few outlying Early period villages, though some of these may actually pre-date the Vijayanagara period. In the fifteenth century, or Middle Vijayanagara period, few new settlements were established and indeed few (dateable) structures of any kind were built at this time. This tempo is entirely consistent with inscriptional and paleobotanical data (see Morrison this volume, and Morrison and Lycett 1994) and suggests that the dynamic settlement expansion of the fourteenth century had slowed by the fifteenth century. Throughout the first 200 years of the Vijayanagara empire in this region, population was concentrated in and near the city; smaller walled towns and villages were strung out along major roadways connecting the city with a few nearby towns and, ultimately, with far-off markets and ports.

In the sixteenth century there were significant changes in regional settlement distributions and overall regional population. There appears to have been a major influx of population into the region, reflected in massive building programmes throughout the survey area. Not only was there a regional boom in the construction of monumental architecture, well-attested to in the city itself (manifest in outlying areas primarily in terms of temples and reservoirs), but there were also many new settlements established. Some of these filled in areas in between older villages and towns, especially on the outskirts of the city (Sinopoli 1997). Other settlements appeared in area that had previously been only sparsely occupied and used for more extensive activities such as grazing and collecting. These new settlements are associated with facilities relating to dry farming and often with newly built, runoff-fed reservoirs, facilities which required a considerable amount of resources and labour to construct and maintain, but which helped mitigate the effects of the region's low and variable rainfall. Areas that saw a major sixteenth-century expansion include the Daroji valley and the Dhanaya-

kanakere area southwest of Hospet (Morrison in preparation).

Inhabitants of the Vijayanagara Metropolitan Region included royalty, imperial officers and soldiers, as well as agriculturalists, craft producers, merchants, labourers, even mobile pastoralists and, possibly, foragers. As noted, settlement beyond the urban core of the city was discontinuous, with population mostly clustered into nucleated settlements. Some 73 sites in the intensive survey area were classified as residential. We have already noted the dense zone of settlement within the outer city walls that emerged in the sixteenth century as the Vijayanagara urban core expanded outwards to the south and east. Beyond the core area of urban settlement, the largest settlements such as Malapannagudi and Bukkasagara ranged from 20 to 70 ha in area and were spaced at intervals of 2 to 4 km along major roads. The populations of these towns ranged from a few thousand to possibly as many as 10,000-15,000 inhabitants. They were typically walled and heavily fortified, and contained multiple temples and shrines. At least one (Old Venkata-pur, VMS-2) revealed traces of an elaborate residential compound, similar in plan to structures that archaeologists in the urban core have referred to as "palaces"; surface collection at this settlement also yielded a fragment of Chinese porcelain. Many of these large Vijayanagara settlements are inhabited today, which has resulted in the destruction of many Vijayanagara period features, making precise estimates of site size and content problematic.

Several smaller nucleated villages were also documented in the Vijayanagara Metropolitan Region. These ranged from 1.5 to 6 ha in area and were often located near areas of low-lying agricultural land. Architecture was less elaborate in these sites and largely consisted of rubble wall foundations to structures that would probably have had wattle-and-daub or earthen walls. Small one- or two-room shrines and sculptures were present in most of the sites, as were high densities of domestic artefacts. At least a few of these smaller settlements were enclosed within masonry walls.

Other residential sites documented by the VMS included isolated houses or structures, many of which may have been occupied seasonally. Concentrated surface scatters of ceramics and other artefacts have also been interpreted as being associated with residential activities in the region, as have rock shelters containing domestic artefacts. These last two site categories were probably occupied for brief periods by mobile groups, including pastoralists, local farmers engaged in collecting firewood, plants, etc. Written sources of the Vijayanagara period note that there were large military encampments on the city's outskirts, and some of the diffuse artefact scatters we find in open areas of the Vijayanagara Metropolitan Region may relate to such activities.

The baseline patterns of regional settlement dynamics sketched above help us to address more specific issues of change such as the intensification of production. In tracing the effects of intensification on the Vijayanagara agricultural landscape we expected to see an increasing pace of construction in soil and water control facilities during the early fourteenth and sixteenth centuries, with sixteenth-century changes strongly affected by the nature of existing facilities. In particular, the early focus on intensive forms of wet agriculture such as canals and canal-fed reservoirs was expected to lead to strategies both of intensification proper (increased intensity or frequency of cropping on the same land, including the development of irrigation facilities allowing multi-cropping and labour-intensive forms of cropping such as paddy rice production) and of diversification (addition of new forms of production to the regional repertoire) in the sixteenth century (Morrison 1995a). It was not expected that there would be an orderly chronological progression from dry to wet agriculture or any other single sequence and, indeed, there was not. What we found, in general, was that demographic trends tracked agricultural change relatively closely (that is, in a broad sense, periods of increased population density were associated with agricultural intensification). However, this overall picture masks a significant degree of variability and, importantly, fails to capture the way in which the diverse paths of intensification are contingent on very local histories of land-

scape modification and very local considerations such as the position of roads, temples and towns, as well as the more obvious constraints placed on agriculture itself by water, soils, slopes, etc. Further, we began to appreciate the important role of social and political power in structuring the course of intensification (Morrison in press). Given that the resources and opportunities of producers vary widely, we find that there was a complex sequence of change involving multiple forms of production. Elite investment in and manipulation of production of both agriculture and craft goods (Sinopoli 1998) can be traced through both inscriptional analysis and, indirectly, through architecture; we have found significant differences in the form and tempo of elite-financed activity through time.

To summarize, we found that the fourteenth-century intensification of agricultural production primarily took the form of expanding areas of intensive, irrigated agriculture. This was effected through the construction of river-fed canals and a large canal-fed reservoir (the Kamalapura reservoir). There are few runoff-fed reservoirs associated with the Early period, although there were clearly some areas of dry (rain-fed) agriculture. This early focus on high-cost but productive wet agriculture seems to have involved a focus on paddy rice, a highly esteemed foodstuff, viewed as essential for elite consumption and ritual (Morrison 2001a). The minimal expansion of the fifteenth century involves the construction of at least one large runoff-fed reservoir, but it was in the sixteenth century, as expected, that we saw the greatest expansion and intensification of agricultural production. This took the form, in part, of the extension of canals (intensification proper). However, sixteenth-century canal extension took place primarily in the areas north of the river, where the new canals displaced existing reservoirs, which were built in either the fourteenth or fifteenth centuries. This sequence of change follows, in large part, expected trajectories of change based on the "orthodox" Boserup-inspired model. However, sixteenth-century changes elsewhere in the survey area differed radically from those of the area north of the river. For example, the Daroji and

Dhanayakanakere valleys saw the massive expansion of both cultivation under runoff-fed reservoirs and of dry farming, a more extensive form of production that nevertheless became part of the *regional* strategy of intensification in the Late Vijayanagara period.

What this overall regional picture of changes in agricultural organization does not, however, highlight, is that the differing forms and practises of production and their associated labour demands, scheduling requirements and type and quantities of crops produced were not practised equally by farmers, labourers, landowners and consumers across the region. Intensification on a regional scale meant very different things for different groups of agriculturalists and had differing consequences for the form and tempo of their labour, for their market participation and for their consumption and even participation in temple rituals, which involved food to a significant degree (Morrison in press).

We were also able to document some changes through time within categories of agricultural production. For example, manuring is now sometimes practised on both dry and irrigated fields, though it tends to be concentrated on dry fields very close to villages (where the manure piles are prepared). The practise of manuring may be visible by tracing the distribution and density of trash (particularly low-density slag scatters) across agricultural areas. Present-day agriculturalists spread trash (plastic, sherds, metal, etc.) across manured fields each year since manure piles include household wastes and are collected from houselots. We found that manuring was practised on a much larger spatial scale during the Vijayanagara period than it is today, with manuring signatures found on fields distant from any settlement. This change may partly reflect contemporary use of chemical fertilizers, though chemical fertilizer use is still quite limited in this region, especially for dry crops, and we suspect that the larger regional population of the Vijayanagara period and consequent demands on the productive capacity of even dry lands led to attempts to increase the fertility of dry fields which may have been cultivated more often then they are today, long fallows being the current norm.

Features related to agricultural production accounted for nearly a quarter of all sites recorded; 157 of the 657 sites (24%) documented in the intensive survey area. In the eight blocks of the intensive survey, we recorded 63 reservoir embankments, varying in size from 20 m to more than 2 km in length; longer and larger reservoirs are present in the extensive survey area. Several extensive terrace systems, including VMS-133 which also integrated a small reservoir, were documented in upland regions south of the city; the largest of these extended over 15 to 20 ha. Numerous smaller agricultural features were also recorded, including check dams, erosion control walls, gravel-mulched field and wells. Wells are often associated with reservoirs, taking advantage of the raised water table thus created. In a few cases, wells were later built in the bed of silted-in reservoirs. Permanent irrigation facilities (that is, facilities with the potential to contain water year-round) included numerous canals, *anicuts* (dams that divert river water into canals), two canal-fed reservoirs and a massive sixteenth-century aqueduct that carried canal water onto a large island north of the city.

Changing patterns of production and land use are also reflected in the regional vegetation record. Not only are periods of forest clearance and vegetation disturbance evident, but different broad categories of production (wet crops, dry crops, arboriculture) as indicated by constellations of ecologically specific taxa can also be discerned in pollen profiles (Morrison 2004 and this volume). The analysis of plant microfossils (pollen, spores and microscopic charcoal) and macrofossils from stratified sediment cores has provided important information on the impact of Vijayanagara settlement and agriculture on regional vegetation that complements archaeological evidence of land use. In general, the pollen data indicate that even by the very early part of the Vijayanagara period, the regional vegetation was highly modified, very open, and that production near the city was oriented toward wet rice. The Vijayanagara period saw massive deforestation, on a scale even greater than the present, when forests are almost non-existent. The existence of Vijayanagara-period coconut plantations is now well established, as is the production of edible oils, especially castor oil and ornamentals such as jasmine flowers. New World cultigens are *not* clearly present in the sixteenth century, although chillies (*Capsicum*), maize (*Zea mays*) and several other novel cultigens were introduced to South Asia sometime in this period. New World weeds do, however, appear in the pollen record around the time of or shortly after the decrease in regional population density following the fall of the city in 1565; some of these weeds have since become serious challenges to agriculture.

Fire histories also reflect the intensity of settlement, field clearance and burning for craft production (charcoal for kilns, etc.). Quantitative analyses of microscopic and macroscopic charcoal from reservoir cores (Morrison 1994) reflect the history of burning in the area, burning that may be related to agriculture, craft production and domestic activities. We have documented significant change in fire histories through time, with charcoal particle concentrations tracking vegetation changes documented by pollen analysis in a fairly direct way. Another significant result of this analysis related to a change in post-Vijayanagara fire regimes, beginning around the British period. At this time, particle ubiquity and size distributions indicate that industrial-scale sugarcane production, as is practised in this area today, was first established, replacing, in large part, paddy rice production. Fire histories near the city, such as this one, should reflect a different trajectory of settlement growth, field clearing, etc., than those further way from the city where expansion and intensification came later and took a different course; quantitative charcoal analysis of five more distant reservoir cores has been carried out; these data are still being analysed.

Regional Landscapes: War and Devotion

Other dimensions of regional land use and settlement studied by the VMS include aspects of defense and militarism and ritual and religious features and structures. Clearly, labelling a structure as being primarily military,

agricultural, religious, etc., tends to elide the fact that many of these had (and often continue to have) multiple components, functions and signification. For example, many sites classified for preliminary analysis as being associated with transport were also important to military infrastructures and were key to agricultural production and the movement of resources; settlement sites were often fortified and contained temples and other religious architecture; agricultural features often had religious significance, and so on.

Throughout Vijayanagara history, militarism and warfare played prominent roles in creating and shaping the empire and the Vijayanagara Metropolitan Region. Although the widespread belief that the city of Vijayanagara was enclosed within seven concentric rings of fortifications, a notion based on conventional descriptions in the travel literature, is incorrect, the capital was heavily fortified. We recorded 62 defensive sites in the intensive survey area, and the outermost fortifications documented extend nearly 30 km from the city core (Brubaker 2000 and see this volume), creating a large area of semi-enclosed agricultural land. Sites classified as defensive include fortification walls, hilltop forts, isolated bastions and horse-stones (see below).

The impressive dry stone masonry walls of the Vijayanagara Urban Core, with their core and veneer construction, are well known and were probably largely completed by the early fifteenth century. At this time there may have been extensive open areas, perhaps with gardens and fields, inside the city – these clearly became crowded out by denser settlement. By the early sixteenth century, this locus of dense settlement had expanded through the addition of an outer fortification wall that encompassed the pre-existing walled town of Kamalapura the new settlement of Varadevi-ammana-pattana and the area between them. Extensive archaeological remains of walls, temples and other structures as well as of dense scatters of artefacts documented in the 1990 and 1991 seasons attest to the intensity of settlement in this area during the early sixteenth century.

However, travellers to Vijayanagara encountered the capital's defensive infrastructure long before reaching either the fifteenth- or the sixteenth-century city centre. Merchants, ambassadors, pilgrims and potential invaders alike entered into a highly structured landscape from the moment they arrived in the Vijayanagara Metropolitan Region (Sinopoli and Morrison 2004a and this volume), passing through series of disconnected fortified places ranging from walled passes to walled towns and overseen by elevated forts and bastions. Although only some of the city's walls were plastered and painted, all made use of the naturally hilly terrain and both these defensive features and the troops stationed near them would have provided a powerful reminder of the military power of the city and empire. Along the northern edges of the Vijayanagara Metropolitan Region lay a string of hilltop forts, each with excellent visibility of the others and of the Urban Core and low-lying regions south of the river (see Brubaker this volume). Similar forts are found in strategic locations throughout the region, including the Daroji Valley to the south of the city and the high Sandur Hills that define the southern edge of that valley. Many of these southern forts have long occupational histories, pre-dating the city itself, a fact which points to the multiplicity of factors affecting the locations and forms of forts, walls and other such features.

Throughout the region, fortification walls spanned strategic passes and potential access routes. The builders of these walls were clearly concerned with both utility and visual impact. While all the walls in the Vijayanagara Metropolitan Region were constructed of locally available granite or basalt, not all are similarly constructed. In outlying areas and especially along wall segments located atop remote hills and far from roads, construction is often less formal, with no attempt to shape the constituent boulders making up these massive walls. Elsewhere, more formal dry stone masonry consisting of quarried blocks or split boulders is found only on the exterior face of the wall, with the interior side either unfinished or else having a built-up ledge of earth for defenders to stand on. However, along major roads, walls and gates were often faced with quarried and even dressed stones; many of these were both massive and ornate, designed to impress and intimidate as well as

defend (Sinopoli and Morrison 2004a and this volume). Other defensive features included watch posts and bastions located along roads and near gates. More unusual features are the rows of boulders known as "horse-stones", features often associated with gateways and passes. Horse-stones are alignments of many closely laid parallel rows of large boulders, each usually at least a metre high and a metre across. These features were placed in low-lying areas where they served to slow down or impede movement, particularly by mounted armies.

Control of movement in the Vijayanagara Metropolitan Region was intimately related to defense, as well as to the flow of resources and of people into and out of the capital. Nearly 80 transport related sites were documented in the intensive survey area. These include several broad roads, 30 to 60 m wide, that were the major routes of movement into the city core, as well as numerous smaller routes leading to temples, settlements and agricultural regions. Both topography and cultural features (such as boundary walls) channeled large-scale movement along major roadways; most of the contemporary roads in the area follow older routes. Often such routes are marked by alignments of gateways, bastions, wells, platforms, shrines and what may have been administrative structures. Boundary walls, cobbled road surfaces and worn areas of sheet-rock mark the location of roads. Linear distributions of structures and other features were particularly important for identifying the major routes into the capital, many of which lie underneath or adjacent to modern paved roads. Rock-cut stairways defined routes of movement across steep outcrop areas, and elevated roadbeds skirted the edges of outcrops above low-lying irrigated fields. Gates in fortification walls ranged from large monumental entries to small passages wide enough only for a single person to pass through. In many cases, roads ran along the tops of reservoir embankments, a practical necessity when crops or muddy fields lay below. The embankment of the massive, canal-fed Kamalapura reservoir not only supported a major road leading into the city but also itself constituted part of the outer city wall, even supporting several bastions.

It is also possible to see the Vijayanagara

Metropolitan Region in terms of a complex and shifting sacred geography. Although many landscape features and structures certainly had religious significance, we categorized 143 sites as being primarily religious in function, the second most common site category after agricultural sites. These locations primarily index formal, institutionalized religious practise; in this same category we could also count many additional sacred images and structures found in residential sites and elsewhere. Sacred sites in the Vijayanagara Metropolitan Region include large Hindu temple complexes, most of these associated with more substantial settlements. The sixteenth-century Pattabhi-rama temple, for example, is one of the largest in the region; it lies just outside the village of Kamalapura but inside the outer circuit of city walls in an area that became densely packed with houses and shops in this century. The Pattabhirama temple and several other large complexes in the survey area enclose multiple shrines within a bounding (*prakara*) wall; their towering gateways or *gopuras* are often visible at great distances. Many of these large complexes were elite-sponsored, as is clear from associated inscriptions and, interestingly, many are associated with Vaishnavite deities while a somewhat larger number of small shrines are associated with Shaivism or Goddess worship.

In addition to the large, formal temples complexes, we documented a large number of smaller temple complexes ranging in date from the Early (Sinopoli 1996a) to Late Vijayanagara periods. Even these small complexes follow consistent architectural formats and layouts, though they are also often carefully sited with reference to either natural features such as rockshelters or hilltops, or face roads or settlements. Only one example of a Harihara shrine (a deity incorporating aspects of both Shiva and Vishnu) was recorded, in the village of Kamalapura. Most shrines are identifiable as either Shaivite, Vaishnavite or Goddess-related, although there is also a wide range of more local deities and "folk" images such as the ubiquitous *naga* stones. In addition to formal shrines, we have also documented a large number of isolated images of deities carved on boulders or slabs. One interesting

example is a large rock whose natural shape evokes a coiled cobra with rearing head and extended hood; this likeness was enhanced with a small amount of carving, creating a large and rather alarming figure guarding a narrow paved passage through the outer city wall.

The range of locations with religious sites is immense. Temples, shrines and sculptures are found along roads and in settlements, near gates and bastions, on isolated hilltops, in fields, in the bed of the river and in association with reservoirs and canals. In some cases, we can link their locations to associations in local sacred geography. For example, the small temple complex VMS-83 is located near one of the seven sacred gateways to the capital that is noted in Sanskrit texts (Sinopoli and Morrison in press b, and Morrison in preparation). Images of a heroic form of Hanuman carved on slabs and boulders are extremely common in the survey area and are particularly associated with gateways and entrances. The popularity of Hanuman may be due to his local connections: this region is widely believed to be ancient Kishkindha, the monkey kingdom ruled by Sugriva (whose throne was restored with the help of the god Rama, a form of Vishnu) with the assistance of his loyal lieutenant Hanuman. Kishkindha and its inhabitants figure importantly in the great epic, the *Ramayana*.

The city of Vijayanagara was a cosmopolitan, multi-religious place and so, it seems, was the region surrounding it. Several places near the city were once home to significant numbers of Muslims; in these locations we have documented fifteenth- and sixteenth-century tombs; a mosque and *idgah* (outdoor place of prayer with a wall and niche indicating the direction of Mecca) were also documented in the extensive survey area, indicating the multi-religious nature of the rural as well as urban population. Jainism developed around the same time as Buddhism but although Buddhism largely disappeared from India in the second millennium, Jainism remained important, especially in Karnataka. Interestingly, Jain temples seem to be restricted to the city itself, suggesting that in this region, Jainism was practised primarily by urban dwellers. Even today, many Jains are involved in trade and business and agricultural practice is prohibited to observant Jains.

Before Vijayanagara: Longer-Term Records

Finally, the VMS documented more than 40 previously unknown pre-Vijayanagara sites, ranging from the Neolithic through the Early Historic, enabling us to reconstruct in a general way the occupation and land use history of the study area from about 2400 BC to the present, elucidating for this area a history that was previously entirely absent. Isolated finds of prehistoric artefacts and temporally non-diagnostic lithics were also made throughout the survey region. A small number of the pre-Vijayanagara sites had been previously reported, such as the Neolithic ash mound locally known as Wali Ghat (VMS-26), presumed to be the funeral pyre of Vali (the brother of Sugriva who was killed by Rama). A few others were noted by British officer and antiquarian Robert Bruce Foote in the late nineteenth century; however, the vast majority of these sites have not previously been documented.

The majority of pre-Vijayanagara cultural features date to the late Iron Age and Early Historic periods; we link these periods together intentionally because of the problematic chronology in this region, where it is clear that megalith construction continued well into historic times. The sites typically lie within 1 to 2 km of the Tungabhadra River, most often on the slopes or upper terraces of high outcrops. We expect that many more such sites once existed in the region, particularly in areas south of the river, where many prehistoric remains were probably destroyed by the Vijayanagara-period building boom. Some 33 sites were documented in the intensive survey area. Outside the intensive survey area in the Daroji Valley is VMS-110, a large iron-smelting and settlement site occupied during the Neolithic and then again in the Early Historic period, finally being modified into a reservoir in the Vijayanagara period. In this same general area are megaliths, rock art, artefact scatters and four now largely destroyed Neolithic ash mounds. In many cases, we found Neolithic material (ceramics, ash mounds) in association with later Iron Age or Early Historic deposits, although the pattern in the Daroji Valley suggests less continuity in occupation than that near the river.

Pre-Vijayanagara site types identified include seven megalith mortuary complexes, the largest of which (VMS-643, 645 and 647) may have covered as much as 20 to 30 ha. Features at these complexes included linear cairn megaliths, as well as circular and other stone alignments, petroglyphs and enigmatic features that we have tentatively termed crack features, in which large boulders (some of them chipped) were deliberately placed in fissures in outcrops. Clearly not all of these features are associated with burials; in fact most of them probably are not (many features are built over sheet-rock) and we prefer to refer to these impressive complexes as "commemorative" locations rather than cemeteries (Lycett and Morrison in preparation). Substantial reservoirs are also found at some of these sites; these differ morphologically from Vijayanagara-period facilities and do not seem to be associated with agriculture.

Nine sites contained isolated cairn megaliths. These were typically located on the edges of high outcrops in areas of high visibility. In several instances, a larger cemetery was found within 100 to 200 m of these isolated cairns. Five rock art sites were recorded. These were rock shelters or faces containing painted (red and white) and pecked motifs. In addition, cemetery and settlement sites often contained rock art (rock bruisings) as well as lines of small cupules pecked into sheet-rock, sometimes in intersecting patterns. Several isolated rock art sites were also located and described.

Among our most significant Iron Age/Early Historic discoveries was the identification of seven settlement sites. Although late prehistoric and early historic period settlements are almost certainly under-reported relative to mortuary/commemorative (megalithic) complexes, our systematic survey located settlement sites at about the same frequency as large megalithic complexes. The identification of settlements may be hampered by their lack of standing architecture, a feature which makes them less evident to local inhabitants. Survey work of the village-to-village variety is critically dependent on local under-standing of archaeological distributions, and sites that are small, less obtrusive or simply not adequately described by visiting archaeologists may be missed in this kind of research. Iron Age and Early Historic settlements in the survey area were typically located atop high outcrops and on their slopes though small artifact scatters in low-lying areas suggests that a more complete picture of regional land use is probably obscured by later modifications, especially intensive agriculture. In several cases, settlements were paired with mortuary/com-memorative complexes such as settlement VMS-541, located on the northern slope of the outcrop containing VMS-543. The majority of settlements were small, about 1 to 2 ha. Others, however, were significantly larger, with one of 20 ha and another of 40 ha; these larger settlements show signs of internal spatial differ-entiation, which we are still in the process of analysing.

Settlements were identified by high surface densities of artefacts as well as remains of structures, including rubble wall alignments and brick fragments. Artefacts include Black and Red Ware (BRW), polished and un-polished Red and Black wares, as well as Russet-Coated Painted Ware (RCPW) and a small number of Rouletted Ware (RW) sherds (the latter coming from far-off Bengal, accord-ing to recent XRF work by Gogte). Other materials found on the surface and in test excavations of VMS-110 include stone and ivory beads, lapis lazuli beads and shell ornaments as well as chipped and ground stone artefacts, iron slag and faunal remains. Unfortunately, botanical preservation was poor and we can as yet say little about agricultural practice or food ways. VMS-110 also contained a well-preserved Neolithic component, with a distinctive lithic assemblage and micaceous grey and pink ceramics. Six AMS radiocarbon dates from our text excavations date the Early Historic materials from 175 BC to AD 75 and the Neolithic materials to 2465-2035 BC (two sigma ranges, calibrated; Morrison and Johansen in pre-paration).

Discussion

Although much work of analysis and synthesis remains to be done, the work of the VMS has opened up a heretofore unknown history of land use; vegetation, fire and occupational history; landscape modification; and sets of long-term associations and disjunctions of sacred places in northern Karnataka. We have been able to track human use of and human impact on the Vijayanagara area landscape over the past four thousand years and have been able to shed light on processes of imperial expansion, urbanization, agricultural intensi-fication and the changing organization of craft production.

REPORTS OF THE VIJAYANAGARA METROPOLITAN SURVEY PROJECT: INTRODUCTION

Carla M. Sinopoli and Kathleen D. Morrison

The papers that follow report on four field seasons of the Vijayanagara Metropolitan Survey (VMS): 1992, 1994, 1996 and 1997 (the 1987, 1988 and 1990 field seasons have been previously published: Morrison 1991, Sinopoli and Morrison 1991, Morrison and Sinopoli 1996 respectively).[1]

We conceived the Vijayanagara Metropolitan Survey in the mid-1980s, based on our joint interests in the economic structures, land-use and long term history of the region surrounding the imperial city of Vijayanagara, where we had both conducted previous research in collaboration with John M. Fritz and George Michell's Vijayanagara Research Project. Our project design incorporated developments in the methodologies of systematic regional survey from other regions of the world. Specifically, we designed the survey to assure both systematic and representative coverage of the Vijayanagara hinterland. As discussed in the papers that follow, we employed random sampling techniques and high intensity transect survey focused most intensively on the c. 160 sq km region immediately surrounding the urban core of Vijayanagara. This intensive work was complemented by more extensive and problem oriented coverage of the remainder of the c. 435-sq km Metropolitan Region (which was defined based on a combination of natural topographic and constructed features).[2]

Ultimately, we recorded some 740 archaeological sites in the Vijayanagara Metropolitan Region, dating from the South Indian Neolithic up through and after the Vijayanagara period. As the following papers illustrate, the sites documented vary widely in both

function and scale, and provide evidence for a dense and varied human use of the landscape spanning nearly five millennia. Habitation in the region increased exponentially with the founding of the city of Vijayanagara in the mid-fourteenth century as population flowed into the capital from throughout the peninsular and a dense urban infrastructure was created. Sites associated with this infrastructure include numerous agricultural features, settlements, craft production locales and sacred sites as well as roads and fortifications.

Detailed discussions of our sampling techniques and survey methodologies are included in the reports of each field season and have been published in Morrison (2000; but see also Sinopoli and Morrison in press). Although systematic regional survey had been practised in many regions of the world since the 1960s, these techniques were new to South Asia; to our knowledge, the VMS remains unique in the region in its scale and thoroughness. As such, this project makes methodological as well as substantive contributions to South Asian archaeology.

As with all long-term archaeological projects, there was a learning curve to our work on the VMS. Over time, our familiarity with the landscape and the kinds of archaeological remains in the region increased. We abandoned certain recording techniques that did not work, and refined and formalized others that did. In later seasons we took advantage of new technologies, such as Global Positioning Systems and Geographic Information Systems, which had not existed when we began our work. The final monographs reporting on survey results, currently in preparation, will present all of our data in final synthesized form. The reports presented below are different, appearing essentially as they were written at the end of each of season. We have not significantly modified or updated them for this volume. This was a deliberate choice, as in their present form they convey the history and development of our research, as well as its substantive accomplishments.

Acknowledgements

Over ten years, a project such as ours accumulates many debts. We first and foremost acknowledge the Government of India and the Karnataka Department of Archaeology and Museums for their sponsorship of our research. We wish particularly to acknowledge and remember our sadly lamented dear colleague and friend, Dr C.S. Patil, who provided guidance, assistance and friendship throughout our many years of fruitful collaboration. Our deepest gratitude to the American Institute of Indian Studies, and its director, Dr P.R. Mehendiratta for their support and wise guidance. We also thank the many dozens of student participants who joined us in our fieldwork over the course of the project. We particularly note the many contributions of Drs Mark T. Lycett and Robert Brubaker. Thanks also to U.V. Srinivas, driver and problem solver extraordinaire. We thank our respective universities for their support of our research (and we both moved several times over the course of this project): University of California at Berkeley, University of Hawai'i, Northwestern University, University of Chicago, University of Wisconsin-Milwaukee and University of Michigan. Finally, we acknowledge the many funding agencies that supported our research: the American Institute of Indian Studies, Smithsonian Institution, Wenner Gren Foundation for Anthropological Research, National Geographic Society, National Endowment for the Humanities and the National Science Foundation.

Notes

1. A second field season in November and December 1997 is not reported here. This was an excavation season and thus quite different in emphasis and focus than the survey reports included here. This season has been discussed in Morrison and Johansen (in press).

2. Our original estimate for the Metropolitan Region was approximately 350 sq km, but this has subsequently been revised (see Sinopoli 1997).

Works Cited

Morrison, K.D., 1991, The Vijayanagara Metropolitan Survey: Preliminary Investigation. In, *Vijayanagara: Progress of Research, 1984-1987*, edited by D.V. Devaraj and C.S. Patil, pp. 136-41, Directorate of Archaeology and Museums, Mysore.

——, 2000, *Fields of Victory: Vijayanagara and the course of Intensification*, reprinted, Munshiram Manoharlal, Delhi. Originally published in 1995, Contributions of the University of California Archaeological Research Facility No. 53, Berkeley.

Morrison, K.D. and C.M. Sinopoli, 1996, Archaeological Survey in the Vijayanagara Metropolitan Region: 1990. In, *Vijayanagara: Progress of Research, 1988-1991*, edited by D.V. Devaraj and C.S. Patil, pp. 59-73, Directorate of Archaeology and Museums, Mysore.

Sinopoli, C.M., 1997, Nucleated settlements in the Vijayanagara Metropolitan Region. In, *South Asian Archaeology 1995*, edited by R. and B. Allchin, pp. 475-87, Oxford and IBH, New Delhi.

Sinopoli, C.M. and K.D. Morrison, 1991, The Vijayanagara Metropolitan Survey: The 1988 season. In, *Vijayanagara: Progress of Research, 1987-1988*, edited by D.V. Devaraj and C.S. Patil, pp. 55-69, Directorate of Archaeology and Museums, Mysore.

——, in press, *The Vijayanagara Metropolitan Survey: Monograph 1*, University of Michigan, Museum of Anthropology Monograph Series, Ann Arbor.

THE VIJAYANAGARA METROPOLITAN SURVEY: OVERVIEW OF THE 1992 SEASON

Carla M. Sinopoli and Kathleen D. Morrison

This paper presents preliminary results of the 1992 season of the Vijayanagara Metropolitan Survey (VMS). The VMS is a programme of systematic intensive surface documentation of archaeological remains in the region immediately surrounding the Urban Core of Vijayanagara. In this work, initiated in 1987, we seek to examine the nature and organization of regional settlement, economic activities (agricultural and craft production), transport and defense in the Vijayanagara Metropolitan Region. This is broadly defined to include the c. 350-sq km area delineated by the city's outermost fortifications (see Morrison 1991, Morrison and Sinopoli 1992 and in press, and Sinopoli and Morrison 1991 and 1992). Our research indicates that during the Vijayanagara period, use of this landscape was complex. This was a zone of spatially segregated towns, villages, temples, massive reservoirs and lush agricultural fields, linked by networks of roads and defended by a range of natural and constructed features.

The first phase of survey tᵢ ɪses on documenting archaeological remaɪɪs of a 50 per cent sample of the eight blocks immediately surrounding the Vijayanagara Urban Core (Block N). Each 4.5-km square block is divided into north-south transects, 250 m wide and 4.5 km long. Nine transects per block are randomly selected for survey. Members of the survey team walk along each transect, spaced 20 m apart, and all archaeological sites identified are recorded. Large or significant sites that lie outside of the sample transects are also recorded (see also Sinopoli and Morrison 1991).

The definition of archaeological sites and their boundaries in such a densely utilized area as the Metropolitan Region is not without difficulty, and we largely employ the site concept as a useful heuristic tool to describe archaeological remains, rather than viewing sites as objective, bounded empirical entities. Thus, we define a site as discrete and identifiable remains of past human activities (though isolated artifacts are not recorded as sites). In some cases, the definition of site boundaries is not straightforward and takes into account a variety of practical and distributional factors. Site function is also taken into account in site designations. For example, a temple and nearby step well, or terrace system and associated reservoir embankment, are typically assigned unique site numbers for analytical purposes, rather than being initially grouped together. Further, although we divide the sites into a number of discrete functions, such as settlement, defense, agricultural, sacred sites and so on, it must be kept in mind that many sites had multiple functions. In the discussion that follows, we will talk of primary and secondary site functions. The primary function of a reservoir embankment, for example, is to store water used in agricultural production. Secondary functions of such sites can include their role as defensive barriers, roadbeds, or foci of religious activities.

To date, survey has been completed in three blocks (Figure 1): Block O (1988), Block S (1990, 1992) and Block T (1992), and 370 archaeological sites have been documented. In this report, we present a preliminary summary of the 1992 field season.

437

Archaeological Survey: Block S

The bulk of Block S was surveyed in the 1990 field season and has been previously reported on (Morrison and Sinopoli 1996). This area was densely settled during Vijayanagara times, and contains the early (through late) settlement of Kamalapura, as well as a sixteenth-century Vijayanagara settlement (Varadadevi-ammana-pattana) in the northeastern quadrant of the block. Dense settlement within the block is restricted to the area within the outer city wall (VMS-123). The large canal-fed reservoir (*kere*) west of Kamalapura allowed year round cultivation in much of Block S. Site density in Block S is extremely high, due, no doubt, to a combination of defensive, agricultural and sociopolitical considerations.

Research in Block S in 1992 was limited to completing the coverage of transects not fully surveyed in 1990. Work focused on the gently sloping region in the central portion of the block. Roughly 1.5 sq km were surveyed and eighteen sites were identified (VMS-274 through VMS-291; Figure 2), resulting in a total of 181 sites recorded in the block.

The sites recorded in 1992 support previously documented and reported evidence for intensive land use in this zone during Vijayanagara times and, particularly, intensive agricultural production. Agricultural sites included four extensive terraced field systems (VMS-276, VMS-280, VMS-283, VMS-287, Figure 3), two wells (VMS-281, VMS-291) and a cistern (VMS-277), along with three isolated wall segments (VMS-274, VMS-282, VMS-288) that may have functioned to limit soil erosion. All of these sites are located beyond the area fed by perennial water sources and would have been associated with seasonal rain-fed fields.

Other sites identified in Block S include a shrine situated on a large natural granite boulder amid agricultural fields (VMS-275, possibly modern), an extensive scatter of Vijayanagara ceramics, perhaps the remains of a small settlement (VMS-278), and a small ceramic scatter (VMS-285). Also recorded were two long walls (more than 180 m long), each spanning areas of outcropping boulders that may have served defensive functions (VMS-279, VMS-284), two isolated standing perforated columns (VMS-289), boulders inscribed with snake and other motifs (probably recent, VMS-290) and isolated walls of unknown function (VMS-286). Detailed analysis of Block S sites and artefacts is presently underway.

Archaeological Survey: Block T

The major emphasis of our research in 1992 was the survey of a 50 per cent sample of Block T. Unlike Blocks O and S, Block T lacked perennial water sources during the Vijayanagara period and agricultural production was limited to seasonal reservoir-fed fields and dry farming. Block T is predominantly characterized by sloping land surfaces. The terrain rises up to the north and south, with small outcropping hillocks throughout, and large granitic hills in the north, centre and southern portions of the block. A band of relatively flat, low-lying terrain extends east-west across a roughly 1 km-wide strip in the northern half of the block. The modern paved road runs across this zone, as did a large Vijayanagara period road (see below).

Survey in Block T focused on nine randomly selected transects: 5, 6, 7, 9, 11, 12, 14, 15 and 17 (Figure 4). In addition, a number of sites lying outside of those transects were recorded. Some 77 archaeological sites were recorded in Block T, a significantly lower density than recorded in either Block O or Block S samples (Figure 5). This is most likely a function of the absence of perennial water sources, as well as increasing distances from the Urban Core. Unlike Blocks O and S, no portion of Block T lies within the second ring of defensive walls enclosing the Urban Core. Nonetheless, it is evident that Block T was intensively utilized for agriculture, transport and settlement during Vijayanagara times.

Settlements

Residential sites in the Metropolitan Region include isolated structures and inhabited rock-shelters and small and large residential clusters: hamlets, villages and towns. In Block T, the remains of isolated structures or tent footings occur in isolated areas or in association with terrace systems (e.g. VMS-344) and are difficult to date with any precision. Six sites recorded in Block T were designated as being primarily settlement sites (though may have had other functions as well): VMS-329, VMS-336, VMS-340, VMS-343, VMS-361 and VMS-365 (Sinopoli this volume). In addition, three sites were defined as having had residential components in addition to their primary function: VMS-330 (reservoir with one structure), VMS-344 (terrace system, with three structures) and VMS-317 (temple complex with dense ceramic and slag scatter).

The six primary residential sites vary in size, complexity and length of occupation. As noted, several categories of residential sites can be distinguished in the Metropolitan Region, including short-term encampments, such as field houses or rock-shelters, used by agricultural labourers, herders, hunters and the like; hamlets, or clusters of two or more structures with greater architectural investment and complexity; and permanent nucleated settlements, containing residential and non-residential structures. Examples of each of these settlement types were recorded in Block T (see Table 1).

Short-term Encampments

Site VMS-336 is a short-term encampment in a small rock-shelter. Large quantities of post-Vijayanagara pottery were found in the shelter's four chambers. Site VMS-343 is a small rectangular structure located near terrace system VMS-344. It probably served as a residence for agricultural labourers working in the nearby fields.

Hamlets

Site VMS-340 belongs to the second category of residential sites, and consists of one circular platform and four rectangular structures (Figure 6). The site is situated in a flat area on relatively high ground, with excellent visibility to the north, west and east. The rubble-filled circular platform is *c.* 7 m in diametre and is built on top of a natural outcropping boulder.

It is possible that this structure served as a lookout point or watchtower. Four small residential structures and one isolated wall fragment are found to the west and southwest of the platform. Also found at this site was a small surface scatter of shards and a broken groundstone mortar.

Nucleated Settlements

Sites VMS-329, VMS-361 and VMS-365 consist of the remains of more substantial and durable village settlements. The dense cluster of ceramic and iron slag around the temple complex VMS-317 may also be the remains of a substantial settlement near that feature. VMS-329 and VMS-369 are best considered as portions of a single large settlement that has been disturbed by recent agricultural activities. These sites cluster around a stone outcrop on which sites a circular platform (VMS-327) similar to that described above from VMS-340. A step-well (VMS-328) is also associated with this site cluster. The foundation of a number of structures are best preserved at VMS-361, which is located on an area of relatively flat sheet-rock, and thus has not been subject to damage from farming. This site extends over an area of *c.* 85 x 70 m; at least four rectangular rooms and numerous wall fragments are visible. High densities of ceramics occur in the fields to the south and east of the structures. Local farmers informed us that several standing temples had existed in those fields until quite recently, but these were destroyed when the Tungabhadra reservoir and canal construction transformed the area into productive agricultural lands over the last few decades.

Site VMS-365 is a much better preserved and more extensive walled settlement, approximately 600 x 300 m in extent, located in the south-east quadrant of Block T (see Sinopoli in this volume).

Although isolated structures do occur in the Metropolitan Region, settlement in Block T provides evidence for a concern with defense, manifest by the preference for nucleation and through construction of watchtowers and enclosure walls. Nucleated settlement VMS329/VMS-361 is located *c.* 5 km from

Vijayanagara's Urban Core along a substantial east-west road (VMS-326, VMS-360). This settlement appears to be less heavily defended than the more distant and inaccessible VMS-365, which may have been somewhat more cut-off from the benefits afforded by proximity to the Urban Core.

Fortifications/Defensive Sites

The massive fortifications enclosing Vijayanagara's Urban Core provide ample evidence of its occupants concern with defending the heart of the city. This focus on defense is found throughout the Metropolitan Region and is evident in its many watchtowers or lookouts, defensive walls and fortified gates. However, contrary to the reports of several contemporary travellers to Vijayanagara, the Metropolitan Region was not enclosed within continuous circuits of walls. Instead, access to the city was limited and carefully controlled by large walls spanning potential access routes, often with narrow and easily monitored gates. In addition, the many large reservoir embankments and the pools of water behind them no doubt made most of the low-lying areas of the Metropolitan Region virtually impassable for much of the year. Transport into and out of the city was thus channelled along a number of major and minor routes that could be easily monitored and defended.

Among the defensive features recorded in Block T are the two circular platforms or watchtowers described above (VMS-328, VMS-340) and the square platform or tower associated with the hilltop shrine (VMS-309; see below). At site VMS-359, the very fragmentary remains of a structure on a low outcrop may also have been a lookout point or watchtower of some sort.

The other defensive features documented in Block T are walls (VMS-306, VMS-325, VMS-339, VMS-348, VMS-353). These include the walls that enclose settlement VMS-365 (including, perhaps, VMS-348 and VMS-353). Site VMS-325 is a massive double-faced wall that was traced for *c.* 250 m. It is located near a reservoir embankment (VMS-324) and a Vijayanagara period columned hall (VMS-303),

which may have been part of a gate complex. A broad earthen embankment, VMS-305, in the northwest quadrant of the block may also have had a defensive function.

The most striking of the large defensive walls in Block T is VMS-339 (Plate 1). This is a broad, double-faced rubble wall ranging in width from 2 to 6 m. It was traced for approximately 2 km. The wall is breached at several points by modern cart tracks and footpaths, and thus does not appear to be a recent construction. Site VMS-306, a similarly constructed wall, lies to the north of the modern canal that defines the northern end of VMS-339 and is likely an extension of that site.

Transport Sites

Concomitant with the concern for defending the city, Vijayanagara's occupants were also concerned with controlling movement into and within the Metropolitan Region. Numerous road segments have been identified in our survey, ranging from narrow foot and cart paths to broad streets along which several carts (or many foot soldiers) could pass abreast. Roads may be identified directly through the presence of stone pavements, raised causeways or parallel boundary walls, or can be identified indirectly through the alignment of structures and other features along their path.

Transport routes identified in Block T include: the broad top of reservoir embankment VMS-364 (see below) and the wall and pathway in the outcrops to its north; a route around the base of the outcrop leading toward settlement VMS-365 that is defined by a low terrace or wall (VMS-345, VMS-348, VMS-353); and a wide east-west avenue that runs across the broad valley in the northern portion of the block (VMS-326, VMS-360). Two low, double-faced walls, spaced between 20 and 30 m apart, define this latter route. Segment VMS-326 was traced for approximately 1,200 m, and segment VMS-360 for approximately 800 m. The large unrecorded embankment in the western part of the block (not in a sample transect) was probably also part of this road, which may well have passed through the Penukonda gate complex in Block S (VMS-217) and into the city core.

Sacred Sites

Twelve of the 77 sites recorded in Block T (15.6%) were religious in nature, including temples, shrines and isolated sculptures. In addition, shrines and sculptures were found in settlement VMS-365 and near settlement site VMS-361. As in Blocks O and S, these sites exhibit a range of variation in scale and architectural complexity. They occur in several spatial contexts: within settlements, along roadsides, on hilltops and in association with agricultural sites, such as reservoir embankments.

Site VMS-309 is a shrine dramatically situated on a high boulder that provides a panoramic view to the north. The site is reached by scaling a *c.* 8-m high, almost vertical outcrop. No traces of footholds or stairways to ease access to this shrine are discernible. A small rectangular platform (watchtower) is located on the flat stone surface below this outcropping boulder. The shrine is defined by the natural configuration of the boulders, with only a small retaining wall constructed around the edges of the horizontal ledge on which the site is located. Images of Shiva and Parvati seated cross-legged beneath an arch are sculpted on the sloping face of a boulder, below a large overhang. An inscription is carved above the arch and three human skulls are inscribed below it. A pair of feet encircled by a *naga* are inscribed into the flat bedrock in front of the images. A worshipper at this site would have had an excellent view to the broad low valley to the north containing the large Vijayanagara road (VMS-326, VMS-360). It is not unlikely that lookouts were posted at or near this site to monitor for potential intruders. Indeed, the gods themselves may have been seen as defenders of this route into the city core.

Several more accessible shrines and temples were also recorded in Block T. Many of these cluster along the above-mentioned road. These include: VMS-317, VMS-293 and VMS-292 (Plate 2); inscribed slabs VMS-295 and VMS-296; and a Muslim tomb, VMS-297.

VMS-293 is located to the east of the modern settlement of Sitaram Tanda and consists of a multi-chambered Shaivite temple with a lamp column and carved stone basin in front of it (Figure 7). The structure is oriented to the east of north and consists of an open, 4 by 2 column roofed porch, and a 2 by 2 column ante-chamber in front of a sanctuary of the same size. The columns are unsculpted. A small image of Ganapati is sculpted on the lintel above the antechamber and a *naga* is carved on the inner wall of the sanctuary. A *lingam* is presently in worship in the sanctuary, though this is clearly not the original image; in fact, it appears to be a damaged Vijayanagara period Nandi that has been remodelled to a *lingam* form and placed on a modern image base. The *shikhara* is plastered brick with poorly preserved floral and other motifs. In front of this temple is a stone casket set on a low informal stone platform. This casket, constructed from a single block of stone, is *c.* 2 m long x 1.5 m wide x 1.5 m high, and has a stone slab lid. Sculpted on one long face, from right to left, are a *lingam* within a frame, a Nandi and three devotees with folded hands. Two pairs of small circular perforations are found on this face, above and below the sculpted figures. A crescent moon and sun occur in the upper left and right, respectively. Finally, a tall lamp-column on a modern pedestal is located on line with the sanctuary, 13 m in front of the temple. The Vijayanagara period column is *c.* 4 m tall, with six square panels separated by octagonal insets. A small Nandi image is sculpted on the lowermost panel facing the temple.

Not all of the religious sites in the Metropolitan Region are associated with Hinduism. VMS-297 is an Islamic tomb located amid modern agricultural fields (Figure 8, Plate 3). A rubble mound of stone, brick and plaster architectural fragments that lies to its south may be the remains of a second tomb or other associated architectural feature. The tomb is square, *c.* 4 m on a side, and is symmetrical in plan, with each side containing an arched entrance. A small hemispherical plastered dome roofs the structure. Niche-shaped motifs occur on the dome exterior and interior. Although smaller and somewhat simpler in plan than most of the tombs in Vijayanagara's Islamic quarter or the suburb of Kadirampura, this structure generally conforms to the plan of tombs that Michell has tentatively dated to the fifteenth century (Michell 1985: 108).

The large numbers and broad range of religious sites found throughout the Metropolitan Region provide graphic evidence that, like the Urban Core, this was a sacred landscape. Protector deities are found at points of entry into the city, and hilltop shrines abound across the landscape. Vijaya-nagara shrines and temples vary widely in architectural complexity and productive investment, from small rural goddess shrines to massive temple centres. No doubt their makers and users were similarly diverse, from individual sponsors to royal institutions.

Agricultural Features

Agricultural activities and investment in Block T during Vijayanagara times were intensive. Thirty-three (42.8%) of the sites recorded in Block T are in some way related to agricultural activities (Table 2).

Terrace Systems

Six terrace systems were recorded and mapped in Block T. However, it must be noted that much of the gently sloping upland areas in the block are currently being farmed, and chronologically ambiguous terrace systems are found elsewhere in the block. Terrace systems were recorded by us if they were: (1) clearly associated with Vijayanagara period reservoirs or other dated features; (2) if there were significant soil accumulations in or behind the terrace walls indicating that they had been in use for some time; or (3) if they occurred in areas with no evidence of recent farming. Terrace systems that did not meet these criteria were recorded in field notes, but were not given site designations.

The extent of recorded terrace systems varied considerably from *c.* 560 sq m (VMS-362) to 90,000 sq m (VMS-344) (Table 3). Each consisted of a number of low walls, constructed of unmodified cobbles and boulders, typically no more than two courses high. These walls served to slow the rate of erosion and runoff in the sloping terrain where fields were located, and may also have served to define field boundaries.

Reservoir Embankments

Only one of the fifteen runoff-fed reservoir embankments recorded in Block T still functions to retain water. This is VMS-315, a stone-faced earthen embankment approximately 5 m long x 20 m wide x 7 m high (Figure 9). A single sluice gate, no longer in use, is located near the centre of the embankment. A small shrine containing a lingam (VMS-316) is located near the northern end of the embankment, and a modern goddess shrine is found in the roots of the massive *banyan* tree that grows at its base. This reservoir is associated with an upslope terrace system (VMS-344) that most likely helped to retard silt accumulation in the reservoir bed. Even today, standing water is present in this reservoir for much of the year; however, the original sluice channel is no longer in use and there appears to be little effort to funnel this water into nearby agricultural fields.

No other reservoir recorded in Block T still successfully retains water. In fact, roads, canals or other features have breached many of the embankments. Among the most dramatic of the embankments recorded is VMS-364, located in the southeastern quadrant of the block. This embankment, now breached by a cart track, is *c.* 190 m long by 45 m wide and stands 11 m high (Figure 10). It spans a narrow valley that slopes down to the north and incorporates natural outcropping boulders on either end. Up to 21 courses of large, unmodified and shaped angular boulders are visible, and flat stone steps project out into the tank bed at irregular intervals. The stones used in the construction of this reservoir are massive, especially near the base, with many well over 1 m across. Several have characteristic Vijayanagara period quarry marks. The top of the embankment is quite broad, nearly 15 m across, and likely served as a transport route across the valley when the reservoir was in use. Low stone walls define the base of the earthen face of the embankment, as well as the northern boundary of the embankment, defining a path through the outcrop hill. The sluice channel can still be traced on both faces of the embankment, but no sluice gate is present.

Other agricultural sites recorded in Block T include step-wells (n = 4), (Figure 11) and isolated soil or run-off control walls (n = 8). In addition, a number of sites whose function could not easily be determined may also have been related to agricultural activities.

The distribution of agricultural sites in Block T expands and confirms patterns identified during the 1988 and 1990 field seasons. Agricultural activity in the Metropolitan Region was both intensive and diverse. With the exception of settled areas and transport routes, virtually all arable land with the region appears to have been farmed through a variety of wet and dry farming regimes. Runoff-fed farming, in terraced areas or through reservoirs, predominated in Block T. These sites were often linked in a complex network that required considerable skill and labour investment to construct and maintain.

Pollen Analysis

An additional avenue to understanding Vijayanagara agricultural production and organization is the study of micro- and macrobotanical remains from the Vijayanagara period. During 1992, Morrison spent a month at the French Institute in Pondicherry analysing pollen samples collected in 1990 from the large, canal-fed Kamalapura reservoir. The pollen curves reveal a complex cycle of change in vegetation patterns in the region from Vijayanagara times to the present (see Morrison this volume).

Craft Production Sites

Little evidence of non-agricultural productive activities was found in Block T. Site VMS-341 is a stone quarrying locale with evidence for cutting and shaping of granite blocks. Large quantities of iron slag were found amidst the structures in temple complex, VMS-317. Feature 7 at that site is a low mound (6 x 3 m in dimension), which may have been associated with metalworking. In general, though, craft production evidence in Block T, as in Blocks O and S, is surprisingly scarce.

Artefacts

A systematic walkover of each archaeological site identified in the Metropolitan Region is conducted in order to identify and collect for analysis artefacts visible on the ground surface. Most of the artefacts recovered are earthenware ceramics, though ground and flaked stone artefacts, steatite "pencils" and imported porcelain and stoneware shards are sometimes found. Non-diagnostic artefacts are sorted, counted and left at their site of recovery, while diagnostic artefacts are removed for more detailed analysis. All diagnostic materials are deposited with the Karnataka Department of Archaeology and Museums.

During the 1992 season, 676 diagnostic ceramics were measured and drawn, and several hundred non-measurable rim sherds were sorted and counted. Non-ceramic diagnostics were drawn, measured and photographed. Quantitative analysis of ceramics are currently underway and will provide information on activities carried out at different sites and, perhaps, on chronological and economic associations between sites and site types.

Discussion

The systematic archaeological survey we are conducting in the Metropolitan Region reveals a complex and densely utilized urban landscape. Settlement, religious features and agricultural sites are distributed in a complex mosaic, belying simplistic models for urban land use and organization.

Agricultural production was extremely important in the Metropolitan Region and irrigation and land-use systems were extremely sophisticated. Vijayanagara's rulers, temples and non-elite inhabitants invested large amounts of labour and resources into assuring a secure food supply for the capital, and produced a wide range of foodstuffs within the fortified Metropolitan Region.

With the exception of short-term occupations in isolated structures or rock-shelters, settlement in the Metropolitan Region tended to be clustered within heavily fortified communities. Block S settlements lay within the massive outer ring of city walls, while in Blocks O and T, settlements were found along roads with easy access to the city core. These and more distant settlements, such as VMS-365, were enclosed within walls, often with associated watchtowers. Roads and transport routes were also defended. Large numbers of religious sites are found throughout the Metropolitan Region in a broad range of spatial contexts. These vary considerably in size and architectural complexity, and were no doubt sponsored by a range of patrons, ranging from small groups of villagers to royal donors.

The excellent state of preservation of a range of archaeological sites from the Vijayanagara period makes the area an important laboratory for examining ancient urban organization, with significance for expanding understandings of pre-modern South Asian cities and urban centres in general. As analysis and survey of the Metropolitan Region continues, we will continue to examine the complex inter-relations and accommodations between the various political, economic, religious and military factors that structured the urban form of the great imperial city of Vijaya-nagara.

Acknowledgements

We would like to thank the Government of India for granting us permission to work at Vijayanagara and the Department of Archaeology and Museums of the Government of Karnataka for sponsoring and supporting our research. Our special thanks to Mr Bala-subrahmanyam and Dr C.S. Patil. Our deepest gratitude also to the American Institute of Indian Studies, and especially Dr P.R. Mehendiratta, for their sponsorship and support of our research. The 1992 Field Season was supported by grants from the Smithsonian Institution (FR00627500), the National Geographic Society (4679-91) and the Wenner Gren Foundation for Anthropological Research (5397). Support for Sinopoli also comes from the National Endowment for the Humanities and the University of Wisconsin-Milwaukee. We would like to thank the members of 1992 field crew: Shinu Abraham, Janice Bailey and Robert Brubaker, as well as volunteers, Tridib Sarma, Pravin Kenkre, S.K. Aruni and Succhi Dayal. Thanks also to U.V. Srinivas for getting us where we needed to go.

Works Cited

Michell, G., 1985, Architecture of the Muslim Quarters of Vijayanagara. In, *Vijaya-nagara: Progress of Research, 1983-1984*, edited by M.S. Nagaraja Rao, pp. 101-18, Directorate of Archaeology and Museums, Mysore.

Morrison, K.D., 1991, The Vijayanagara Metropolitan Survey: Preliminary Invest-igation. In, *Vijayanagara: Progress of Research, 1984-1987*, edited by C.S. Patil and D.V. Devaraj, pp. 136-41, Directorate of Archaeology and Museums, Mysore.

——, 1995, *Fields of Victory: Vijayanagara and the Course of Intensification.* Contributions of the University of California Archaeological Research Facility No. 53, Berkeley.

Morrison, K.D. and C.M. Sinopoli, 1996, Archaeological Survey in the Vijaya-nagara Metropolitan Region: 1990. In, *Vijayanagara: Progress of Research, 1988-1991*, edited by D.V. Devaraj and C.S. Patil, pp. 59-73, Directorate of Archaeology and Museums, Mysore.

Sinopoli, C.M. and K.D. Morrison, 1991, The Vijayanagara Metropolitan Survey: The 1988 Season. In, *Vijayanagara: Progress of Research, 1984-1987*, edited by D.V. Devaraj and C.S. Patil, pp. 55-69, Directorate of Archaeology and Museums, Mysore.

——, 1992, Archaeological survey at Vijaya-nagara. *Research and Exploration*, 8: 237-39.

Table 1. Residential Sites in Block T

Function/site type	Primary site use	Secondary site use
1. Short-term encampment	VMS-336, VMS-343	VMS-344
2. Hamlet	VMS-340	
3. Nucleated settlement	VMS-329, VMS-361, VMS-365	VMS-317

Table 2. Agricultural Sites

Site type	# of sites
Terrace systems	6
Reservoir embankments	15
Soil control walls	8
Step wells	4

Table 3. Dimensions of Terrace Systems and Reservoirs in Block T

Site	Description	Dimensions		
VMS-299	Terrace system	210	x	75 m
VMS-300	Terrace system	150	x	30 m
VMS-310	Terrace system	120	x	35 m
VMS-320	Terrace system	60	x	40 m
VMS-344	Terrace system	280	x	320 m
VMS-362	Terrace system	40	x	14 m
VMS-301	Reservoir embankment	125	x	10 m
VMS-302	Reservoir embankment	75	x	26 m
VMS-315	Reservoir embankment	500	x	20 m
VMS-318	Reservoir embankment	240	x	35 m
VMS-322	Reservoir embankment	170	x	15 m
VMS-324	Reservoir embankment	65	x	15 m
VMS-330	Reservoir embankment	650	x	60 m
VMS-335	Reservoir embankment	135	x	23 m
VMS-342	Reservoir embankment	62	x	13 m
VMS-346	Reservoir embankment	72	x	20 m
VMS-349	Reservoir embankment	300	x	20 m
VMS-355	Reservoir embankment	120	x	8 m
VMS-364	Reservoir embankment	190	x	45 m
VMS-369	Reservoir embankment	260	x	30 m

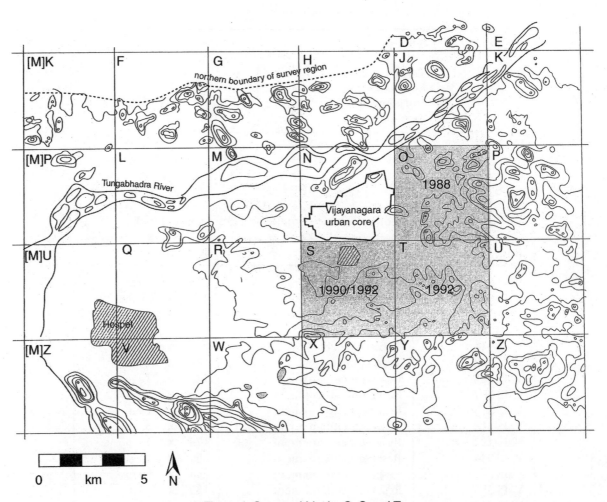

Figure 1. Surveyed blocks O, S and T.

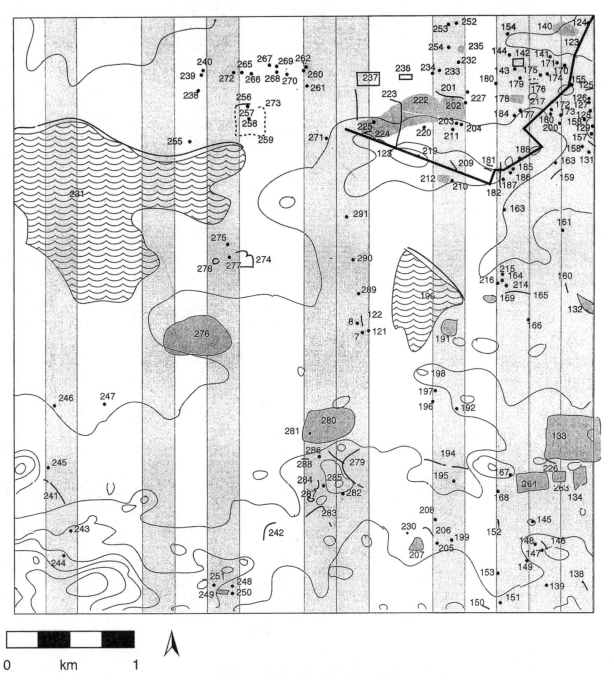

Figure 2. Block S, site distribution.

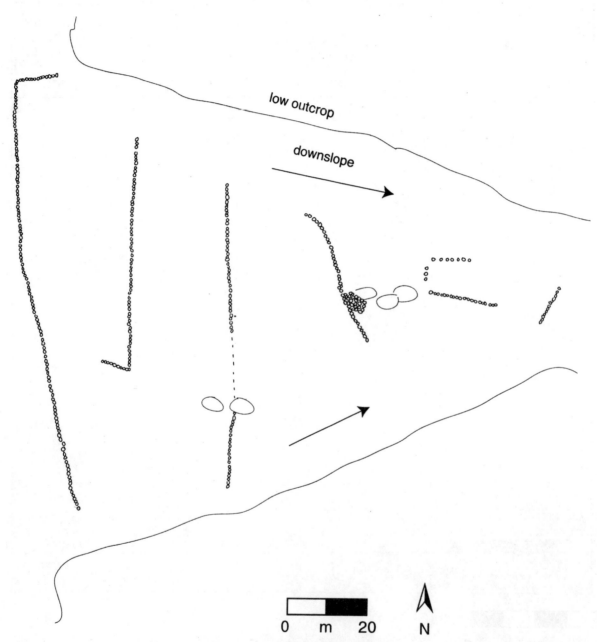

low outcrop

downslope

0   m   20

N

Figure 3. VMS-283, terrace system.

Figure 4. Block T, sample transects.

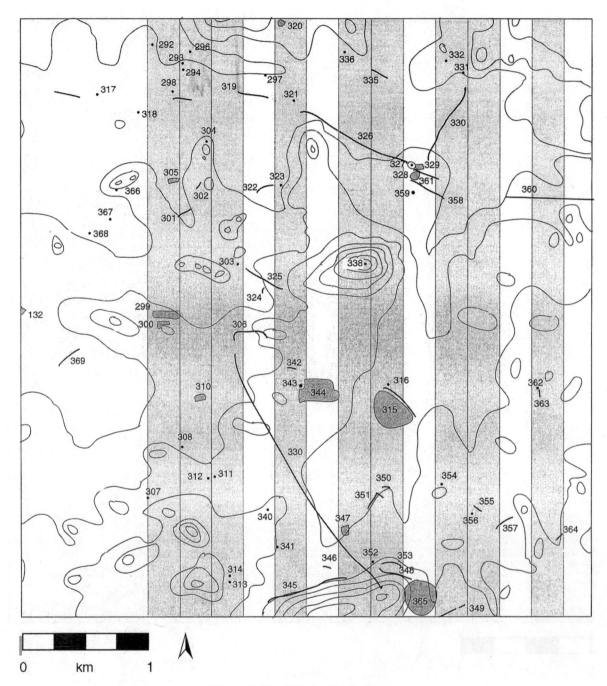

Figure 5. Block T, site distribution.

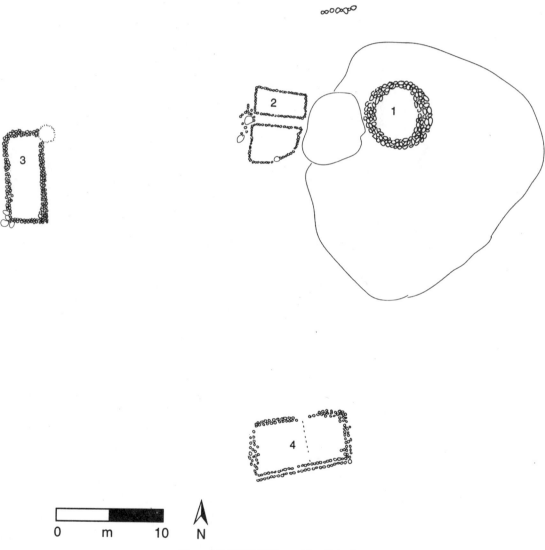

0 m 10 N

Figure 6. VMS-340, residential site.

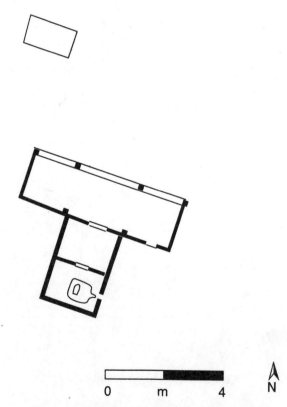

Figure 7. VMS-293, Shaivite temple complex.

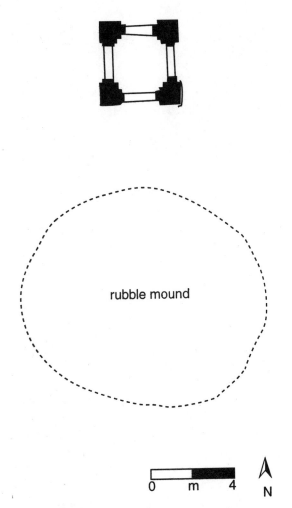

Figure 8. VMS-296, Islamic tomb.

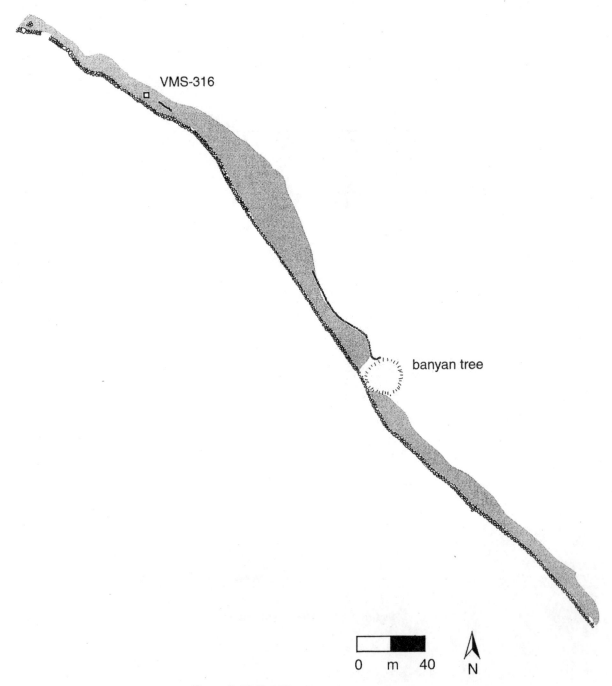

VMS-316

banyan tree

0   m   40   N

Figure 9. VMS-315, reservoir embankment.

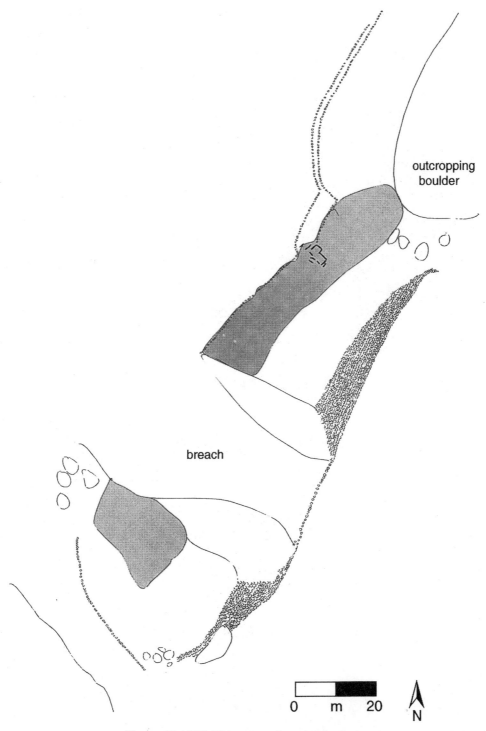

outcropping
boulder

breach

0   m   20

N

Figure 10. VMS-364, reservoir embankment.

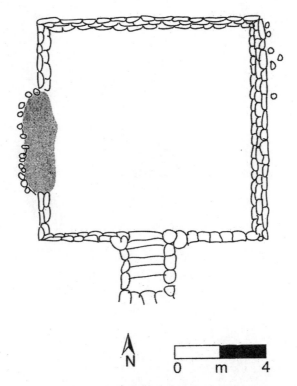

Figure 11. VMS-298, step-well.

Plate 1. VMS-339, fortification wall, looking north from southern end.

Plate 2. VMS-297 Islamic tomb with mounded rubble to the south.

Plate 3. VMS-292, roadside shrine.

THE VIJAYANAGARA METROPOLITAN SURVEY: OVERVIEW OF THE 1994 SEASON

Kathleen D. Morrison and Carla M. Sinopoli

This paper reports preliminary results of the 1994 season of the Vijayanagara Metropolitan Survey (VMS). The project is designed to investigate the operation and structure of imperial economies as they are manifest in the urban and periurban archaeological landscape. Research is focused both on the organization of production of a range of goods – food, other agricultural produce, ceramics and metal goods – and on the ways in which agricultural and craft production changed through time. The city of Vijayanagara – the capital of a vast empire that claimed hegemony over much of peninsular India between the fourteenth and sixteenth centuries – was established in an area that had never been politically central or densely occupied. Its rapid expansion prompted dramatic changes in the organization and scale of production of agriculture and craft goods, and in the regional layout of settlement, fortification and transportation.

Research reported here is directed toward studying the structure of production, settlement, transportation and fortification in the region outside and immediately surrounding the city of Vijayanagara, an area termed the Greater Metropolitan Region. Multiple lines of evidence are combined in an analysis of this area. These forms of evidence are based on archaeological survey and test excavation, analysis of historical data, observation of contemporary craft production and the analysis of fossil pollen and charcoal. Here we report on the 1994 archaeological results.

The VMS consists of a programme of systematic intensive surface survey in the hinterland of the city of Vijayanagara. To date we have been able to identify a complex landscape of settlements, roads, temples and agricultural facilities. During the 1994 season 144 new archaeological sites were located and examined and 140 recorded in some detail. Allied with our surface investigation is a programme of small-scale test excavations in several locations of agricultural and craft production. Profiles from one agricultural terrace system were examined during the 1994 season.

Archaeological Survey

The VMS consists of two major components; intensive survey of the area immediately surrounding the city and more extensive examination of a larger area. The intensive survey universe consists of eight arbitrarily defined blocks of land, each approximately 20 sq km. Blocks are divided into 250 m wide north-south transects. We selected a 50 per cent random sample of transects from the block and survey each selected transect. Survey is accomplished by a crew of three to six archaeologists spaced 20 m apart, who walk systematically across the transect and record all archaeological occurrences. When time permits, we also record archaeological sites outside the sample transects, but we recognize that our sample of such areas is not complete. Each site is mapped, described and photographed, and controlled surface collections of artefacts are made (compare Sinopoli and Morrison 1991).

In the 1994 season, all of Block R was surveyed and approximately three-quarters of Block M was surveyed (Figure 1). 144 archaeological sites were located and 140 described in detail, bringing the total to 511. Thus, with the exception of a part of Block J, all of the intensive survey universe south of the Tunga-bhadra River has been surveyed. The following sections describe firstly, the areas surveyed in 1994 and, secondly, a few of the archaeological sites recorded.

Block R

Block R (Figure 2) lies to the south and west of the city and consists primarily of flat or gently sloping red soils. Although a few granitic outcrops emerge from the mostly level surface of this block, particularly in the northwest and southeast, only the southeastern corner of the block displays a hilly and dissected topography. At present, there is a very sharp distinction between the irrigated and non-irrigated parts of Block R and this distinction appears to be relevant to understanding Vijayanagara period landuse as well. Although sections of the modern Tungabhadra canals run through this block, they are deeply entrenched and water only a very small area in the block itself compared to the larger contribution of the Vijayanagara period Raya canal and the Kamalapura reservoir. The Raya canal feeds the Kamalapura reservoir as well as providing water for extensive areas of cane and paddy rice. In the northwestern quarter of the block, the Raya canal snakes around several high granitic outcrops, watering areas of lower elevation, and in this area the contrast between wet and dry is the most pronounced.

The dominant archaeological feature of Block R is the northeast-southwest oriented roadway stretching between the city of Vijayanagara and a string of settlements to the southwest. A large number of the sites identified in this block was located in these roadside settlements or along the course of the road. A section of the outer city wall, also recorded in Blocks O and S (Morrison and Sinopoli 1996, Sinopoli and Morrison 1991), arcs across the northeastern corner of the block, where it joins the embankment of the Kamalapura reservoir (VMS-231).

Block M

Block M to the west of the city is dominated by irrigated fields out of which granitic outcrops emerge like high islands (Figure 3). Only the part of Block M south of the Tungabhadra River was surveyed in the 1994 season. The southwestern corner of Block M displays the highest relief. Low lying areas in the eastern half of the block are crossed by a maze of Vijayanagara canals which still water vast tracts of sugarcane, bananas and some paddy rice.

Notable cultural features in Block M include the northern portion of the outer city wall. Curiously, this outer fortification ends rather abruptly in Block M, as a parallel to its termination east of the city on Block O (Sinopoli and Morrison 1991). Thus, the entire outer fortification can be conceived as an upright U-shape, running primarily through dry areas and ending in areas of canal irrigation. Most of the portion of Block M surveyed in 1994 appears to have been under cultivation during the Vijayanagara period, but there are also several settlements, roads, shrines and other structures in the block.

Other Areas

A number of other areas was also studied in the 1994 season. VMS-6 is a site complex that includes a settlement area and a fortified hilltop. This site had been located and briefly described (Morrison 1991). In the 1994 season we made more detailed descriptions, maps, and surface artefact collections. Several other sites in the vicinity of VMS-6 (Block W) were described at the same time (see Dega and Brubaker this volume).

Two sites in Block O, east of the city, were also recorded. The sites, a small Shaivite temple (VMS-371) and associated step-well (VMS-372), had been obscured by heavy vegetation in previous seasons.

Transportation

In both Blocks R and M, a great many sites that structured movement of people, animals and wheeled traffic were identified. These sites include roads, paths, bridges and stairways.

Structures that blocked movement or channelled it, such as walls and gates, are also relevant to understanding transportation in the Metropolitan Region. As noted, the largest transportation feature in Block R is the major roadway joining the city of Vijayanagara with towns and villages to the southwest. Mallapannagudi, a substantial settlement during the Vijayanagara period, was located along this roadway, as were many other smaller settlements. Apart from this route, however, a number of other roads were identified. Table 1 contains summary information on these sites; locations are indicated in Figures 2 and 3.

Settlement

Block R was densely settled, containing the remains of at least three areas of nucleated settlement. In the northeastern corner of the block, the embankment of the Kamalapura reservoir serves not only as a dam, but also as a road and fortification (Morrison and Sinopoli 1996). The embankment ends on the west with a gateway (VMS-450). Abutting VMS-450 is a continuation of the outer ring of the city wall (VMS-10, VMS-123), here recorded as VMS-451 and VMS-455. Although the area inside this wall did not fall in the sample universe, it seems probable that it served at least some domestic function. VMS-454 is a badly disturbed, but very substantial north-south wall that runs approximately parallel to VMS-451/455. Adjacent to VMS-454 is VMS-432, a dense ceramic scatter, which would have lay inside the area guarded by the massive wall. Thus, it appears that there were areas of settlement, still not very well defined, in the northeast corner of Block R.

The modern village of Malapannagudi lies astride the Hospet-Kamalapura road. This pattern is not new. Malapannagudi was a larger settlement during the Vijayanagara period and, like its modern counterpart, it lay along the major northeast-southwest roadway. Malapannagudi is bounded by a very regularly shaped rectangular enclosure wall, VMS-383. The latter is 555 m east-west by 360 m north-south. Two identical gateways constitute the only openings into the town, VMS-384 on the west and VMS-385 on the east. Within the

settlement is a monumental Shaivite temple complex, VMS-487, (Plate 2) as well as a smaller shrine, VMS-489, and an elaborate octagonal step-well, VMS-488. Built into an extension of the town wall is a large reservoir, VMS-4. Near the edge of the water contained within this reservoir is an area of iron production, VMS-5 (see also Morrison 1991). VMS-5 consists of an extensive (280 x 200 m) slag scatter, possibly representing the remains of multiple, short or medium term, small-scale episodes of iron working or smelting. The spatial association of this smelting/working area with the settlement of Malapannagudi and the major roadway leading to the city is of note.

The third potential locus of permanent settlement in Block R is the area around the contemporary village of Kondanayakanahalli. A bastion (VMS-494), gateway (VMS-497), rock-cut well (VMS-445), temple (VMS-496) and sculpted Nandi (VMS-419) are all located in or near Kondanayakanahalli. However, there are no definite traces of Vijayanagara period settlement and it is difficult to be sure if there was actually a permanent settlement here.

In Block M, permanent settlement may have extended out from the city itself to the eastern edge of the block. However, this area did not fall in the sample universe. Further, there is at present very dense irrigated vegetation in this area and the exact locations of Vijayanagara residence are thus conjectural. The contemporary village of Kadirampura abuts a well-known complex of Muslim tombs (VMS-504), and this settlement may also have roots in the Vijayanagara period. Finally, an abandoned village identified by the Survey of India as Kalaghatti, was located along the western edge of Block M, just south of the Tungabhadra River. It was not recorded in the 1994 season.

Temples and Shrines

As elsewhere in the survey area, temples and shrines are ubiquitous. Religious sites range from relatively modest depictions of sacred images such as *lingam* to large complexes of structures. Table 2 provides summary information on religious structures from Blocks R

461

and M recorded during the 1994 season.

Agriculture

A diverse array of facilities related to agriculture was located during the 1994 season. As elsewhere in the study area, there is a sharp distinction between areas under perennial wet irrigation (canals and canal-fed reservoirs) and those farmed under either a rainfall-dependent regime or more seasonal form of irrigation. The southern half of Block R is quite dry, with only modest topographic relief (except for the southeast corner). However, these dry portions of the block appear to have been very intensively farmed in the past. Block R contains a cluster of large reservoirs dating to the Vijayanagara period. The largest of these, VMS-4 (Plate 5, see also Morrison 1991), is associated with the settlement at Malapannagudi. To the northeast of VMS-4 is another reservoir, VMS-417, that has been superseded by the relatively recent expansion of the Basavanna canal. However, these two reservoirs were apparently once linked in terms of water flow. Further east from VMS-4 and also associated with it is VMS-412, another large reservoir. VMS-400 lies in the southeastern corner of the block. This reservoir is not connected to any others but is associated with a number of smaller scale agricultural facilities such as erosion control walls and check-dams.

The relative paucity of reservoirs in Block R contrasts markedly with their abundance in other dry parts of the study area. However, dry farmed areas in Block R also exhibited unusually high surface densities of slag and slightly lighter than usual densities of earthenware ceramic shards. It is suggested here that these extensive slag and sherd scatters are, at least in part, the product of manuring of fields and indicate a very long history for manuring in the region. Fields in this area are still intensively manured and this practice leaves a low-density, but continuous scatter of modern debris on the fields (glass, plastic, etc.). Slag and shard densities away from settlements are, in general, lower in other dry farmed portions of the study area than they are in portions of Block R. Thus, it is suggested that this area was previously under intensive

dry cultivation that involved at least periodic manuring.

The dominant Vijayanagara period agricultural regime in the areas studied during the 1994 season was, however, canal irrigation. Because all of the Vijayanagara canals in this area are still in use today, it is very difficult to make statements about their construction and age from archaeological evidence alone. Repairs and renovations have taken place more or less continuously since the construction of each canal and, thus, only a little constructional information can be gleaned from the facilities themselves. Analysis of the distribution of archaeological sites on and near the canals, however, confirms their chronological placement, even if it does not allow precise dates to be assigned to each canal.

The Raya canal (VMS-486) extends through both Blocks M and R, making its way from its source in the Tungabhadra River (now submerged by a recent dam) to the northwest to the Kamalapura reservoir on the east. The date of the Raya canal cannot be fixed with any degree of certainty (cf. Morrison 1995). However, there is some reason to believe that it dates to the earlier part of the Vijayanagara period. In Block M a cluster of temples is located atop a high outcrop, around which the Raya canal makes a sharp turn. These temples may date to the early Vijayanagara period, but because there is no surviving bridge or other structure directly linking the canal with the temple complex the association of the features is unclear. Several other sites are located along the course of the Raya canal, including VMS-434, a one-room structure, and VMS-425, a group of displaced architectural elements. Modern irrigation in areas watered by the canal may have displaced other structures and certainly obscures artefact distributions.

The Kalaghatta (VMS-485) and Turtha (VMS-496) canals dominate the surveyed portions of Block M. Like the Raya canal, these facilities are still in use and water large tracts of sugarcane, bananas and some paddy rice. The Kalaghatta has its origin upstream, to the west of Block M, and it flows into the Turtha canal, joining it near the centre of the block. The Kalaghatta splits into several discrete channels before merging with the Turtha; it is not known if these channels are recent modifications or not. The Turtha canal, in contrast, has its origin in Block M, where a more than 270 m-long series of *anicuts* or diversion weirs (VMS-472, VMS-473) diverts water from one channel of the braided Tungabhadra River. Although the Turtha *anicuts* have been continuously maintained and repaired, much of the original structure is evident. The Turtha canal makes its way into the city of Vijayanagara and emerges on the east into Block O (Sinopoli and Morrison 1991) and eventually back into the river. Structures along VMS-496 located and described in the 1994 season include VMS-449, a raised road segment; VMS-477, a ceramic scatter; and VMS-496, a shrine with a large Hanuman sculpture.

Craft Production

Two sites related to the procurement and processing of stone and iron were located during the 1994 season. The first of these, VMS-5 (cf. Morrison 1991), is in block R approximately 250 m south of the town of Malapannagudi. VMS-5 is a large scatter (280 x 200 m) of iron slag, droplets, brick fragments and ceramics. The distribution of slag and artefacts is more highly concentrated in a few areas. One of the high density areas also contains a high density of brick fragments. This area is currently being dry-farmed and has been subject to considerable disturbance by plowing. In the raised boundary between two fields several bricks appear to be in alignment; this may be a furnace.

VMS-423, in the northwestern corner of Block R, is a quarry area that appears to date to both the recent and the Vijayanagara periods. A number of blocks that has been marked for removal remain in situ, but the strings of rectangular quarry marks, quite unlike the traces of modern quarrying, indicate that many other blocks were removed from this area. One interesting feature of this site is a group of sixteen vertical tick marks incised in the side of a large boulder (for record keeping?). Other areas of craft production may have been located in the settlements.

Fortification

Several features related to defense and boundary definition were located in Blocks R and M. Most prominent among these are the sections of the outer ring of the city wall (VMS-451, VMS-455 that extends across the northeast corner of Block R and into Block M (Plate 6). The other notable defensive feature is the walled settlement of Malapanna-gudi itself. As discussed above, Malapannagudi is enclosed within a well-built rectangular fortification wall (VMS-383), broken only by a pair of matched gateways (VMS-384 and VMS-385) on the west and east. Like the walls of the city itself, VMS-383 is constructed of dry masonry consisting of two faces of wedge-shaped blocks joined by earth and rubble fill.

The outer ring of the city wall does not completely enclose the city. Instead, it curves around the southern edge of the city, ending at the transition zone between areas of dry and wet agriculture on both east and west. The outer wall appears to have been constructed and/or repaired incrementally, inasmuch as different segments were constructed in quite different styles and using different materials (blocks vs boulders, for example). In areas to the south and east of the city, this wall appears to be a late development and was perhaps designed to protect and define the expanding areas of population in the sixteenth century (Morrison 1995). On the west, in the areas surveyed in the 1994 season, the chronology is less clear. The wall, which was built into the embankment of the Kamalapura reservoir, is broken by a gateway (VMS-450) on the western edge of the reservoir. The major southwest-northeast road would have passed through this gateway. One other large gateway (VMS-452) indicates the location of an alternate entryway into the city. The wall is well constructed of shaped granite blocks fit closely together without mortar. The construction of this fortification wall may post-date the existence of irrigated fields in the area, since provision was made in the structure of the wall (e.g. VMS-456/F1) for the movement of water underneath it. The wall ends in an embankment, VMS-456.

In addition to the walled settlement of Malapannagudi and the sections of the outer ring of the city wall just described, there were also a number of other features located in the 1994 season that appears to relate to defensive concerns. These include VMS-454, a 285-m long section of wall constructed of large (*c.* 1.5 m diameter) split boulders that runs roughly parallel to the course of the outer city wall (VMS-451) at a distance of *c.* 750 m. The southeast corner of Block R also contains evidence of fortification, in the form of strongly constructed, but more informal walls of large boulders and cobbles. VMS-399 is a U-shaped wall that partly encloses an area of *c.* 100 x 60 m; this feature may be related to the cluster of agricultural facilities found nearby.

Results of the 1994 Season

Coring and Testing

Coring and testing were largely confined to VMS-133, which is a large system of inter-related agricultural terraces located in the southern portion of Block S. This dry area of moderate to rugged topography is not now regularly cultivated, supporting an occasional dry field, grazing by sheep and goats, and firewood collection. There are no modern settlements in the vicinity not indeed have any Vijayanagara period settlements been located in proximity to the terrace system. The terrace covers an area approximately 375 x 375 m and includes a small reservoir, VMS-126. Many terrace walls consist of two widely separated faces, resulting in some walls that are more than a metre wide. However, the terraces are not high, with two courses the maximum present height. Terrace walls are placed both perpendicular to and parallel to the direction of drainage, suggesting that the control of soil and water was only one aspect of their function.

This terrace system was recorded in 1990 (Morrison 1995 and Morrison and Sinopoli 1996), and was slated for test excavation. In 1994, we revisited the site and found that subsequent to the acquisition of the land by Kannada University, they had dug several hundred tree-planting holes, each *c.* 50 x 50 cm, spaced more or less regularly across the site. With the kind permission of the university, these tree-planting-holes allowed us to make observations of sediment profiles across a portion of the site. Some 61 profiles were drawn from the exposed faces made by the tree planters. This information will allow us to refine our strategies for further excavation in agricultural facilities.

Other Research

Although no studies of contemporary pottery production were carried out this season, we did make some preliminary observations on the process of brick making. Brick manufacture is carried out on a small to medium scale throughout the area and leaves a significant mark on the landscape. Inasmuch as brick production was also important during the Vijayanagara period – and the abundant remains of bricks suggest that it was – it is useful to consider both the technology and organization of brick making today (see Fogelin this volume).

Acknowledgements

We would like to acknowledge the Government of India and the Archaeological Survey of India for their permission to carry out this research. Research was facilitated by the American Institute of Indian Studies. We thank the AIIS and, in particular, Dr Pradeep Mehendiratta, its Director-General and Vice-President, as well as the entire staff. We are affiliated with the Karnataka State Directorate of Archaeology and Museums and acknowledge their hospitality and invaluable contribution to the research. Thanks also to Deccan College, Dr V.N. Misra, and all of the Deccan College students who worked with us and to Kannada University for permission to examine the tree-planting squares. Fieldwork in the 1994 season was supported by the Smithsonian Foreign Currency Program, the National Geographic Society, and by additional support to the Social Science Research Institute, University of Hawai'i. Finally, we acknowledge the heroic efforts of all of the team members.

Works Cited

Morrison, K.D., 1991, The Vijayanagara Metropolitan Survey: Preliminary

Investigation. In, *Vijayanagara: Progress of Research, 1984-1987,* edited by C.S. Patil and D.V. Devaraj, pp. 136-41, Directorate of Archaeology and Museums, Mysore.

——, 1995, *Fields of Victory: Vijayanagara and the Course of Intensification,* Contributions of the University of California Archaeological Research Facility, No. 53, Berkeley.

Morrison, K.D. and C.M. Sinopoli, 1996, Archaeological Survey in the Vijaya-nagara Metropolitan Region: 1990. In, *Vijayanagara: Progress of Research, 1988-1991,* edited by C.S. Patil and D.V. Devaraj, pp. 59-73, Directorate of Archaeology and Museums, Mysore.

Sinopoli, C.M. and K.D. Morrison, 1991, The Vijayanagara Metropolitan Survey: The 1988 Season. In, *Vijayanagara: Progress of Research, 1984-1987,* edited by C.S. Patil and D.V. Devaraj, pp. 55-69, Directorate of Archaeology and Museums, Mysore.

Table 1. Sites Related to Transportation

Site	Block	Transect	Description
Roadways			
VMS-392	R	14-16	This long (ca 865 m long x 10 m wide) double wall skirts the edge of an outcrop, running primarily east-west. It creates an elevated roadway high above the dry farmed south-east corner of Block R. It probably connected with VMS-393.
VMS-393	R	17	Starting at the eastern end of VMS-392, this ramp-cum-staircase (40 x 7 m) leads up the side of an outcrop.
VMS-396	R	13	This is a narrow but well-defined passageway (10.4 x 3 m) cleared through the saddle of an outcrop.
VMS-426	R	9	This short (26.4 x 2.6 m) segment is bounded by parallel walls.
VMS-429	R	9	Skirting the north edge of an outcrop, this road segment (25 x 0.4 m) consists of terrace walls and a raised earthen pathway.
VMS-430	R	9-10	This roadway (78 m long) is a continuation of VMS-429 east of the outcrop. It is defined by worn sheet-rock, a possible paved surface and quarried road walls.
VMS-431	R	8-9	This roadway (255 m long) is a continuation of VMS-429 to the west. Like VMS-429 it consists of a raised road surface bounded by walls that hug the north edge of an outcrop. The western end consists of a cleared passageway in the boulders.
VMS-435	R	12	This roadway (120 x 0.75 m) is defined by parallel walls and may be a continuation of VMS-426.
VMS-449	M	9	Running perpendicular to the road along the Turtha canal, this raised roadway (82 x 5 m) stands 2 m above the present ground surface. It may have connected sites on a low outcrop to the canal road.
VMS-465	M	13	This roadway (50 x 2 m) is defined by parallel walls; probably related to VMS-467, 468, a complex of temples and a *mandapa*.
VMS-466	M	13	This short (7 x 1.2 m) roadway was probably once connected to VMS-465.
VMS-470	M	10	This elaborate cobbled road surface (250 x 15 m) runs up over an outcrop and is associated with a small columned structure base (F1) and several pecked figures (Plate 1).
VMS-471	M	9-10	The car street associated with the temple VMS-448, this straight (95 x 19 m) roadway is associated with a Nandi, other Shaivite imagery, and a small room.
VMS-495	M	12-13	This roadway (55 x 2.5 m) is bounded by parallel walls.
VMS-501	M	3	A short (12 x 8 m) paved surface that runs from an area of sheet-rock to the river, this pathway may have been associated with the settlement of Kalaghatti.
VMS-502	M	3	This roadway (16 x 1 m) consists of walls placed along the side of an outcrop, creating a raised terrace.
Bridges			
VMS-480	M	15	This two-section masonry bridge (17 x 5 m) spans the Turtha canal outlet channel.
VMS-472	M	8	The Turtha canal diversion weirs, or *anicuts*, could also have been used as foot-bridges over the Tungabhadra.
VMS-473	M	7	The Turtha canal diversion weirs, or *anicuts*, could also have been used as foot-bridges over the Tungabhadra.

Table 2. Sites with Religious Associations

Site	Block	Transect	Affiliation	Description
VMS-387	R	7	Shaivite (?)	Shrine, modern with Vijayanagara elements
VMS-389	R	8	Unknown	Shrine, 2 by 2 columns
VMS-395	R	16	Shaivite	Shrine, 2 by 2 columns on platform
VMS-414	R	11	Vaishnavite	Shrine, 2 by 2 columns with brick superstructure
VMS-415	R	14	Vaishnavite	Anjaneya Hanuman sculpture
VMS-416	R	10	Unknown	Shrine, 2 by 2 columns
VMS-418	R	4	Shaivite	Displaced Nandi sculpture
VMS-419	R	3	Vaishnavite	Anjaneya Hanuman and possible structure
VMS-421	R	13	Vaishnavite	Anjaneya Hanuman in 2 by 2 column shrine
VMS-433	R	14	Shaivite	Large sculpted Nandi on platform
VMS-437	M	6	Unknown	2 by 2 column, possibly not a shrine
VMS-438	M	6	Unknown	Small temple, 24 x 20 m
VMS-439	M	6	Shaivite	Temple tank, *lingam,* and associated small structures and pathway
VMS-440	M	6	Shaivite	Temple complex, on raised platform (Plate 3)
VMS-441	M	6	Unknown	3 by 2 column *mandapa* on high platform
VMS-442	M	2	Vaishnavite	Small temple, Anjaneya Hanuman image, lamp column
VMS-444	M	2	Other	Rock-shelter, Nagamma images, wall
VMS-446	R	1	Vaishnavite	2 by 2 column shrine
VMS-447	M	6	Vaishnavite (?)	Ornate small temple, badly disturbed
VMS-448	M	11	Shaivite (?)	Small temple, 12.5 x 7.5 m
VMS-453	R	16	Vaishnavite	3 by 2 column shrine with Anjaneya Hanuman
VMS-457	M	13	Other	*Sati* stone
VMS-458	M	12	Vaishnavite	Anjaneya Hanuman and platform
VMS-462	M	15	Unknown	Large shrine on hillside platform with associated walls and stairs
VMS-463	M	15	Shaivite	Sculpted boulder with footings and peg holes
VMS-467	M	13	Unknown	2 small shrines, rock shelter, and terrace walls
VMS-469	M	15	Unknown	2 *mandapas,* together 120 x 34 m, may not be temples
VMS-478	M	15	Unknown	2 by 2 column shrine
VMS-479	M	15	Unknown	2 by 2 column shrine
VMS-487	R	7	Shaivite	Large walled temple complex with multiple subsidiary shrines and structures
VMS-489	R	7	Unknown	Small temple
VMS-492	R	16	Unknown	Small shrine, 7 x 5 m
VMS-493	R	16	Shaivite	2.1 x 2.1 m shrine
VMS-496	M	18	Vaishnavite	4 by 3 column shrine with Anjaneya Hanuman
VMS-498	R	2	Vaishnavite	6 x 6 m temple
VMS-499	R	2	Shaivite	Temple complex with modern additions and inscription
VMS-500	M	16	Shaivite	10 x 5.5 m shrine
VMS-504	M	15	Muslim	Kadirampura tombs and cemetery (Plate 4)
VMS-508	M	8	Unknown	3 by 2 column shrine
VMS-511	R	2	Shaivite	2 by 2 column shrine

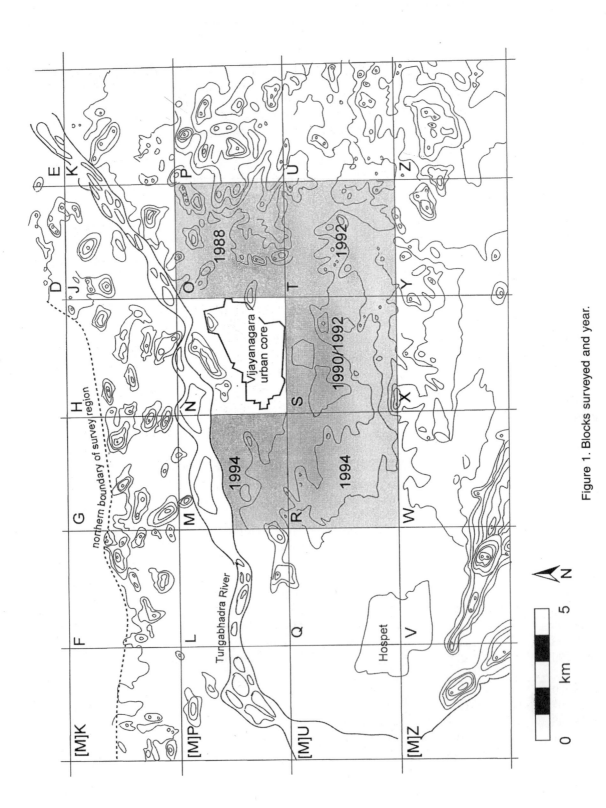

Figure 1. Blocks surveyed and year.

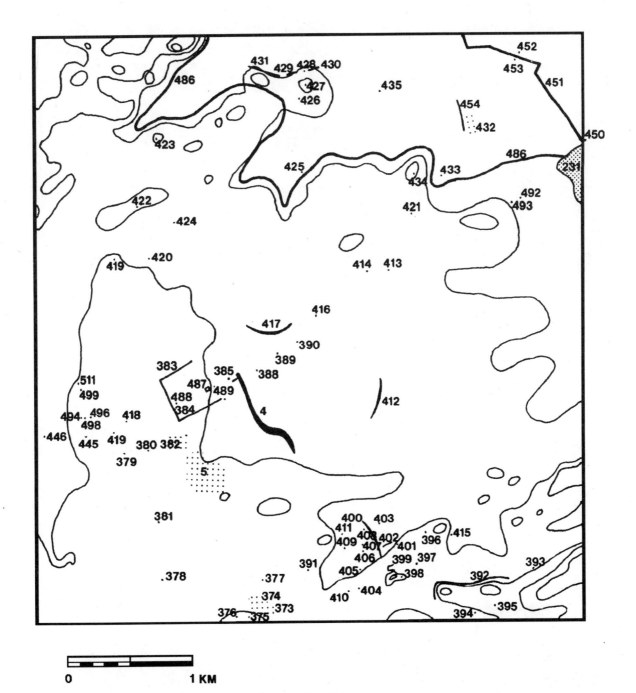

Figure 2. Block R map.

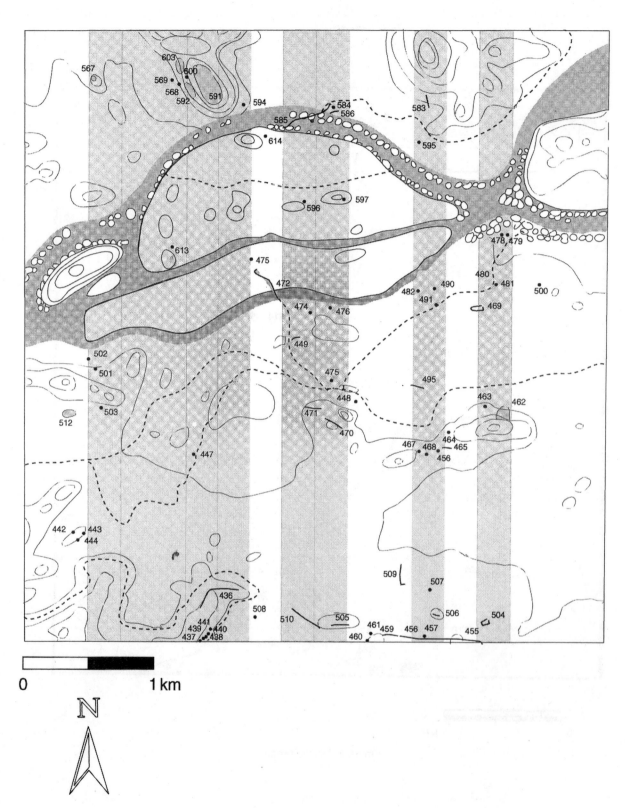

Figure 3. Block M map.

Plate 1. VMS-470, cobble road segment.

Plate 2. VMS-487, Malapannagudi temple *gopura*.

Plate 3. VMS-440, temple complex.

Plate 4. VMS-504, Kadirampura tombs and cemetery.

Plate 5. VMS-4, reservoir embankment.

Plate 6. VMS-451, outer city wall segment.

THE VIJAYANAGARA METROPOLITAN SURVEY: OVERVIEW OF THE 1996 SEASON

Kathleen D. Morrison and Carla M. Sinopoli

Introduction

The Vijayanagara Metropolitan Survey (VMS), directed by Drs Kathleen D. Morrison and Carla M. Sinopoli conducted its sixth season of field research from January through March 1996. The VMS project is a multi-phased project focusing on the documentation of archaeological remains in the ca 350-sq km Metropolitan Region of the imperial capital of Vijayanagara. Our project seeks to examine the economic and political development and organization of Vijayanagara through an understanding of the distribution, growth and nature of settlement, productive activities and infrastructure in the Vijayanagara urban landscape.

We have defined the Vijayanagara Metropolitan Region according to a combination of topographic and cultural features as the area contained within the outermost fortifications of the capital. Since fortification walls do not form a continuous ring around the city, but instead span low-lying regions or routes of access into the capital, topographic features were also taken into account in defining the bounds of the metropolitan region. This is especially the case to the north of the Tungabhadra River, where the extremely rugged Raichur Hills provide an effective barrier to occupation and movement.

In the VMS research design, the survey area is subdivided into arbitrary blocks, each 4.5 km on a side, following the map system of Fritz and Michell (1985; see also Morrison and Sinopoli 1996, and Sinopoli and Morrison 1991). The research strategy consists of three inter-related phases or aspects of research: (1) systematic, intensive transect survey in the eight blocks immediately surrounding the Urban Core (Blocks G, H, J, M, O, R, S and T); (2) extensive survey in the remaining blocks of the Metropolitan Region; and (3) test excavations in six small, primarily agricultural sites identified through systematic survey. In this paper we report on some preliminary results of the 1996 season of field research, with special emphasis on the systematic survey.

Along with the project directors, 1996 VMS participants included: Dr Mark T. Lycett, Jennifer Lundal and Anwen Tormey of Northwestern University; Jane Jalutkewicz and John Norder of the University of Michigan; Kalyani Bhave, Neena Jhanjee, Shivendra Kadjaonkar, Varada Khaladkar, Shyamanajali Mansingh and Ditamalu Vasa of Deccan College, Pune; and Renu Bhatlekar and Subuhi Sayed of Bombay University.

Strategy I: Intensive Survey

During 1996, intensive transect survey focused on areas located to the north of the Tungabhadra River in Blocks M, G, H, and J, as well as on a large island in the river in Block M (Figure 1). This region in general consists of a narrow low-lying alluvial band located along the banks of the river that ranges in width from less than 100 m to up to c. 2.5 km. This highly fertile zone is now largely under intensive wet cultivation, primarily of rice, sugarcane and bananas. As we note below, these areas were also important for agriculture in the Vijayanagara period, but the nature of their use also changed through time within this period. In places, isolated granite outcrops and hills, some quite high, rise up from the fields. To the north of this zone, a broad band of steep granitic hills rises steeply. These hills define the northern boundary of the survey region and, in fact, we have found a marked reduction in the density of structures and artefacts as these steep hills are approached.

In each of the eight intensively surveyed blocks, a total of nine 250 m-wide transects was randomly selected to define a 50 per cent sample. Ideally, transects are surveyed by teams of three to six archaeologists spaced at intervals of 20 m who cover the area in a north-south direction. However, the terrain of the 1996 survey area made this strategy difficult to adhere to at times. When transect survey was not possible, two alternate survey strategies were employed. The first was relevant to areas dominated by rice or sugarcane cultivation. In these areas, survey crews walked along the edges of irrigation canals and paths that provided access to fields. When fallow fields or surveyable agricultural areas (such as banana fields) were discovered, these were covered using our standard methods. Attempts were made to survey non-arable areas located amid fields, such as granite inselbergs or hills. The second survey strategy was used in the extremely rugged outcrops that dominate the northern part of this region. In these zones it was typically impossible to maintain transect spacing and orientation. Instead, members scaled the hills through whatever route possible and attempted to cover all accessible areas. Where relatively flat terraces were discovered on outcrops these were systematically surveyed. In some cases, the outcrops were so steep and sheer that only their lower portions could be examined.

A total of 97 sites was recorded in the four blocks. The general characteristics of each block are described below, along with a list of identified sites.

Block M

Block M is located due west of the Vijayanagara Urban Core (Figure 2). The Tungabhadra River crosses across the upper portion of the block. Areas to the south of the river were surveyed in the 1994 field season (Morrison and Sinopoli this volume). During 1996, we concentrated on the area north of the river

and on the large island in the central part of the block. Low-lying areas near the river were typically in rice or sugarcane agriculture. The Anegondi canal *anicut* is located in the centre of the block, and extends east, providing evidence for irrigated agriculture extending back to the Vijayanagara period. Two areas of high granitic outcrops dominate the northern portion of Block M. The western outcrop located south of the Anegondi-Gangavati road was fully surveyed, though the area of this outcrop located to the north of the road was largely inaccessible. The eastern outcrop was surveyed where possible. The transects randomly selected for survey were Transects 3, 4, 5, 6, 7, 9, 10, 13 and 15 (Figure 2). Twenty sites were recorded in Block M during 1996 (Table 1).

Block G

Located to the north of Block M, Block G is characterized by extremely rugged topography (Figure 3). There are few low-lying areas in this block and these are primarily restricted to the southern part of the block, the southwest corner and, to a lesser extent, in the southeastern quadrant. Based on our topographically defined boundary of the Metropolitan Region only the southern portion of the block (ranging from 1.0 to 1.5 km from the southern block boundary) fell within the survey area (Figure 3). Even in this region, a modern dam located to the northwest of Sanapur has submerged a significant area of transects 4-8. Randomly selected survey transects in Block G were 1, 2, 3, 4, 5, 6, 12, 14 and 15. Not surprisingly given the terrain, site density was extremely low in this area and only six sites were identified (Table 2).

Block H

Block H is located due north of the Vijayanagara Urban Core (Block N) (Figure 4). The ancient and modern settlement of Anegondi extends over the southeast quadrant of the block. The archaeological remains of Anegondi have been thoroughly documented in the doctoral dissertation of Sugandha Purandare (1986; Deccan College, Pune), who recorded more than 300 archaeological features within the walls of the settlement. Our work therefore focused largely on documenting remains beyond the outer walls of Anegondi and in the area between the inner and outer city walls. The outer wall themselves were mapped and described, as they did not appear to have been a focus of Purandare's work. The northwest corner of the block also fell outside of the Metropolitan Region, based on our topographic definition. Transects selected for survey in Block H were 1, 3, 4, 7, 10, 13, 14, 15 and 16. A total of 26 sites were documented (Table 3).

Block J

The Tungabhadra River extends north-east from the southwest corner of Block J, bisecting the block (Figure 5). In 1996, we surveyed the area of the block located north of the river, leaving the area south of the river for the 1997 season. Low-lying irrigated land is common in the survey area, with steep outcrops on the western side of the block and in the northeast corner. As in other areas north of the river, lower elevations are intensively farmed and many areas were inaccessible. Modern quarrying activities in the northwestern corner of the block, as elsewhere in the Metropolitan Region, also pose an imminent threat to many of the archaeological sites on higher terrain. Transects selected for survey in Block J were 2, 5, 6, 7, 8, 11, 14, 15 and 17; 48 sites were recorded in the surveyed area (Table 4).

Site Summary

Sites recorded in the four blocks during the 1996 season encompass a broad array of site types, relating to agricultural production, transportation, settlement, craft production and defense, among others. In the discussion and tables below, we consider only those sites whose functions can be securely determined. A number of sites of unknown function (e.g. isolated walls or architectural elements) are not discussed.

Transportation

Sites related to transportation were found in Blocks H and J (Table 5). They include road

segments and gates. While other routes can be identified on the basis of site alignments, here we limit discussion to only those sites which can themselves be directly related to transport. It is likely that several ancient routes followed canals or modern roads and are not clearly visible today; others may have been obscured by recent agricultural expansion and quarrying in the region.

Three gates were documented along the outer city walls of Anegondi. Two (VMS-529/F3 and VMS-529/F5) are located in the continuous wall segment to the northeast and east of the modern town (VMS-529). VMS-529/F5 lies along the Gangavati-Anegondi road, on the eastern edge of the modern village of Kadebakele (Kannada for "Last Gate"). A third gate, not yet documented, is found near the river on the southern extent of this wall. These are relatively simple gates, lacking the elaborate columned platforms and complex changes of direction known from other gates of the Vijayanagara period, and are instead essentially faced gaps in the fortification wall. A road paved with well worn cobbles runs through gate VMS-529/F3, though it is no longer preserved outside of the gate. Site VMS-549 is located in the wall segment to the northwest of Anegondi, c. 40 m to the west of the modern road. This gate consists of two columned platforms, and is c. 9 x 6 m in dimension. A modern irrigation canal now runs through the centre of the gate.

Eight roads or road segments were documented. Most skirt the base of outcrops, allowing access to agricultural fields and/or settlements. The most substantial road recorded in 1996 is site VMS-524, located in the northwest quadrant of Block J. This broad road was traced for 980 m; both the northern and southern ends have been destroyed by recent agricultural activities and the original road was certainly longer. The road ranges in width from 10 to 20 m, and is flanked on both sides by low walls that define narrow platforms. Artefact densities were, however, low, suggesting that these platforms may have served more to define the road than as basements for the small shops and/or residences of a bazaar street, as we have found elsewhere in the survey area. Traces of pavement are preserved in some areas. Two step-wells, one near each end, were found along the road. A small Anjaneya Hanuman shrine lies near the well at the road's present southern end.

Settlement

Twelve sites that can be categorized as having served primarily as settlement locales were recorded in the 1996 field season (Table 6). Settlements were identified in Blocks M, H, and J; none were recorded in the rugged terrain of Block G. Nucleated communities of a dozen or more structural complexes are the most common form of settlements in the surveyed area. Two factors appear to have most strongly affected settlement location. This first is a concern for defense; settlements are often walled and several contain bastions or watchtowers. The second factor affecting settlement location is a concern to avoid settlement on prime agricultural lands while retaining access to them. The preferred location for settlements seemed, therefore, to be on sheet-rock or outcrops above, but proximate to, agricultural fields. It is possible that some substantial settlements were built in low-lying areas and are now obliterated by recent agricultural activities, but we have not located any artefactual traces of such settlements. Low-lying areas were almost certainly occupied on a short-term basis, but for the most part traces of these more ephemeral sites have been destroyed by intensive agriculture.

The modern village of Kadebakele located to the east of Anegondi contained several badly disturbed, Vijayanagara structures and probably also had an earlier occupation. The contemporary settlements of Anegondi and Gangavati, to the east of the survey area, are also well known as locales of Vijayanagara period settlement and contain numerous Vijayanagara architectural and artefactual remains. In general, however, Vijayanagara period remains were scarce in other modern villages in the area (e.g. Timmalapur, Sonapur and Mallapur). This pattern differs markedly from that observed south of the river (particularly in Blocks M, S, and R) where modern settlements are often located in the same areas as (continuously occupied?) Vijayanagara period settlements.

Site VMS-513 is among the more substantial settlements recorded. The present site area is 6 ha (300 x 200 m) and it is clear that ongoing quarrying and agricultural activities have destroyed large parts of the settlement. The site is located along the eastern slope of a high outcrop. A massive double-faced wall, *c.* 2.5 m in width and constructed of small to large unmodified boulders, borders the settlement on the north while other walls bound the site intermittently on other sides and define occupational terraces on the steeply sloping sheet-rock. Dense structural remains are visible in the flat central area of the site, with at least ten multi-room structures built around court-yards evident. Other evidence for domestic occupation includes the presence of several sheet-rock and block mortars. Artefact density is variable and is highest on the southern edge of the site where storage pits containing high densities of ceramics have been exposed by recent digging.

Temples and Shrines

Fourteen sites can be classed as having a primary function as sacred sites (Table 7). sacred images and shrines are also found in other sites, such as settlements. Small shrines or sculpted slabs were most common in the area surveyed. No large temple complexes were identified in the survey area, although several are located in Anegondi. Six of the fourteen sacred sites contained Vaishnava images; all of the latter were of the Anjaneya form of Hanuman. Six sites were devoted to Shaiva deities and contained *lingams*, Nandi and Ganesha images, or Shaiva door guardians. Site VMS-560 was a small single chamber shrine containing a hero stone. VMS-525 presently contains modern Durga images, though its original affiliation is unknown.

Agriculture

24 of the 97 sites recorded in 1996 (24.7%) can be linked in whole or part to agricultural activities. Agricultural sites were found in all four blocks and attest to the intensive investment in diverse agricultural regimes that occurred during the Vijayanagara period. Several sites also provide evidence for temporal

changes in Vijayanagara agricultural practices. A variety of agricultural sites was recorded. These include: reservoir embankments, terrace systems, step-wells, erosion control walls and check dams, and the Anegondi canal *anicut*, outlet and a small canal section that was abandoned when the course of the canal was altered. Agricultural sites are summarized in Table 8.

A large *anicut* (VMS-585) diverts water from the river in Block M and serves as the source of the Anegondi canal. This large canal runs through the northeast quadrant of Block M, and then and winds to the northeast through Blocks H and J before diverting back toward the river south of Gangavati, where it joins with another canal that originates near Singanagandu. A massive aqueduct (VMS-3) located on the northern edge of Block N transported water from the Anegundi canal to a large island in the Tungabhadra River. Although modern construction has considerably modified the Vijayanagara period Anegondi *anicut*, traces of the original construction are evident.

The construction of the canal significantly altered earlier Vijayanagara agricultural practices in this area. At least two reservoirs were made obsolete by the canal's construction. Reservoir embankments VMS-517 and VMS-573 in Block J were both cut by the canal, rendering them ineffective. Their construction must therefore date to earlier in the Vijayanagara period, or perhaps pre-Vijayanagara. Reservoir VMS-563 in Block H may also have been dramatically affected by the canal construction. The canal itself was also modified over time. Site VMS-564 in the southwest quadrant of Block H is a 140 m long section of canal that fell out of use when the canal's path was diverted further to the east. In this section of the canal, there is a significant difference in slope on each side of the site, with terrain to the east of the canal 6 to 8 m below the canal and the area to its west. The canal thus served as a significant barrier to movement across the area. A square bastion on the northern end of VMS-564 provides evidence that it was protected and had a defensive function.

Craft Production

Craft production evidence was sparse in the surveyed area. Only two sites had clear evidence for craft activities, both involving sculpting of sacred images. These were sites VMS-538 and VMS-567. Site VMS-538 consisted of a large quarried slab (*c.* 2.0 x 1.5 x 0.15 m) that had been removed from a nearby outcrop. An image of a striding Hanuman was in the process of being carved on the slab when it cracked and was abandoned. This image is located less than 100 m west of settlement VMS-537, where there is a large Hanuman shrine. It is possible that this shrine is was the intended destination for the slab suggesting that, as we have observed elsewhere in the Metropolitan Region, sculptors produced images near to their location of use. The second example of image sculpting is also the production of a striding Hanuman image. This is at the settlement site VMS-567. The outlines of the deity were lightly pecked onto the boulder, but no details had been carved. The reasons for the abandonment of this carving prior to completion are unknown.

Defense/Fortification

A concern with defense was a common feature in sites recorded in the survey area in 1996 (Table 9). As discussed earlier, the predominant mode of settlement in the area was in walled communities, several of which had associated bastions or watch towers. In addition, portions of the Anegondi canal were fortified. Undoubtedly, the most heavily fortified settlement was the centre of Anegondi. As noted above, while we did not document the inner walls and internal features of the town, we did map and document the town's outer fortification walls on the northwest and northeast side of the town. The northwest section was designated VMS-548. The southern end of the wall begins on the slope of a large outcrop. From there the wall extends to the northeast across a narrow valley and up a steep outcrop. A modern road run through this valley providing the major access to Anegondi from the north; a gate in the wall (VMS-548) suggests an earlier road (slightly to the west of the modern one) followed a similar route. Three square bastions project from the wall, which is constructed of up to ten courses of irregularly laid wedge shaped blocks. The large outcrop that defines the eastern edge of this wall extends for more than a kilometer to the east and is 700 to 800 m wide. This steep outcrop is in itself an extremely effective barrier to movement and the fortification wall picks up on its eastern edge and wraps around the town to the southeast. Sections of this wall were assigned site numbers VMS-527, VMS-528, and VMS-529. The well constructed wall includes a number of bastions and has many changes of direction as its orientation follows that of the stone outcrops on its southern border. In many places, outcrops are incorporated into the wall, or it rests on them. Two gates are located along the wall, *c.* 750 m from its western end in the village of Kadebakele. To the south and east of Kadebakele, wall segments wrap around the high outcrop in the southwest corner of Block J.

Pre-Vijayanagara Sites

Raichur District (north of the Tungabhadra River) is well known for its many prehistoric and early historic sites, with sites from the Palaeolithic to the Early Historic being reported. Our survey confirmed this previously reported pattern. Prehistoric sites, dating mostly to the Iron Age and Early Historic, were found in all four blocks. Sites identified in the 1996 season are listed in Table 10. Included among them are three painted rock-shelters (VMS-568, VMS-574, VMS-601). Motifs are typically painted in red and white and include stylized humans, structures, plants, and geometrics. A painted boulder (VMS-574) and large boulder with bruisings (VMS-600) were also documented. Sites with megalithic mortuary features included a number of isolated linear cairns, and two small cemetery sites (VMS-543, VMS-603) containing stone alignments and walled rock-shelters or gaps in sheet-rock sealed by small stones. Pre-medieval settlement sites (VMS-530, VMS-541, VMS-579) were located on terraces on top of outcrops and contained surface scatters of prehistoric ceramics, and stone alignments and terraces.

Strategy II: Extensive Survey

Intensive transect survey focuses on the eight blocks of the Metropolitan Region that surround the Urban Core. In the remainder of the region, a more extensive approach to site documentation is practised, focusing on documenting major sites of particular relevance to our research, rather than systematic coverage of the area. In 1996, extensive survey focused on documenting sites located in the Daroji Valley to the southeast of the Urban Core in Blocks W and X, where Morrison has been conducting a long-term study of a network of Vijayanagara period, irrigation reservoirs. Fieldwork this season focused on completing the documentation of a number of reservoirs that had been partly documented in earlier seasons. Several additional sites were also documented, including a small fort on the outskirts of the village of Papinayakanahalli and the large temple complex in the village, a walled settlement, two shrines, an Islamic prayer wall, or *idgah,* and two step-wells.

Strategy III: Test Excavations

The third component of the VMS involves excavations at several sites identified in earlier season of survey. The Government of India and Archaeological Survey of India have granted permission for excavation at six sites. All of these sites are agricultural features, though one, a large reservoir (VMS-101), also has surface remains of iron smelting activity. Through the excavations, we seek to expand our knowledge of land use and agricultural practices during the Vijayanagara period. In 1996, excavations were conducted at site VMS-133, an extensive dry-farmed terrace system (*c.* 375 x 375 m) located in Block S that was discovered and recorded in the 1990 field season. A number of sediment profiles had been recorded in 1994, through documentation of a series of tree planting holes that had been dug as part of a reforestation program in the area. In 1996, we excavated six 1.0 x 1.0 m square units that were placed along an east-west axis across the terraces. The units were excavated in 10 cm levels until bedrock was reached. Information was recorded on stratigraphy and sediment and matrix composition. Soil colours were recorded using Munsell Charts. Profiles were drawn of the north and east walls of all units. Unit depths ranged from 17 to 83 cm. The deepest unit was located immediately to the west of a terrace wall, and the depth of soil accumulation attests to the effectiveness of terrace walls in soil retention and transforming this semi-arid area to one with agricultural potential. Sediment and flotation cores were collected from two units. Grain size analysis was conducted by Morrison, and flotation yielded botanical materials. Small samples were retained for pollen analysis.

Other Research

In addition to the archaeological research, Sinopoli conducted a brief study of a potter's workshop in Papinayakanahalli, one of four traditional pottery workshops in that village. Interviews were carried out with members of the potter's family, and approximately three dozen vessels were acquired for study. These vessels were drawn and measured, with detailed information recorded on diameters, thicknesses, heights and composition. This is part of an ongoing study to examine inter- and intra-workshop ceramic variability in a modern context, with a goal of better understanding ceramic variability of the Vijayanagara period.

Acknowledgements

We would like to gratefully acknowledge the Government of India and the Archaeological Survey of India for permission to carry out this research. Research was facilitated by the American Institute of Indian Studies. We thank the AIIS, and in particular, Dr Pradeep Mehendiratta, Director-General and Vice-President, as well as the entire staff. Our project is affiliated with the Government of Karnataka, Directorate of Archaeology and Museums, and we acknowledge with thanks their hospitality and generous contributions to our research. Thanks also to Deccan College, Dr V.N. Misra and all of the Deccan College and Bombay University students who worked with us. The 1996 field season was supported by the National Science Foundation, National Endowment for the Humanities and the Wenner Gren Foundation for Anthropological Research, and by Northwestern University and the University of Michigan. Finally, we acknowledge the contributions of all of the VMS team members.

Works Cited

Morrison, K.D. and C.M. Sinopoli, 1996, Archaeological Survey in the Vijayanagara Metropolitan Region: 1990. In, *Vijayanagara: Progress of Research, 1988-1991*, edited by C.S. Patil and D.V. Devaraj, pp. 59-73, Directorate of Archaeology and Museums, Mysore.

Sinopoli, C.M. and K.D. Morrison, 1991, The Vijayanagara Metropolitan Survey: The 1988 Season. In, *Vijayanagara: Progress of Research, 1987-1988*, edited by C.S. Patil and D.V. Devaraj, pp. 55-69, Directorate of Archaeology and Museums, Mysore.

Table 1. Sites Documented in Block M

Site	Block	Transect	Description
VMS-512	M	2	Settlement
VMS-567	M	3	Settlement, shrine
VMS-568	M	5	Rock-shelter
VMS-569	M	5	Megalith
VMS-570	M	6	Water catchment basin
VMS-583	M	13	Reservoir embankment
VMS-584	M	10	Hanuman shrine and bastion
VMS-585	M	8-10	*Anicut* (Anegondi canal)
VMS-586	M	10	Anegondi canal outlet and embankment
VMS-587	M	9	Isolated wall
VMS-591	M	6-7	Fort
VMS-592	M	6	Settlement
VMS-594	M	7	Displaced sculptures
VMS-595	M	13	Hanuman shrine
VMS-596	M	9	Game
VMS-597	M	10	Artefact scatter
VMS-600	M	5	Petroglyph
VMS-603	M	5	Megalithic cemetery
VMS-613	M	5	Shrines
VMS-614	M	8	Wall

Table 2. Sites Documented in Block G

Site	Block	Transect	Description
VMS-575	G	2	Terraces
VMS-576	G	3	Reservoir embankment
VMS-577	G	3	Reservoir embankment
VMS-578	G	3	Rock-shelter
VMS-582	G	15	Lithic scatter
VMS-611	G	3	Wall-alignments

Table 3. Sites Documented in Block H

Site	Block	Transect	Description
VMS-527	H	14	Fortification wall (Anegondi)
VMS-528	H	14	Embankment/wall
VMS-529	H/J	14-18/ 1-3	Fortification wall (Anegondi)
VMS-547	H	5	Reservoir
VMS-548	H	10	Fortification wall (Anegondi)
VMS-549	H	9	Gate
VMS-550	H	10	Settlement
VMS-562	H	14	Temple
VMS-563	H	15	Reservoir embankment
VMS-564	H	7	Fortification
VMS-565	H	7	Road segment
VMS-566	H	7	Temple
VMS-572	H	1	Catchment tank/embankment wall
VMS-573	H	15-16	Reservoir
VMS-574	H	16	Pictograph
VMS-579	H	11	Settlement
VMS-580	H	10	Fortification wall
VMS-588	H	10	Wall and room
VMS-589	H	12	Painted rock shelter
VMS-590	H	11	Reservoir
VMS-593	H	4	Step-well
VMS-598	H	11	Megalith
VMS-599	H	12	Megalith
VMS-601	H	11	Rock-shelter with paintings
VMS-602	H	12	Megalith

Table 4. Sites documented in Block J

Site	Block	Transect	Description
VMS-513	J	7-8	Settlement
VMS-514	J	8	Temples in compound
VMS-515	J	7	Artefact scatter
VMS-516	J	7	Shrine (Shaivite)
VMS-517	J	5	Reservoir embankment
VMS-518	J	4	Settlement
VMS-519	J	4	Bastion
VMS-520	J	4	Bastion and wall
VMS-521	J	4	Bastion
VMS-522	J	2	Step-well
VMS-523	J	1	Reservoir embankment
VMS-524	J	1	Road
VMS-525	J	2	Temple (Durga)
VMS-526	J	2	Images on boulder
VMS-519	J	4	Bastion
VMS-520	J	4	Bastion and wall
VMS-521	J	4	Bastion
VMS-529	H/J	14-18/1-3	Fortification wall (Anegondi)
VMS-530	J	2-3	Settlement
VMS-531	J	1	*Mandapa*/displaced elements
VMS-532	J	4-6	Road segment
VMS-533	J	5	Artefact scatter
VMS-534	J	7-9	Anicut
VMS-535	J	3	Reservoir embankment
VMS-536	J	15	Road segment
VMS-537	J	15	Settlement, with shrine
VMS-538	J	15	Hanuman slab
VMS-539	J	15	Road wall
VMS-540	J	16	Step-well
VMS-541	H	11	Settlement
VMS-542	J	7	Wall segment
VMS-543	H	8	Megalithic cemetery/platforms
VMS-544	J	14	Temple/terrace/structure
VMS-545	J	14	Artefact scatter/settlement
VMS-546	J	14	Fortification wall and peg holes
VMS-551	J	8	Erosion control wall
VMS-552	J	8	Road segment
VMS-553	J	8	Horse stones
VMS-554	J	7	Road wall
VMS-555	J	7	Wall and platform
VMS-556	J	7	Displaced image and columns
VMS-557	J	6-7	Wall/road
VMS-558	J	6	Horse-stones
VMS-559	J	6	Inscription
VMS-560	J	10	Shrine
VMS-561	J	11	Single room structure
VMS-571	J	7	Ceramic scatter
VMS-581	J	17	Platform

Table 5. Sites Related to Transportation

Site	Block	Transect	Description
VMS-529/F1	H	17	This is a small stairway constructed of boulders placed along a well-worn area of sheet-rock (*c.* 3 x 2 m) located along a path to the south of the outer wall of Anegondi (VMS-529).
VMS-529/F3	H	17	Simple linear gate in outer wall of Anegondi, ca 9 m long x 8 m wide, narrowing to the south.
VMS-529/F5	J	2	Simple linear gate in outer wall of Anegondi, located on Gangavati-Anegondi road, *c.* 15 m long x 8 m wide, faced with large stone blocks, 2 platforms or bastions on interior.
VMS-549	H	9	Two platform columned gateway on high basement located outer wall of Anegondi in a narrow valley between two high hills. Central columns are square with octagonal insets, remaining columns are simple rectangular blocks.
VMS-565	H	7	This is a small (30 x 14 m) road segment defined by a boulder alignment on sheet-rock, skirting the base of an outcrop.
VMS-524	J	1	Large road (980 x 20 m) oriented 20 east of north, in a valley between two high outcrops. Low walls line either side, and traces of pavement are preserved in some areas.
VMS-532	J	4-6	This long road (300 x 12 m) extends south from Kadebakele toward the Anegondi *anicut.* It is lined on one or both sides by a low wall constructed of large unmodified boulders; a small platform (Feature 1) is located on western edge of road.
VMS-536	J	15	This small road fragment (36 m long) is flanked by two walls, and extends along the base of an outcrop.
VMS-539	J	15	This 22 m long segment of double-faced wall is probably associated with VMS-536.
VMS-552	J	8	This is a small segment (40 x 6 m) of paved road bed extending along a low outcrop and incorporating worn sheet-rock in sections.
VMS-554	J	7	Skirting the southern face of an outcrop, this long wall of 1-2 courses forms a flat terrace, *c.* 80 m long x 2 m wide.
VMS-557	J	6-7	This road is likely a continuation of VMS-554. A low wall ranging from 1-5 courses skirts the southern edge of an outcrop; a small platform is located near western end of wall.

Table 6. Sites Related to Settlement

Site	Block	Transect	Description
VMS-512	M	2	This is a nucleated settlement bounded by a large enclosure wall, and with a Hanuman shrine. Traces of several small structures evident within this *c.* 135 x 130 m settlement; southern part of site has been recently ploughed, destroying structural remains and contributing to dense artefact scatter.
VMS-567	M	3	A small settlement (75 x 60 m) located on a low rising outcrop above rice fields; some modern artefacts and structures, but displaced Vijayanagara elements present, and traces of at least 5 rectangular structures, unfinished Hanuman sculpture on boulder near small circular stone tower or bastion.
VMS-592 (Figure 6)	M	6	This is a fortified area of *c.* 14 rooms (180 x 40 m) located on the southwest slope of the outcrop below fort VMS-591, with which it is most likely associated.
VMS-550	H	10	This is a nucleated settlement (190 m north-south x 230 m east-west, minimal estimate) built against the west face of a large outcrop, to the north of the outer wall of Anegondi. Despite extensive disturbance by modern agricultural activities and quarrying, the remains of many rectilinear structures placed opportunistically among the outcrops are evident, as are traces of an enclosure wall.
VMS-588	H	10	This site consists of wall alignments and small structure located *c.* 100 m north of VMS-550; small room or terrace of unknown date.
VMS-513	J	7-8	A nucleated walled settlement, *c.* 300 x 200 m located on the eastern slope of a moderately high outcrop. Heavily disturbed by quarrying. Enclosure walls are constructed of large unmodified boulders, with entry to the settlement through broad gaps. In some areas, traces of dense rectilinear structures are preserved, some situated around courtyards. Storage pit profiles are evident in modern soil excavations.
VMS-515	J	7	This is a surface scatter of ceramics (60 x 60 m) located ca 150 m southwest of VMS-513 and probably associated with that large settlement.
VMS-518 (Figure 7)	J	4	This is a walled settlement protected by four bastions located on a level terrace on the north face of an outcrop, *c.* 120 m east-west x 60 m north-south. A minimum of 8 rectilinear structures are visible within the walls. This area also contains several ground stone mortars and high ceramic density. Some modern modification, but some Vijayanagara elements are present.
VMS-537 (Figure 8)	J	15	This settlement is presently *c.* 120 x 60 m in dimension, though has been disturbed by agricultural activities. The settlement contains a small Hanuman shrine and several displaced sculptural elements. Remains of at least 12 structures are visible within a large enclosure wall.

Table 6. Continued

Site	Block	Transect	Description
VMS-544	J	14	This site contains a small temple located on a terraced area of sheet rock located on the north bank of the Tungabhadra River. A scatter of rubble, artefacts and ground stone suggests that residential structures may once have been present in this area.
VMS-545	J	14	This is an extensive (84 x 76 m) sparse to moderate ceramic scatter in a heavily disturbed area on the north bank of the Tungabhadra River, probably associated with VMS-544. Rubble concentrations in agricultural fields may be the remains of disturbed structures.
VMS-561	J	11	This site consists of a small (3.6 x 3.6 m) single room structure of uncertain date located on a flat area near agricultural fields.

Table 7. Sites with Religious Associations

Site	Block	Transect	Affiliation	Description
VMS-584 (Figure 9)	M	10	Vaishnava	This site, located on the southern edge of the Anegondi canal, consists of an Anjaneya Hanuman carved on a large boulder and an associated round bastion.
VMS-594	M	7	Shaiva	This site consists of two Vijayanagara period sculptures in a modern shrine. They include a Nandi image facing the shrine entry and a seated god, wearing a tall crown and pendant earrings.
VMS-595	M	13	Vaishnava	This site consists of a large Anjaneya Hanuman slab on a modern platform.
VMS-613	M	5	Shaiva	This site, on an island in the Tungabhadra, consists of a small shrine built under a boulder overhang containing a natural *lingam*, and three associated platforms, with a natural Nandi and image base.
VMS-562	H	14	Shaiva	This is a south-facing two-chamber Hanuman temple located in the modern settlement of Mallapur. While much of the structure seems recent, the central image of Hanuman, and smaller images of Nandi and Garuda are of Vijayanagara style.
VMS-566	H	7	Shaiva	This heavily modified early Vijayanagara temple with Shaiva door guardians is situated on the sheet-rock slopes below Anjanadri Hill.
VMS-514	J	8	Shaiva	This is walled temple complex containing 2 two-chambered shrines that abut each other. Associated displaced slabs include an elaborately sculpted doorway, with Shaiva door guardians; possibly late Vijayanagara.
VMS-516	J	7	Shaiva	This shrine consists of a modified rock-shelter and associated terrace. Inside a small walled-off chamber in the shelter are images of a *lingam* and Nandi. A large Ganesha is a carved on a boulder on the terrace as is a seven-headed *naga*.
VMS-525	J	2	Unknown	This is a Vijayanagara period two-chambered shrine that has been incorporated into a modern Durga shrine; original affiliation unknown.
VMS-526	J	2	Shaiva, Vaishnava	This large granite boulder located near the Kadebakele gate is carved with images of a *lingam* and Nandi image, Anjaneya Hanuman, and two humans.
VMS-538	J	15	Vaishnava	This is an unfinished image of an Anjaneya Hanuman on a large stone slab found at its sculpting location.

Table 7. Continued

Site	Block	Transect	Affiliation	Description
VMS-544	J	14	Vaishnava	This is a small single-chambered Hanuman temple located on a terraced area, and probably associated with a much disturbed Vijayanagara period settlement.
VMS-556	J	7	Vaishnava	Vijayanagara period Anjaneya Hanuman in modern structure, fallen lamp-column lies nearby.
VMS-560	J	10	Hero stone	This is a single chamber (2 x 2 column) shrine containing a carved slab on which is depicted a male figure on horseback. The horse is led by a turbaned male figure; a female stands behind the horse. An image of a dog is seen between the horse's legs.

Table 8. Sites Associated with Agricultural Activities

Site	Block	Transect	Description
VMS-570	M	6	This finely built square (11.5 x 9 m) water catchment basin is located in a natural depression on sheet-rock and captured run off from the north and east. The south and west faces are constructed of up to six stepped courses of angular unmodified and split stones.
VMS-583	M	13	This c. 52 m long reservoir has a runoff sluice on its southern end and is located near the mouth of a narrow valley. No formal sluice gate is present.
VMS-585	M	8-10	This 250 m long x 15 m wide site is the *anicut* that provides water to the Anegondi canal. Much of the *anicut* is modern, though several elements date to the Vijayanagara construction.
VMS-586	M	10	This site is a stepped stone canal embankment and outlet of the Anegondi canal that parallels the Tungabhadra River for c. 120 m. The embankment is up to 20 m wide. The modern canal is located slightly to the north of this site.
VMS-575	G	2	This small (16 x 10 m) site consists of three walls that served to limit erosion from agricultural fields in an area of sloping terrain.
VMS-576	G	3	This heavily overgrown and damaged reservoir embankment (60 x 10 m) is located between granitic hills and channelled water to the southwest. It is constructed of up to 10 courses of medium to large unmodified and split boulders.
VMS-577	G	3	This small reservoir embankment (100 x 7.5 m) is similar to VMS-576 and likewise spans a narrow valley. It is constructed of up to 10 irregular courses of small to medium unmodified and split boulders.
VMS-611	G	3	This site consists of two parallel wall alignments located near reservoir VMS-576. It may have served to control erosion.
VMS-528	H	14	This 185-m long stepped stone embankment is incorporated in the outer fortification wall of Anegondi. It spans an east facing valley. The east face is a well constructed Vijayanagara fortification wall of wedge-shaped blocks; the west face is stepped and constructed of up to 11 courses of medium to large unmodified and split boulders. It would have impounded water from slopes to the west in a catchment c. 100 x 140 m in area.
VMS-547	H	5	This 270-m long north south reservoir embankment is located between two large outcrops. One sluice gate is preserved near the south end and a sluice outlet is visible in the north. This tall and steep embankment is faced on both sides, with between 13-15 courses of dressed slabs.

490

Table 8. Continued

Site	Block	Transect	Description
VMS-563	H	15	This site is a northeast-southwest oriented reservoir embankment that spans a narrow valley between two outcrops. The eastern side is faced with five to seven courses of medium to large unmodified and split boulders. Two standing columns mark the existence of a disturbed sluice gate.
VMS-564	H	7	This site is a 140-m long segment of the Anegondi canal that fell out of use when the canal was diverted to its present course. In sections there is a significant difference in elevation on either side of the canal, with the terrain to the east 6 to 8 m below the western face. The eastern embankment is faced with up to 12 courses of stepped stones. A stone platform is located near the south end of the site, and a square bastion is located on the north.
VMS-572	H	1	This stepped, north-south oriented, 340 m-long embankment spans a valley between two steep outcrops. The western side is faced with 5-13 regular courses of medium to large unmodified boulders. A square outlet basin is located near the south end.
VMS-573	H	15-16	This site consists of a highly disturbed 320+ m long reservoir embankment located amid irrigated rice and peanut fields. One sluice gate is extant with a single angled bevel moulding. Embankment construction is of 5-7 irregular courses of medium to large unmodified boulders.
VMS-590	H	11	This site consists of a reservoir or water catchment feature (39 x 36 m) and associated walls that bound a natural depression on an outcrop. May be prehistoric in date, as black and red ware sherds were found on nearby terraces.
VMS-593	H	4	This small heavily overgrown step-well is located in a low lying area amid modern fields.
VMS-612	H	1	This is a small (85 x 8 m) reservoir embankment that encloses a narrow valley between two east-west trending outcrops. It is constructed of up to 8 courses of medium to large unmodified and split boulders and most likely served to impound water, not to distribute it. No sluices are present.
VMS-517	J	5	This poorly preserved, 250 x 15 m north-south reservoir embankment spanned a low-lying area between two outcrops. 5 to 7 stepped courses of medium large unmodified and split boulders are preserved. The embankment was cut by the Anegondi canal and must therefore predate canal construction. A sluice outlet is preserved, though no gate is present.

Table 8. Continued

Site	Block	Transect	Description
VMS-522	J	2	This site consists of a small shrine and associated step-well. The water basin of the well is *c.* 10 x 10 m, with steps on the west and a water drawing platform on the east. The walls of the well are constructed of well dressed cut granite slabs and blocks; coursing is regular and Vijayanagara quarry marks are visible.
VMS-523	J	1	This heavily disturbed, north south oriented reservoir embankment extends north from the Kadebakele gateway on the outer wall of Vijayanagara. It was made obsolete during Vijayanagara times by the construction of the Anegondi canal. The western face of the embankment is faced with 3 to 7 course of unmodified medium boulders. A sluice gate is preserved near the southern end.
VMS-534	J	7-9	This long *anicut* (1,100 m) snakes along the Tungabhadra River from the northern bank to the southeast. Large parts are fully submerged. The *anicut* diverts part of the river flow to a natural channel between large boulders that ultimately leads to the Ramasagara channel on the southern river bank.
VMS-535	J	3	This *c.* 200 m long reservoir embankment spans a valley between two outcrops, and is oriented 10° east of north. The western face is constructed of up to seven courses of unmodified and split medium boulders. No sluice gate is preserved.
VMS-540	J	16	This rectangular step-well is associated with settlement VMS-537 located 30 m to its north. The well is constructed of up to four visible courses of masonry. There are no stairs.
VMS-551	J	8	This site consists of a doubled-faced wall that extends for 58 m along the southern edge of an outcropping area. Incorporating natural boulders in parts, the wall likely served to limit erosion in the fields to the south of the wall, though it may also have defined a foot path.

Table 9. Sites Related to Fortification and Defense

Site	Block	Transect	Description
VMS-584 (Figure 9)	M	10	This site located on the southern edge of the Anegondi canal, consists of an Anjaneya Hanuman carved on a large boulder and an round bastion. The bastion is *c.* 6 m in diameter and was *c.* 1.6 m high.
VMS-591	M	6-7	This is a large fort located atop a high outcrop overlooking the Tungabhadra River and affording excellent views to the south, west and east. The *c.* 310 x 100 m fort follows the contours of the outcrop, with two main levels of room blocks, containing residential space, storage structures and water basins.
VMS-527	H	14	This is a 40 m-long segment of the outer fortification wall of Anegondi that spans an open area between two outcrops. The exterior of this double-faced wall is constructed of large wedge-shaped blocks, while the interior is of large unmodified boulders. This site is associated with VMS-528 and VMS-529.
VMS-528	H	14	This 185-m long stepped stone embankment is incorporated in the outer fortification wall of Anegondi. It spans an east-facing valley. The east face is a well constructed Vijayanagara fortification wall of wedge-shaped blocks; the west face is stepped and constructed of up to 11 courses of medium to large unmodified and split boulders. It would have impounded water from slopes to the west in a catchment *c.* 100 x 140 m in area.
VMS-529	H/J	14-18/1-3	This is a *c.* 2-km long section of the outer fortification wall of Anegondi, which wraps around the settlement on the north and east. The wall incorporates three gates and has several square bastions. Its orientation follows the path of outcrops on which it rests. It is constructed of well-fitted wedge-shaped blocks and is mostly double-faced ranging from 4 to 12 m in width.
VMS-548	H	10	This 200-m long section of the outer wall of Anegondi is located to the north-west of the town and spans a narrow valley between two high outcrops. Up to 10 courses of wedge-shaped block masonry are preserved. Gate VMS-549 provided access through this wall.
VMS-580	H	10	This 30-m long, double-faced wall blocks a passage through outcrops that provided access to VMS-550. It is double faced and constructed of large split boulders, with rubble fill.
VMS-519	J	4	This is a small circular bastion or watch tower located atop a high outcrop overlooking settlement VMS-518 and reservoir VMS-517. It is constructed of 14+ courses of small square and rectangular blocks. Possibly post-Vijayanagara.
VMS-520	J	4	This small square bastion is situated on a small boulder overlooking settlement VMS-517. Possibly post-Vijayanagara.

Table 9. Continued

Site	Block	Transect	Description
VMS-521	J	4	This round bastion guards the western approach to settlement VMS-517. It is constructed of small square to rectangular blocks, with up to 11 courses preserved.
VMS-546	J	14	This is a small section of fortification wall (12 x 7 m) spanning a gap in an outcrop on the north bank of the Tungabhadra River. The wall is composed of medium to large granite blocks and split boulders, with some wedge-shaped blocks. Four courses are visible.
VMS-553	J	8	This site is a 12-m long section of four parallel rows of boulders, with a width of 6 m. The boulders stand 0.8 to 1.0 m high and are spaced less than 1 m apart. Modern quarrying in the area has probably destroyed much of this site. The stones probably served as horse-stones, a defensive feature designed to impede the movement of cavalry, and were part of the defensive system of Anegondi.
VMS-558	J	6	This 110-m long site consists of two sets of parallel rows of large boulders. The northern set consists of three rows of boulder alignments, with distance between rows c. 1.5 m, while in the southern set lines are spaced at 1.0 m apart. The rows are heavily disturbed by wet agriculture and the original extent was undoubtedly much longer. The stones probably served as horse-stones.

Table 10. Prehistoric Sites Documented

Site	Block	Transect	Description
VMS-568	M	5	The rear wall of this 27-m long, northwest-facing rock shelter is painted with numerous naturalistic and geometric motifs in red and white pigment. Depictions include human figures, animals, and structures.
VMS-569	M	5	This linear cairn is located on an outcrop above VMS-568 and is associated with cemetery site VMS-603.
VMS-600	M	·5	Several circular petroglyphs of uncertain date are inscribed on the eastern face of a large (*c.* 15 m high) boulder, located near megalithic sites VMS-568 and VMS-603.
VMS-603	M	5	Located on a terrace on the northern side of a steep outcrop, this site contains a number of circular and linear stone alignments, and possible cairns spreading over an area *c.* 80 x 40 m.
VMS-578	G	3	This is a two-chambered north-facing rock-shelter located on the western slope of an outcrop. The shelter contains sparse scatter of highly eroded ceramics of unknown date (but most likely prehistoric).
VMS-582	G	15	This is a small scatter of quartzite lithic debris, including cores, shatter and flakes. Date unknown.
VMS-574	H	16	This site consists of two superimposed painted images on a large vertical boulder. Designs are geometric and while the topmost image appears modern, the lower image may be Prehistoric in date.
VMS-579 (Figure 10)	H	11	This settlement site is located on the slopes of a large outcrop. Surface remains include terrace walls, and room blocks. Surface remains include black and red ware and polished red ware ceramics, slag, granite debris, and bone, ash and charcoal, associated with water catchment basin/ reservoir VMS-590.
VMS-589	H	12	This west-southwest-facing rock overhang contains red and white painted geometric and stylized human images. Rock shelter.
VMS-590	H	11	This site consists of a reservoir or water catchment feature (39 x 36 m) and associated walls that bound a natural depression on an outcrop. May be prehistoric in date, as black and red ware sherds were found nearby, and it appears to be associated with settlement VMS-579.
VMS-598	H	11	This site is an isolated linear cairn megalith (4.7 x 1.9 m).
VMS-599	H	12	This is an isolated linear cairn megalith (6.7 x 2.7 m).

Table 10. Continued.

Site	Block	Transect	Description
VMS-601	H	11	This south-facing rock-shelter is located in a narrow passage in a large outcrop, and contains red and white painted images of humans, animals, plants (?) and geometric motifs.
VMS-602	H	12	This is an isolated linear cairn megalith (4.55 x 2.5 m).
VMS-530	J	2-3	This settlement site is located on terraces on a high outcrop above the Tungabhadra River. Surface remains include black and red ware, polished red, polished black and russet-coated painted ware ceramics, lithics, bone and ash. Terrace walls and wall alignments are visible.
VMS-541 (Figure 11)	J	11	This settlement site is located on the northern terraces of a high outcrop and consists of stone alignments and a surface scatter of iron age ceramics. Modern quarrying has probably destroyed much of this site.
VMS-543 (Figure 12, Plate 1)	J	8	Located on the southern end of the same outcrop containing settlement VMS-541, this mortuary site contains a number of stone alignments and linear cairns. Walls were built in many of the small rock shelters on the outcrop creating small chambers.

Plate 1. VMS-543, close up of Feature 5, linear cairn.

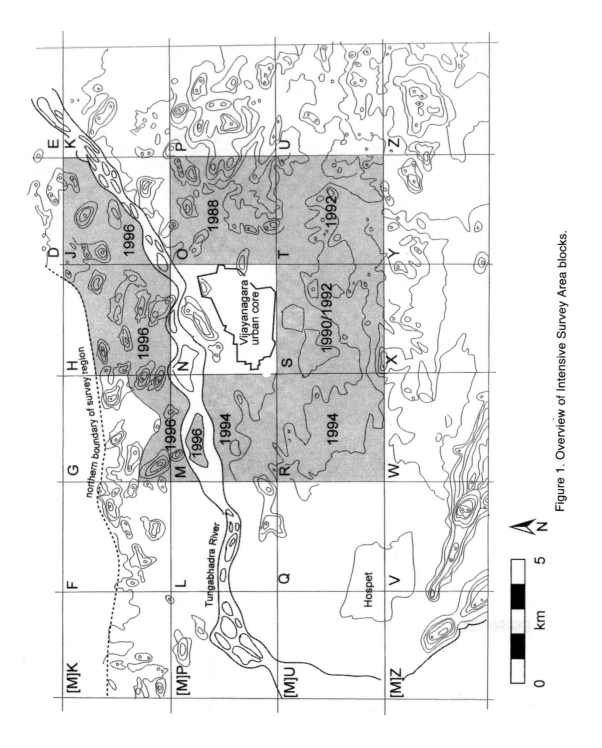

Figure 1. Overview of Intensive Survey Area blocks.

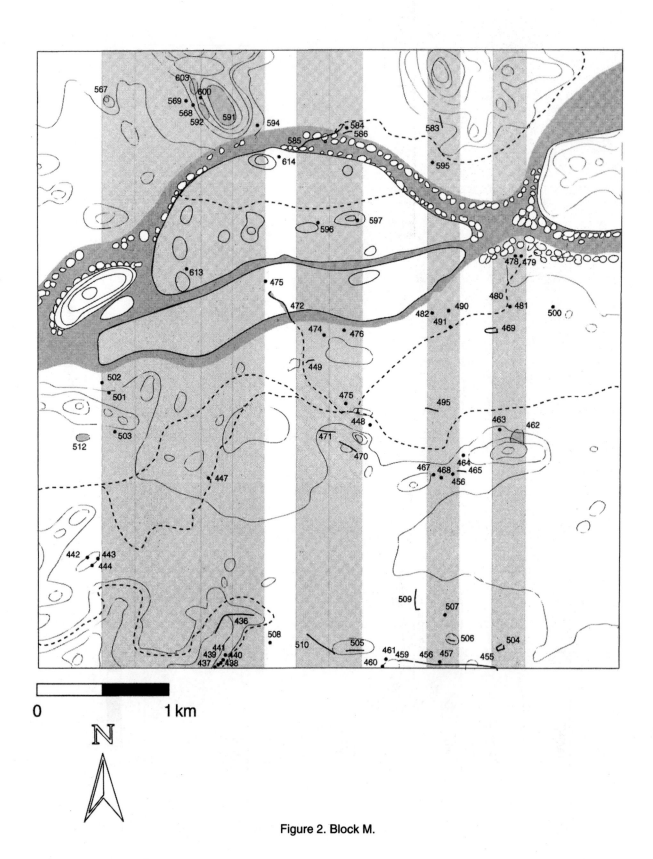

Figure 2. Block M.

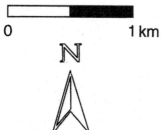

0   1 km

N

Figure 3. Block G.

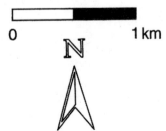

Figure 4. Block H.

Figure 5. Block J.

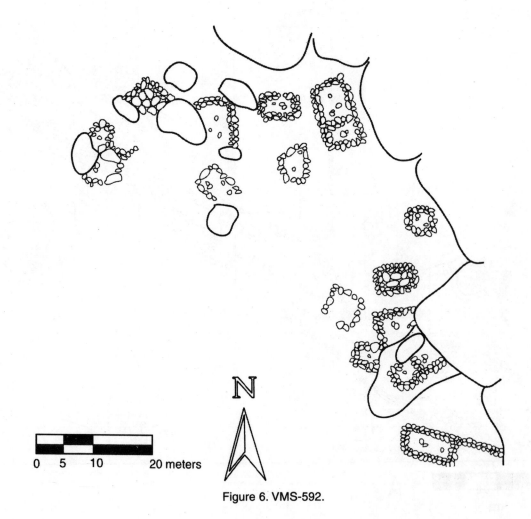

N

0   5   10   20 meters

Figure 6. VMS-592.

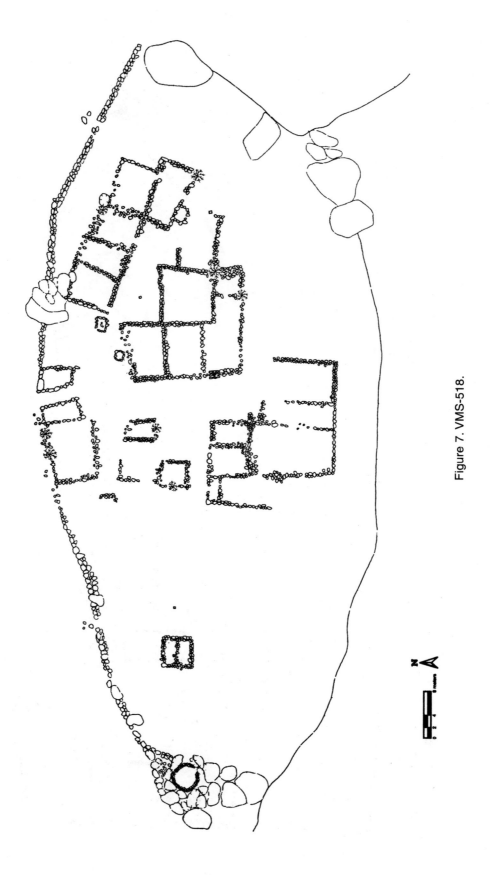

Figure 7. VMS-518.

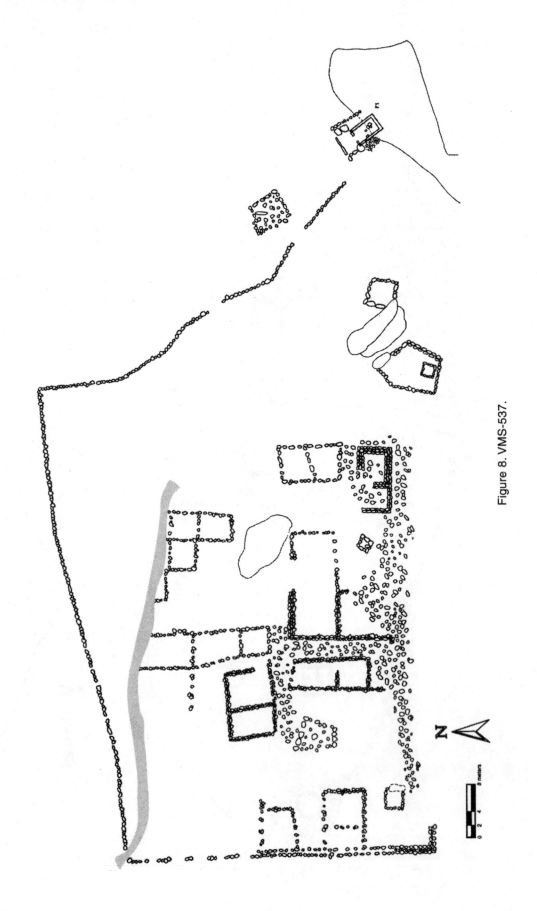

Figure 8. VMS-537.

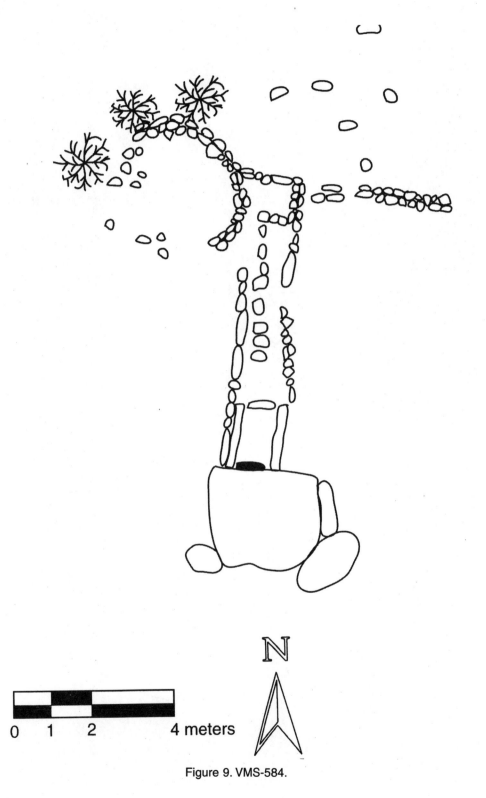

Figure 9. VMS-584.

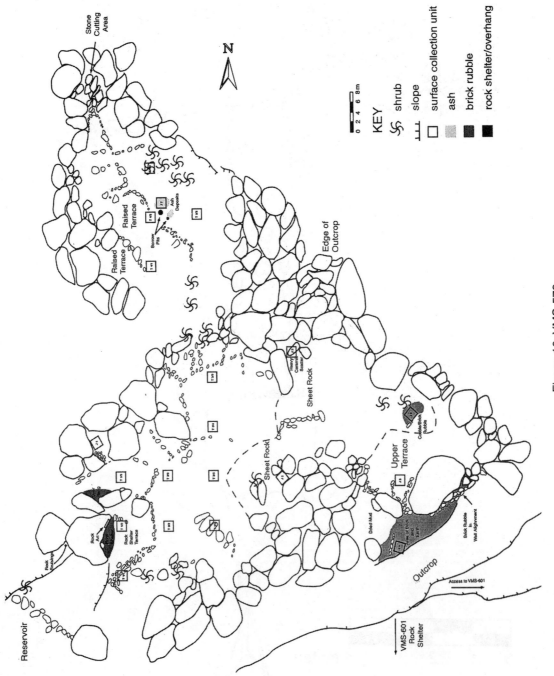

Figure 10. VMS-579.

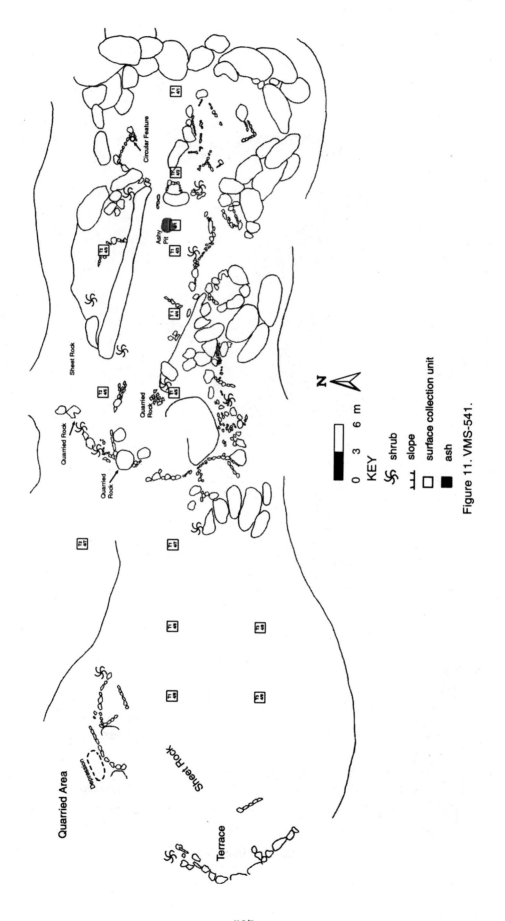

Figure 11. VMS-541.

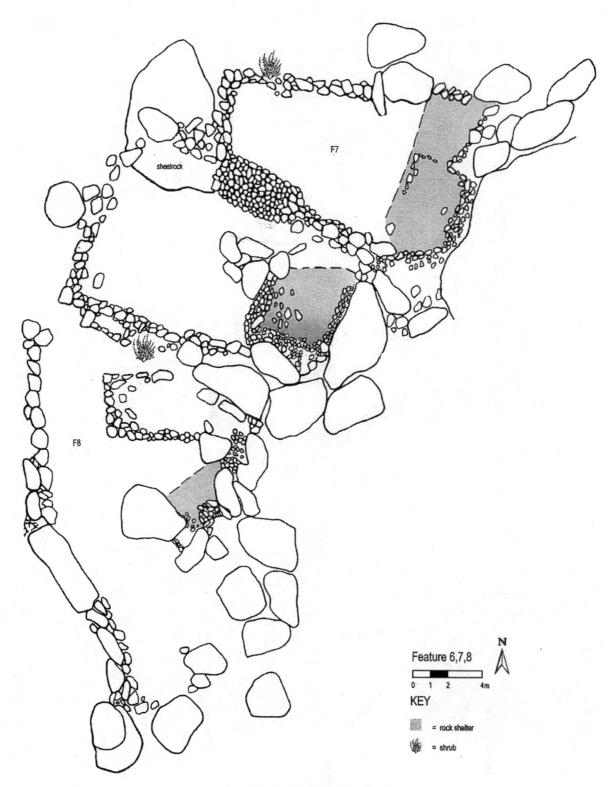

Figure 12. VMS-543.

THE VIJAYANAGARA METROPOLITAN SURVEY: OVERVIEW OF THE 1997 SEASON

Carla M. Sinopoli and Kathleen D. Morrison

Fieldwork of the Vijayanagara Metropolitan Survey (VMS) entails three components: (1) intensive survey in the eight sample blocks immediately surrounding the city core; (2) extensive survey in the remaining areas of the Vijayanagara Metropolitan Region; and (3) test excavations at several sites dating to the Vijayanagara period. In this paper, we report on our fieldwork in February-March 1997, which focused on the first two components of this research.

In addition to Professors Sinopoli and Morrison, the 1997 project participants included Robert Brubaker, Daniel M. Bass and Lynn Rainville of the University of Michigan, Jennifer L. Lundal of the University of Chicago, and Allison I. Ziff of La Crosse, WI, USA.

Intensive Survey

Survey Methodology

Intensive transect survey of a 50 per cent random sample in each of the eight blocks surrounding the Urban Core of Vijayanagara was initiated in 1988, with subsequent field seasons in 1990, 1992, 1994 and 1996. During February-March 1997 this phase of the project was fully completed. Survey was carried out in the southern portion of Block J, south of the Tungabhadra River (the northern portion of this block had been surveyed in 1996). The intensive survey covered a 50 per cent sample of the block in nine randomly selected 250-m wide sample transects (Transects 2, 5, 6, 7, 8, 11, 14, 15 and 17) (Figure 1). The transects were surveyed according to the methodology developed in previous field seasons (see

Morrison 1995 and Morrison and Sinopoli 1996). A crew of three to six individuals systematically walked each transect in a north-south orientation, with crew members spaced 20 m apart. This spacing allows recovery of even very small sites. All archaeological features identified by the survey team were noted (including small features such as isolated bedrock mortars or quarry marks that were not given site designations), and all archaeological sites were documented.

Sites identified were assigned a sequential site number and were located on the 1:25,000 base map series developed for the region; latitude and longitude locational information was recorded using a hand-held global positioning system (GPS). The VMS strategy for site recording is comprehensive, with information on each site recorded on standardized forms for eventual entry into a computerized database and Geographic Information System (GIS). Data are recorded on environmental setting (slope, vegetation, natural resources and water sources), modern land use and disturbances, artefact distributions and site plan and layout. Interpretations of site function and chronology are made. Sites are mapped and photographed in black and white and colour. Where relevant, systematic surface collections of artefacts are made. Nondiagnostic artifacts are sorted and counted in the field, while diagnostics are taken back to the field camp for more detailed morphological studies. After analysis, artefacts remain in the custody of the Karnataka Department of Archaeology and Museums and are stored in their Kamalapura facilities.

Block J Sites

The surveyed terrain of Block J is varied and encompasses much of the topographic variability evident across the Metropolitan Region. The northern boundary of the area surveyed in 1997 is the Tungabhadra River, with its many braided channels. Along the river shore, the low-lying terrain is marshy and covered by thick grasses, resulting in poor surface visibility. The Ramasagara canal emerges from the river in the eastern part of the block (Transect 13) and merges with the Turtha canal, which originated several kilometres to the west (on the far side of the Urban Core). Both of these Vijayanagara period canals remain in use today and have undergone modifications since their construction. To the south of the river are low-lying areas that are today the focus of wet agriculture (bananas, rice, sugarcane and vegetables). Several areas of high granitic outcrops are also found in the survey area, particularly in the southeastern portion of the surveyed area. These large areas of outcrops are easily accessible from the settlement of Bukkasagara and are presently the focus of intensive quarrying activities, which has no doubt resulted in the destruction or disturbance of a number of archaeological sites. Bukkasagara lies in the southeastern corner of the block. Still occupied, the town also contains several temples and a fort that date to the Vijayanagara period.

In the 1997 field season, a total of 43 archaeological sites were recorded in the southern section of Block J. These sites include a wide range of site types that span a long chronological range, from late prehistoric Iron Age or Early Historic times to Vijayanagara and post-Vijayanagara periods. In addition, four sites were recorded in Block O (to the south of Block J) and two sites were documented in Block S (the latter include VMS-258, a bastion in Kamalapura that was revisited in 1997). In Block J, sites were especially densely clustered on or along the edges of outcrop areas in the eastern third of the block. This is not surprising given that the lower-lying areas have been subject to intensive land modification related to recent agricultural activities, and were no doubt also farmed during Vijayanagara times.

In general, site density is much greater south of the river than in the portion of the block found to its north. This is probably a function of the southern zone's greater ease of access to the Vijayanagara Urban Core and its importance as a transport route linking the capital with the contemporary settlement at Kampli. There are, however, similarities between both sides of the river in site distributions, particularly in the relatively high densities of prehistoric sites identified. The numbers and kinds of sites recorded in the 1997 season are summarized in Table 1.

Vijayanagara Period Sites

Sites of the Vijayanagara period recorded in 1997 belong to a number of functional categories, including transport sites (n = 12), shrines and temples (n = 8), agricultural sites (n = 4), defensive and fortification sites (n = 3) and three sites of unknown function. In addition, the modern settlement of Bukkasagara overlays a substantial Vijayanagara period settlement of the same name. Given the considerable disturbance of the settlement site its original extent could not be documented, though its associated fort was recorded (VMS-655) and several temples within Bukkasagara were recorded in the 1988 field season (VMS-116, VMS-118, VMS-119). Summaries of sites by broad functional categories are presented below.

Transportation

Sites defining routes of movement across the Vijayanagara landscape comprise the most numerous category of sites recorded in the area surveyed in the 1997 season. Twelve transport-related sites were documented (see Table 2). Vijayanagara period roads take several forms. Sites VMS-627, VMS-640 and VMS-654 are each small sections of stone pavement, ranging from 20 to 50 m in preserved length and between 3 to 5 m in width. Site VMS-650 is a possible bridge defined by standing columns and a mounded area bordered by two parallel walls. The largest and most complex of the roads recorded was designated with two site numbers, VMS-631 and VMS-644. This raised roadbed winds around the base of an outcrop in Transects 16 and 17, in places as much as 6 to 8 m above the fields which surround the outcrop. The road bed is defined by a terraced outer wall, constructed of large unmodified and split boulders and ranges in width from 3 to 5 m. At places, one or two inner walls support the raised road surface. Some Vijayanagara quarry marks are evident on boulders in this area, though the outcrop which the road surrounds is also the site of megalithic cemetery VMS-643 and VMS-645, and the builders of the road may have taken advantage of earlier alignments and building materials in their construction.

Temples and Shrines

Eight sites classed as temples, shrines or sacred sculptures were recorded in the 1997 field season (Table 3). Two of these are located in Block O. The first, VMS-607, is a displaced structure of two male devotees with hands folded in front of them, found in a modern structure; while the second, VMS-653, is a large boulder sculpted with an image of Ganesha and with small niches that is located along the main Vijayanagara-Kampli road (Plate 1). The largest temple complex recorded in the 1997 season is VMS-630. This Shaivite temple is still in worship and has undergone many modifications since its original construction early in the Vijayanagara period, as evidenced by the early style columns with disc-shaped capitals. The temple lies near the confluence of the Turtha and Ramasagara canals and is *c.* 150 m south of the Tungabhadra River. The raised road bed discussed above (VMS-631 and VMS-644) runs near the temple. Modern *mandapas* have been constructed to the west and southeast of the temple, and a later structure abuts the original construction on the north, attesting to the long history of this complex.

Agriculture

Only four sites clearly associated with agricultural activities were recorded in the surveyed area (see Table 4), though this low number does not include the Ramasagara and Bukkasagara canals that played a major role in determining the agricultural regimes of this area which was dominated by wet farming. Perhaps most interesting of the agricultural sites documented is VMS-623, a 180-m long low reservoir embankment that spans a broad valley between two low outcrops. This earthen embankment is faced with up to eight steeply stepped courses of masonry on its southern side, and has a single sluice gate with a roughly dressed rectangular lintel. During the Vijayanagara period, the eastern end of the reservoir was breached by the Turtha canal, rendering the reservoir obsolete. In addition, a smaller masonry lined canal (VMS-625) diverged off from the Turtha canal and passed through the reservoir's defunct sluice channel. Both the Turtha canal and its feeder canal are still in use.

Defense/Fortification

Three sites recorded in the southern portion of Block J are related to Vijayanagara defensive practices (Table 5). A fourth site, VMS-648, a *mandapa* with sanctuary located atop a high outcrop in the southeast corner of the block, also no doubt had a defensive role, and afforded excellent visibility to the north and west. Site VMS-639 consists of a 61-m long alignment of up to five parallel rows of large boulders. The site lies along the northern edge of a low outcrop, north of a saddle in the outcrop that could afford easy passage across it. The linear alignments of large boulders, ranging up to 1.5 m across and 1 m high, with many set on edge, could have served to impede foot, animal and vehicle movement across the outcrop.

Site VMS-655 is a fort located on the low outcrop adjacent to the Vijayanagara period settlement of Bukkasagara (Figure 2). The 210 x 130 m fort makes opportunistic use of the hilly outcrop on which it is situated, and is borderer by segments of low, double-faced stone walls that form two contiguous enclosures around the central relatively flat terraces on top of the outcrop. The northern enclosure is located about four meters above the lower southern enclosure; access between them was through a gate (Feature 3) defined by two rectangular platforms that flank a 2-m wide paved passage. Ten circular bastions are located at irregular intervals around the site's edges; these are usually constructed on top of large boulders, and are built of smaller quarried stones than the wall segments; which they may postdate. The upper enclosure of the fort contains a three-roomed structure (Feature 1) and a plastered cistern (Feature 2), as well as a crude stairway that extends up to the boulder ridge that defines the site's northern boundary. No surface features were evident in the southern enclosure.

Sites of Unknown Function

Table 6 lists four sites of unknown function recorded in 1997. These include sites that consist of displaced architectural elements of the Vijayanagara period (VMS-605), as well as small walls or terraces of unknown date.

Prehistoric and Early Historic Sites

Karnataka's Bellary and Raichur Districts are widely known for their many Neolithic, Iron Age (Megalithic) and Early Historic period sites. Numerous sites in this region have been documented by many generations of Indian archaeologists (e.g. Nagaraja Rao 1965 and 1971, Allchin 1963, Ansari and Nagaraja Rao 1969, Majumdar and Rajaguru 1966, among others). Although the primary focus of the VMS has been to document sites of the Vijayanagara period, when non-Vijayanagara sites (both earlier and later) are identified, they are recorded and documented according to the same protocols developed for Vijayanagara period remains. In general, prehistoric sites tend to be located close to the Tungabhadra River, often on outcrop areas in sight of the river. Given the proximity to the river of the 1997 VMS sample transects, it is therefore not surprising that several prehistoric sites were identified. The fourteen prehistoric sites recorded include thirteen found in Block J and one (VMS-604) in Block O; site types are summarized in Table 7. Most common are isolated megaliths. These include linear cairns, stone circles and other alignments, and "crack features" (locations where rocks have been wedged into cracks in outcrops to define mortuary spaces). VMS-634 located in Transect 11 is a *c.* 1.8 ha settlement area (Figure 3). The

site is located in a relatively flat open space amid an outcrop. Portions of the site have been disturbed by modern quarrying and ash mining, and its original extent cannot be determined. Surface densities of ceramics (Black and Red Ware, polished black ware, polished red ware) range from moderate to high; other materials observed on the surface and in pitted include bone, iron ore and slag, ground stone and a bead. The site was mapped and eighteen 1 x 1 m surface collection units were laid out systematically, along north-south transects that were spaced at 30 m intervals (with collection units along each transect spaced at 15 m intervals). Diagnostic collections of ceramics were also made for morphological study. VMS-633 is a rock-shelter located just to the northeast of the settlement site and associated with it; VMS-637 a small embankment wall at the edge of a valley to the south of the settlement may also have been associated with the prehistoric settlement.

Another interesting prehistoric remains recorded in 1997 include sites VMS-643, VMS-645 and VMS-647. Although in parts discontinuous (and hence given discrete site numbers), these three sites actually probably once comprised part of a single extensive megalithic cemetery that extended across two low outcrops and the low-lying area between them (though any remains that may once have existed in this lower area have been destroyed by later agricultural activities). Mortuary features in these sites include numerous stone alignments, including stone circles ranging from *c.* 2.5 to 10 m in diameter, rectangular alignments and a boundary wall that runs along the western base of the outcrop (Site VMS-645). These alignments are extensive, found in widely spaced flat areas along the outcrop, often with gaps of 30-40 m between them. A single linear cairn megalith was noted in site VMS-645.

Extensive Survey

A second component of the VMS is the extensive survey that has been carried out in the area beyond the eight blocks that have been subject to intensive random sample survey. In this outer portion of the Metropolitan Region our focus has not been to document every archaeological site. Instead, in this area survey has focused on particular kinds of sites or regions that are of particular interest to the broader goals of project members. Such focused research has included Morrison's ongoing study of the network of irrigation reservoirs of the Daroji system on the southeastern edge of the Metropolitan Region. With a few exceptions, site numbers in the extensive survey area were arbitrarily begun at VMS-1000, so as not to overlap with numbers with numbers assigned in the intensively surveyed area.

In 1997, extensive survey focused on sites related to Vijayanagara's defensive infrastructure and on locating the defended boundaries of the Metropolitan Region. This work was carried out under the supervision of Robert Brubaker as part of his doctoral dissertation research. In 1997, we documented 38 sites of diverse types associated with bounding and securing the protection of the Metropolitan Region. These include hilltop *mandapas* or watch posts, fortification walls, alignments of large stone boulders (horse-stones) spread across valleys to impede horse or cart movement, and forts, typically located atop high outcrops in areas with excellent visibility of surrounding terrain. Sites recorded in 1997 are summarized in Table 8.

The diverse defensive sites documented are strategically placed both to protect and monitor possible routes of transport into the Vijayanagara capital, and to create a network of sites that are visually linked, a not in-considerable challenge in the highly dissected landscape of the Metropolitan Region. Although the modern Tungabhadra Reservoir (to the west of Hospet) has destroyed many sites on the western and southwestern bound-aries of the region, traces of fortification walls remain along the Chitradurga road to indicate their former location. The VMS has also been successful in identifying sites on the north, northeast, east and southeast edges of the Metropolitan Region that define the defended boundaries of the capital. These are not the seven concentric rings of walls reported by Niccolo Conti, a fifteenth-century Italian visitor to Vijayanagara, but instead consist of a number of strategically placed walls, hilltop forts, watchtowers, and other features that made effective use of the rugged landscape, incorporating and spanning high hills.

Artefact Analysis

Ceramics collected at Vijayanagara period sites are analysed according to criteria established by Sinopoli (1993). All shards are sorted by ware and colour, and a range of attributes are measured on rim shards, to allow for functional and temporal classification. In 1997 approximately 134 rims from nine sites of the Vijayanagara period were measured. Shards from prehistoric sites are also subject to detailed analysis; body shards are weighed, and information on surface treatment and surface colour is recorded. Diagnostic shards are measured and drawn. More than 3,000 body shards and 340 rims from nine prehistoric sites were documented. Analysis of the ceramic data is currently underway.

Dr D.V. Gogte of Deccan College, Pune, an expert in archaeochemistry and ancient metallurgy, visited Vijayanagara for a brief period to advise on some of the metallurgical sites identified in previous seasons. Gogte will be conducting chemical analyses of small samples of slag, bloom and tuyeres from some of these sites.

Ethnoarchaeological Research

As part of our interest in craft production, in 1997 we continued our study of contemporary pottery producing workshops in the Metropolitan Region. Because of the brevity of our field season, only one workshop was visited. This workshop is located on the eastern edge of the village of Venkatapur to the northeast of Vijayanagara. A single adult male potter, his wife and children all assist in pottery manufacture and distribution in the workshop. As part of the ethnoarchaeological research, Sinopoli interviewed the male potter (his wife was visiting relatives) and observed him at work. Photographs of the workshop area were taken, and a sketch map prepared. Approximately two dozen vessels were purchased for more detailed analysis. A series of measurements were taken on each vessel, and each was drawn. These data will be combined with data collected in previous seasons and in the subsequent Fall 1997 season in order to examine inter-workshop differences in production technology and final products. Such work will be useful in developing models for the study of ceramic variability during the Vijayanagara period.

Acknowledgements

We acknowledge with gratitude the Government of India and the Archaeological Survey of India for permission to conduct this research. Our thanks also to the Karnataka Department of Archaeology and Museums, and particularly to Dr D.V. Devaraj, Director, and Dr C.S. Patil, Deputy Director, and T.M. Manjunathaiah. Our most sincere gratitude to the American Institute of Indian Studies, and its Director-General and President Dr Pradeep Mehendiratta for supporting our research. Thanks also to Suri and Raghavan of the AIIS for their kind help.

Research of the VMS is supported by grants from the National Science Foundation (Morrison), the Wenner Gren Foundation for Anthropological Research and National Endowment for the Humanities (Sinopoli), the George F. Dales Foundation, the James B. Griffin Fund, Museum of Anthropology University of Michigan and the Department of Anthropology, University of Michigan (Brubaker). The University of Chicago has provided additional support to Morrison, and the University of Michigan has provided additional support to Sinopoli.

Works Cited

Allchin, F.R., 1963, *Neolithic Cattle Keepers of South India*, Cambridge University Press, Cambridge.

Ansari, Z.D. and M.S. Nagaraja Rao, 1969, *Excavations at Sangankallu, 1964-65: Early Neolithic House at Bellary*, Deccan College Postgraduate and Research Institute, Poona.

Majumdar, G.G. and S.N. Rajaguru, 1966, *Ashmound Excavations at Kupgal*, Deccan College Postgraduate and Research Institute, Poona.

Morrison, K.D., 1995, *Fields of Victory: Vijayanagara and the Course of Intensification*, Contributions of the University of California Archaeological Research Facility No. 53, Berkeley.

Morrison, K.D. and C.M. Sinopoli, 1996, Archaeological Survey in the Vijayanagara Metropolitan Region: 1990. In, *Vijayanagara: Progress of Research, 1988-1991*, edited by D.V. Devaraj and C.S. Patil, pp. 59-73, Directorate of Archaeology and Museums, Mysore.

Nagaraja Rao, M.S., 1965, *Stone Age Hill Dwellers of Tekkalakota*, Deccan College Postgraduate and Research Institute, Poona.

———, 1971, *Protohistoric Cultures of the Tungabhadra Valley (A report on the Hallur Excavations)*, Karnatak University, Dharwar.

Sinopoli, C.M., 1993, *Pots and Palaces: The Earthenware Ceramics of the Noblemen's Quarter of Vijayanagara*, Manohar and American Institute of Indian Studies, New Delhi.

Table 1. Intensive Survey: Sites Recorded

Site	Block	Transect	Description
VMS-604	O	5	Rock-shelter with megalith
VMS-605	J	6	Structural debris
VMS-606	J	8	Structural remains with prehistoric pottery
VMS-607	O	13	Sculpture
VMS-608	J	14	Wall
VMS-609	J	14	Road segment/stairway
VMS-610	J	14	Terraced platform
VMS-615	J	14	Megalith and associated features
VMS-616	J	13	Rock-shelter with megalith
VMS-617	J	14	Rock-shelter with megalith and associated features
VMS-618	J	13	Terrace
VMS-619	J	14	Megalithic stone circle and associated features
VMS-620	J	14	Megalithic features
VMS-621	J	14	Megalithic features
VMS-622	J	14	Circular enclosure
VMS-623	J	15	Reservoir
VMS-624	J	15	Wall/road wall
VMS-625	J	15	Canal: masonry faced
VMS-626	J	15	Ramasagara canal
VMS-627	J	15	Road segment
VMS-628	J	15	Durga shrine
VMS-629	J	15	Road segment and horse tie
VMS-630	J	15-16	Temple complex
VMS-631	J	16	Road
VMS-632	J	16	Shrine
VMS-633	J	11	Rock-shelter with ceramics and rock art
VMS-634	J	11	Neolithic/Iron Age settlement
VMS-635	J	12-13	Road
VMS-636	J	13	Well
VMS-637	J	11	Embankment/reservoir
VMS-638	J	11	Platform
VMS-639	J	11	Stone alignments (horse-stones)
VMS-640	J	17	Road
VMS-641	J	17	Shrine: pecked boulder (trident)
VMS-642	J	17	Shrine: Hanuman
VMS-643	J	17	Mortuary site
VMS-644	J	17	Road
VMS-645	J	17	Megalithic mortuary site
VMS-646	J	17	Terrace wall and artifact scatter
VMS-647	J	17-18	Megalithic mortuary site/enclosures
VMS-648	J	18	*Mandapa*
VMS-649	J	17	Megaliths
VMS-650	J	16	Standing columns and walls (transport?)
VMS-651	S	18	Gate (in wall VMS-123)
VMS-652	O	12-13	Road Wall
VMS-653	O	2	Ganesha sculpture on boulder
VMS-654	J	17	Road segment
VMS-655	J	16	Fort (Bukkasagara)

Table 2. Sites Associated with Transport

Site	Block	Transect	Description
VMS-608	J	14	Single course wall of large boulders (14.5 x 1 m) located along the base of an outcrop, may define transport route, associated with VMS-609.
VMS-609	J	14	Stairway and cleared road segment (*c.* 18 x 1.5 m) extending up an outcrop to the northwest. Stairs are constructed of medium granite blocks, sheet-rock above them is worn and polished.
VMS-624	J	15	40-m long, single course wall located along the edge of an outcrop, incorporating large outcropping boulders, perhaps defining a transport route.
VMS-627	J	15	20 x 3-m long road segment along southern base of an outcrop; formal pavement of unmodified heavily worn medium to large boulders and area of worn sheet-rock to south.
VMS-629	J	15	Road segment (96 m long) defined by two single course walls of large unmodified and split boulders, located along the edge of an outcrop area between Bukkasagara and the Turtha canal. A horse tie is pecked into the outcrop, *c.* 18 m from the southern end of the site.
VMS-631	J	16	1.25-km long road wall that winds around the base of an outcrop above an area of irrigated fields. The road is constructed of up to 8 courses of large unmodified boulders, many of which may have derived from the nearby megalithic cemetery sites VMS-543, VMS-545 and VMS-547. The date of this site is unknown; it may be a Vijayanagara period road following an earlier route or boundary wall.
VMS-635	J	12-13	250-m long x 27-m wide road segment paralleling the western edge of an outcrop. The road is defined by parallel double-faced walls constructed of one-two courses of unmodified medium boulders with earthen fill.
VMS-640	J	17	50 x 3 m road segment consisting of heavily worn pavement of small-large split stones; bordered on both sides by natural granite boulders, some of which may have been displaced to clear the route.
VMS-644	J	16-17	350 x 5 m road segment, continuation of VMS-631, similarly follows along the edge of a large outcrop.
VMS-650	J	16	Possible bridge, consisting of 2 parallel three-course high north-south walls joined by a raised rubble fill and spaced 4.5 m apart. At the north end are three Vijayanagara columns. Located south of the Ramasagara canal and north of road VMS-644, with which it may be associated.
VMS-652	O	12-13	Road wall parallel to the modern Kamalapura-Venkatapur road, with single-face wall construction of 1-2 courses of large unmodified and split boulders.
VMS-654	J	17	28 x 8-m long paved road segment; associated with VMS-640 to its south.

Table 3. Shrines and Temples Recorded in 1997

Site	Block	Transect	Description
VMS-607	O	13	Sculpted panel (0.5 x 0.6 m) of two male devotees with folded hands; in modern structure.
VMS-628	J	15	Sculptures beneath a large overhanging boulder, include small (0.3 x 0.4 m) image of Durga slaying the buffalo demon, and *naga* stone. Currently in worship.
VMS-630	J	15-16	Heavily modified temple complex located near the confluence of the Turtha and Ramasagara canals. Still in worship, though original construction dates to the early Vijayanagara period; Shaivite.
VMS-632	J	17	2 by 2 column *mandapa* located atop a high outcrop; no images present, but panel from lotus medallion ceiling lies nearby.
VMS-641	J	17	Trident image (0.9 m high x 0.4 m wide) pecked into a large boulder along the modern Bukkasagara-Kampli road.
VMS-642	J	17	Small Hanuman image (0.7 m high x 0.4 m wide) sculpted on large boulder along modern Bukkasagara-Kampli road, enclosed by modern structure. Sculpture is consistent with Vijayanagara period style.
VMS-648	J	18	North-facing 4 by 3 column *mandapa* located on a 38 x 10 m terrace on high outcrop overlooking the Bukkasagara-Kampli road; sanctuary in northeast corner; may also have had defensive function given excellent visibility from this locale.
VMS-653 (Plate 1)	O	2	Ganesha sculpture and seven small niches pecked on to 3 x 2 m boulder.

Table 4. Agricultural Sites Recorded in 1997

Site	Block	Transect	Description
VMS-618	J	13	25 x 22 m natural sandy terrace in outcrop area; bordered by a low wall of roughly piled cobbles on three sides.
VMS-623	J	15	Reservoir embankment, 180 x 15 m, spanning a broad colluvial valley between two low outcrops; was superseded by Turtha canal, probably during Vijayanagara times.
VMS-625	J	15	Masonry faced canal, *c.* 130 x 3 m, feeder channel from the Turtha canal; passes through the defunct sluice channel of reservoir VMS-623 which it replaced; faced with large unmodified rounded boulders and split blocks, of up to 8 courses.
VMS-646	J	17	Terrace wall and artifact scatter; 48-m long terrace wall in a low dry-farmed valley between sites VMS-643 and VMS-645. Terrain is *c.* 1 m higher to east of the four course wall then to the west.

Table 5. Sites Associated with Defense and Fortifications Recorded in 1997

Site	Block	Transect	Description
VMS-610	J	14	4 x 5 m platform forming a small terrace on an outcrop overlooking a flat area to the west. unknown date.
VMS-639	J	11	Stone alignments (horse-stones?), 61 x 10 m, up to 5 parallel alignments of large boulders oriented parallel to the base of an outcrop near a saddle across the outcrop. Constructed of large unmodified rounded boulders (up to 1.2 m high), many set on edge. Rows are spaced 1.0-1.5 m apart.
VMS-655 (Figure 2)	J	16	210 x 130 m fort located on outcrop overlooking Bukkasagara settlement; fortification walls link large boulders along outcrop; 10 circular bastions spaced around perimeters of site. Several rectangular structures are found on two level terraces within the site, as is a large cistern. The southern lower terrace and northern upper terrace are linked by a large gate.

Table 6. Sites of Unknown Function Recorded in 1997

Site	Block	Transect	Description
VMS-605	J	6	Structural remains, Vijayanagara period architectural elements incorporated into modern structures, original functions unknown.
VMS-622	J	14	Large semi-circular, single-course wall constructed at the northern edge of a large outcrop; 50 x 25 m, constructed of a single course of large unmodified stones; near prehistoric site VMS-621, date unknown.
VMS-636	J	13	Small (6 x 4 m) informal wall terrace constructed of large unmodified and split boulders situated in an uncultivated flat area; located 20 m to the west of road VMS-635, with which it may have been associated.
VMS-638	J	11	4.5 x 4 m platform in irrigated area, 1 element high.

Table 7. Prehistoric and Early Historic Sites Recorded in the 1997 Season

Site	Block	Transect	Description
VMS-604	O	5	Rock-shelter with megalith
VMS-606	J	8	Structural remains with prehistoric pottery
VMS-615	J	14	Megalith and associated features
VMS-616	J	13	Rock-shelter with megalith
VMS-617	J	14	Rock-shelter with megalith and associated features
VMS-619	J	14	Megalithic stone circle and associated features
VMS-620	J	14	Megalithic features
VMS-621	J	14	Megalithic features
VMS-633	J	11	Rock-shelter with ceramics and rock-art
VMS-634	J	11	Neolithic/Iron Age settlement (Figure 3)
VMS-637	J	11	Embankment/reservoir (19 x 5 m) bounding southern end of large internal drainage basin in the valley to the south of settlement VMS-634
VMS-643	J	17	Mortuary site
VMS-645	J	17	Megalithic mortuary site
VMS-647	J	17-18	Megalithic mortuary site/enclosures
VMS-649	J	17	Megaliths

Table 8. Extensive Survey Sites Recorded in 1997

Site	Block	Description
VMS-1020	[O]W	Daroji fort
VMS-1025		Walls north of Sultanpur
VMS-1042	[M]P	Fort on Tungabhadra island
VMS-1043	K	Hilltop *mandapa*/watch post
VMS-1044	K	Horse-stones
VMS-1045	K	Fortification wall
VMS-1046	P	Fortification wall
VMS-1047	P	Fortification wall
VMS-1048	K/P	Settlement
VMS-1049	K	Road segment (east of VMS-VMS-1045)
VMS-1050	K	Cobble wall west of VMS-VMS-1045
VMS-1051	K	Walls in pass
VMS-1052	K	Wall segment north of VMS-VMS-1044
VMS-1053	K	Ramasagara fort
VMS-1054	P	Walls atop outcrop
VMS-1055	K	Wall
VMS-1056	[O]A	Kampli fort
VMS-1057	[N]D	Hire Jantakallu fort
VMS-1058	[N]D	Hire Jantakallu shrine
VMS-1059	[O]A	Chikka Jantakallu fort
VMS-1060	[O]R	Fort (w of Daroji fort)
VMS-1061	[O]R	Walls, at end of valley east of VMS-370
VMS-1062	[T]M	Lingadahalli bastion and tank
VMS-1063	[T]H/N	Fortification wall, across pass northwest of Kodalu
VMS-1064	[T]H	Fortification wall, across pass north of Kodalu
VMS-1065	[T]H	Fortification wall, across pass northeast of Kodalu
VMS-1066	[T]H/J	Fortification wall, long "Sultanpur" wall
VMS-1067	[T]J	Fortification wall, northeast of VMS-1066
VMS-1068	[T]D	Fortification wall, across valley, 50 m east of Kudatini ash mound
VMS-1069	[T]D	Fortification wall, across valley, north of Kudatini ash mound
VMS-1070	[T]J	Fortification wall
VMS-1071	[T]C	Fortification wall, across gap east-northeast of Toranagallu
VMS-1072	[T]C	Fortification wall, across gap east of Toranagallu
VMS-1073	[T]D	Fortification wall, running northwest-southeast across gap south of Suji Gudda
VMS-1074	[M]Z	Fortification wall, southwest of Hospet
VMS-1075	[M]T	Fort, Shivapur
VMS-1076	[M]U	Bastion and inscription, southwest of Ningapur
VMS-1077	[T]C	Fort and shrine, Toranagallu

Note: Block designation not yet determined for some sites.

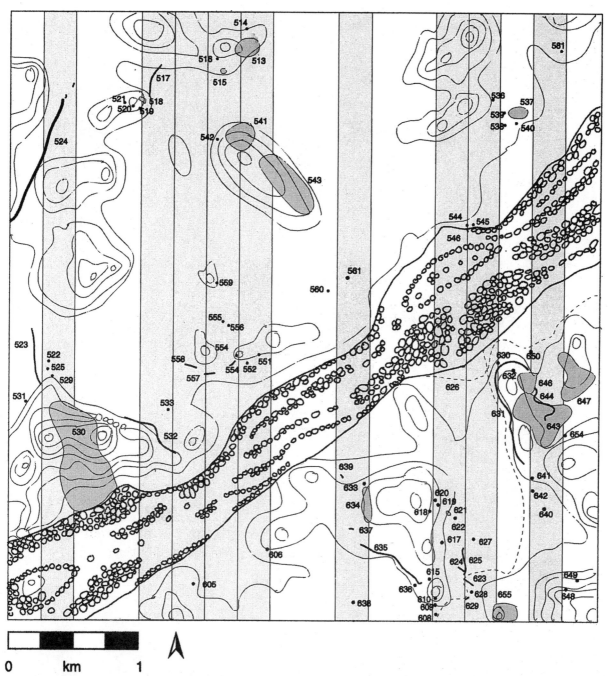

Figure 1. Block J, shaded areas indicate surveyed transects.

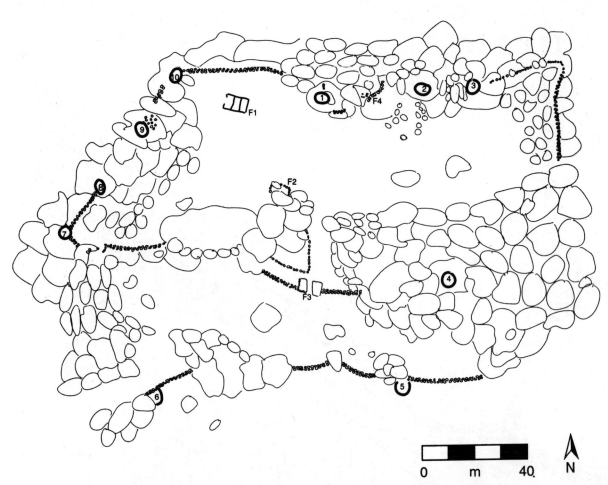

Figure 2. VMS-655, hilltop fort above Bukkasagara, with bastions numbered.

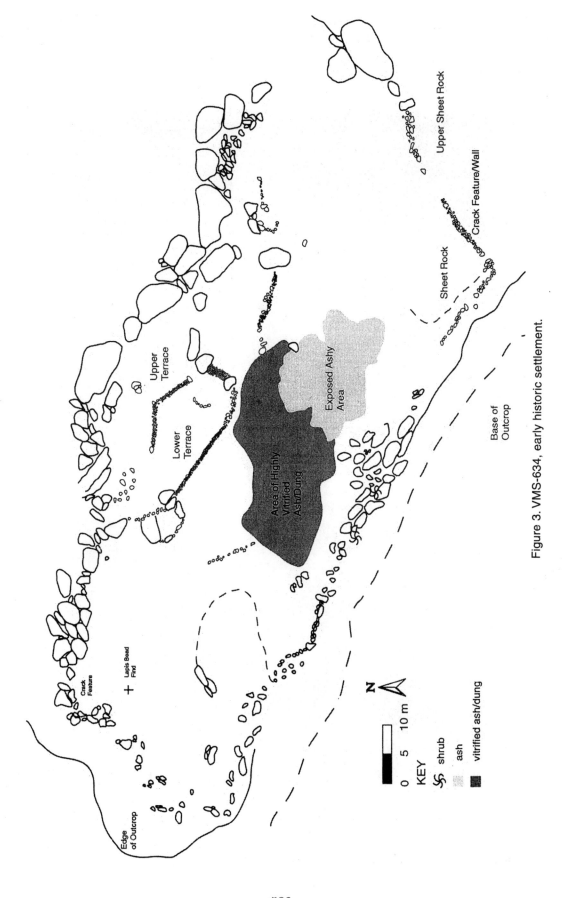

Figure 3. VMS-634, early historic settlement.

Plate 1. VMS-653, Ganesha image on boulder along road.

VMS-365: A WALLED SETTLEMENT SITE

Carla M. Sinopoli

Archaeological survey in the Vijayanagara Metropolitan Region has resulted in the discovery of many previously unreported sites of the Vijayanagara period (see contributions by Morrison and Sinopoli, this volume). These include a diversity of functional types – e.g. terraces, reservoir embankments, workshops, temples, shrines, fortifications (see Brubaker, this volume) and settlements – attesting to the intensive and varied use of the Vijayanagara urban landscape. In this paper I report on an interrelated complex of sites recorded during the 1992 seasons of the Vijayanagara Metropolitan Survey (VMS): a Vijayanagara period, walled settlement (VMS-365) and associated reservoir embankment (VMS-349), and several associated walls (VMS-345, VMS-348, VMS-353) (Figure 1).

Settlement sites in the Metropolitan Region include isolated structures and, more commonly, multi-household villages and towns. Such aggregated settlement sites are predominantly clustered within the shadows of the outer ring of fortifications protecting the city core (e.g. the settlement of Kamalapura VMS-257-59 and the late Vijayanagara period settlement around the Pattabhirama temple). Other settlements are found along major roadways leading into the fortified core (e.g. Bukkasagara, VMS-101, and Venkatapur, VMS-2). A small number of identified settlements occurs in areas more distant from both the Urban Core and major Vijayanagara roads (e.g. VMS-35-37; Means 1991). Site VMS-365, the settlement reported on here, belongs to this last category of aggregated urban sites (Figure 2).

Site VMS-365, known locally as Mittana Hanuman (Sandals of Hanuman) or Chuppan Gudda (Pointed Hill; Balasubramanyam, personal communications), is located in a gentle sloping area immediately to the east of massive outcrop hill. The site incorporates sheet-rock and outcropping boulders as well as lower-lying open spaces. This was a comparatively small settlement, with a residential area of approximately 2 ha. The region is presently an area of dry farming and herding, though the settlement itself was constructed in a non-arable zone. A Vijayanagara period image has been placed in a modern shrine at the eastern edge of the settlement's core. Modern foot and cart paths skirt the site, and some recent stone quarrying has occurred in the area.

Village Plan (VMS-365)

The settlement complex consists of four main zones of construction: (1) a series of long walls that line the northern and eastern face of the large outcrop to the west of the settlement; (2) to the northwest of the major area of settlements, an unenclosed area of long double-faced walls and several rectangular structures; (3) an area of large walled enclosures and a stone and earth embankment; and (4) the core of the settlement, enclosed within circular walls and containing densely packed rubble wall structures (Figures 1 and 3).

Area 1

A large complex of discontinuous walls surrounds the base of the northern face of the outcrop, including sites VMS-345, VMS-348, VMS-353 and VMS-353 (the southern face of the outcrop was not explored). These walls or pairs of walls were traced for a considerable distance. VMS-345 was traced for 750 m, VMS-348 for 260 m, VMS-352 for 16 m and VMS-353 for 170 m. They are all constructed of large unmodified angular or rounded boulders with irregular coursing, and range from one to five courses in height. In some areas, the walls are single-faced and serve as low retaining walls for narrow terraces 1 to 2-m wide. Two faces are visible in other areas. These walls, which skirt the outcrop hill, most likely defined raised pathways or transport routes that ran along the base of the hill. Such routes would have been especially important during the rainy season, when the low-lying valley to the north would have been difficult to traverse (in fact, much of the area was water logged well into the dry season). Although the walls have clearly been in place for some time, and are likely contemporary with the village site, modern footpaths still run along the top of walls VMS-345, VMS-348 and VMS-353.

Area 2

The second zone of construction is located to the northwest of walled core of the settlement. This is a relatively flat area defined by sheet-rock and outcrop. The area is surrounded by terrace and enclosure walls, typically constructed of very large (more than a metre across) unmodified rounded boulders. The walls range from 1.0 to 1.5 m in width and often have two faces. In several areas, the walls are only a few metres long, and span areas between natural outcropping boulders, forming small rectangular enclosures or structures.

Ten rectangular structures are found in this area, with more fragmentary remains indicating the presence of at least three additional structures. The structures are constructed of small to medium unmodified stones (30 to 60 cm across). In all cases, only one course is preserved, suggesting that these were foundation courses for a less durable superstructure. Several of the structures were internally subdivided, with a main rectangular chamber, and one or more subsidiary rooms (perhaps for storage) (Plate 1). The structures range in size

from *c.* 5 x 5 m to *c.* 5 x 11 m. Very few artefacts are visible on the surface in this area. A circular stone mortar carved onto a large slab was noted near one of the structures.

Area 3

Located immediately to the southeast of Area 2, Area 3 consists of several large enclosure walls, one possible structure, and a small embankment spanning a gully. This area is characterized by more open expanses than Areas 2 or 4, and is presently being farmed. Some of the walls in this area are recent field walls, or possibly, recently modified older walls. The enclosure walls are constructed of medium to large angular unmodified boulders with up to six courses preserved in some areas. Coursing is irregular with no chinking.

The small stone embankment on the eastern side of Area 3 is oriented approximately east-west and spans an erosion channel that slopes down from south to north. The embankment is breached and no longer functions to retain water. The embankment stands approximately 1.2-m high, with its southern face supported by up to five courses of unmodified medium to large (30 to 90 cm) boulders. Immediately to the north of the embankment is an area of outcropping sheet-rock. This suggests that this construction was not intended to feed water to downslope fields, but rather served to retain water or control runoff.

High densities of earthenware ceramics and scattered ashy deposits are found in the ploughed fields within the enclosure walls, indicating a probable midden zone. Some low linear mounds are also present, and appear to mark the location of buried walls. Area 3 is bounded in the south by a long east-west wall. Although parts of this wall appear to be original, other segments are recent and cut into structures in the settlement core.

Area 4

The main area of settlement is approximately 140 x 90 m in dimension and is enclosed within a massive, roughly circular enclosure wall. The wall abuts and incorporates the granite hill to the south of the settlement, and extends to the western edge of reservoir VMS-349 in the east. The enclosure wall is quite substantial: 1 to 2-m wide and double-faced with earth infill. A rectangular enclosure (perhaps for livestock?) extends southward from the southern face of the wall on a level area of the stone outcrop.

A large number of rubble mounds and platforms are found within the enclosure wall, with numerous wall segments visible. For the most part, construction is of small to medium unmodified angular stones, although a number of larger modified blocks with Vijayanagara quarry marks is present. There is a considerable amount of rubble and wall fall in the area, and it is not possible to easily discern the plans of structures. A plaster surface is visible in one structure in the northwest quadrant of the settlement core. It is elevated about 60 cm above the lowermost walls of this structure, attesting to the erosion and disturbance that has occurred here. The plaster flooring is laid on a 10-cm thick bed of small pebbles and mortar. A ceramic water pipe was visible on one of the southern platforms.

A modern structure containing a Vijayanagara period Anjaneya Hanuman image is located in a small walled enclosure in the northeast quadrant of Area 4. The shrine is built on a 1.2-m high platform. Although the platform is recently constructed, it incorporates some Vijayanagara period moulding pieces and quarried slabs. The Hanuman image, brightly painted in red and green, is 2.25-m tall, 1.50-m across and 0.20-m deep (Plate 2). A deep pit is located to the east of the shrine and may mark the location of a well. Five *naga* stones are located along the western edge of the pit.

Approximately 40 m to the south of the shrine are several square columnar slabs, with quarry marks. Two of these are inscribed with a small *lingam* below a crescent sun or moon. No other images or inscriptions were observed, and in general, few artefacts are visible in the main settlement area. This is not surprising, given the substantial wall fall and thick grasses in the area. No mortars were noted, although several handstone fragments and grinding slabs were observed.

Reservoir Embankment (VMS-349)

Approximately 200 m south of the walled village is a long reservoir embankment, with a single preserved sluice gate (Figure 4). The reservoir served to capture seasonal runoff from the hills to its south, and channel it through one or more sluices to agricultural field to its north. The earth and stone embankment is approximately 300-m long and 20-m wide, and has been breached on both its west and eastern ends. The embankment stands approximately 8-m tall. Ten to twelve courses of medium to large unmodified boulders (*c.* 50 to 100 cm) are visible on the stepped southern face of the embankment. The earthen face on the north ranges from 10 to 25 m in width. The partial remains of a single sluice gate are found near the embankment's midpoint. It is constructed of two square columns, spaced 1.6 m apart. The lintel and cross-slabs are not *in situ*, although fallen slabs lie nearby.

Artefacts

As noted above, the visibility of ceramic and other artefacts varies widely across the settlement area. Highest surface densities are found in the agricultural fields in Area 3, and it is here that a surface collection of diagnostic ceramics (rims and decorated body shards) was conducted. All diagnostic shards were drawn and measured according to criteria developed in the analysis of ceramics from Vijayanagara's Urban Core (Sinopoli 1986 and 1993). A total of 84 diagnostic shards were sorted into general rim categories (Table 1, Figures 5 and 6).

The relative frequencies of rim and vessel forms are similar to overall ceramic distributions in the Vijayanagara Urban Core. Restricted vessels (jars) outnumber unrestricted vessels (bowls) by more than six to one, and within the restricted vessel category, flange rim forms predominate. Virtually no shards of clearly modern forms were collected in this area; instead the ceramics indicate a clear Vijayanagara period date. Decorative motifs, including stamped motifs, are identical to those found in the Vijayanagara Urban Core. Although most of the shards collected on the surface of the ploughed fields were quite fragmentary, general vessel form could be determined for most. The vessels have been classified into broad vessel-use or functional categories (Sinopoli 1993). It must be noted that this was not a systematic ceramic collection, and therefore the ratios discussed here are not necessarily representative of vessel form frequencies in the site overall. Nonetheless, attempts were made to collect the full range of forms visible on the surface and to collect an unbiased sample. Few non-ceramic artefacts were observed in the area, though one small soft stone (steatite) bowl fragment was collected.

Unrestricted vessels include five shallow bowls and six "other bowls"; no oil lamps were recovered. The shallow bowls are particularly important, as these small round-based vessels are believed to be diagnostic of the Vijaya-nagara period. The bowls collected at VMS-365 had relatively large mean diametres, with shallow bowls averaging 24.4 cm. This is significantly larger than mean vessel diameter of comparable forms within the Urban Core, where shallow bowls averaged 18.02 cm (Sinopoli 1993). With only five shallow bowls from VMS-365, it is difficult to draw any firm conclusions from this difference.

The category "restricted vessels" incorporates a variety of rim and vessel form categories (see Table 2). They have been divided into six functional, or "vessel-use" categories (RV1-RV6), including small serving vessels, medium food preparation vessels, large food preparation vessels and small, medium and large storage or transport vessels. Ratios of restricted vessels forms at VMS-365 differ somewhat from their distributions in the Urban Core. In particular, large vertical-necked storage vessels (RV5 and RV6) occur in higher frequencies in the village settlement (see Table 3). Given the small sample sizes from VMS-365, statistical analyses of these distributions are not feasible, and these differences are suggestive at best. However, patterns at VMS-365 are similar to those in several other village sites in the Metropolitan Region, with higher than expected frequencies of large storage vessels as compared to the Urban Core (Sinopoli 1999). This may related to a greater dependence on

stored, locally produced, foodstuffs in villages, as compared to the Urban Core, where non-agriculturalists acquired their food from daily markets. It could also be correlated with larger commensal units (households?) in village vs. urban contexts. At present, we have little additional evidence to confirm or refute either interpretation.

In addition to the diagnostic collection described above, a total collection of all surface ceramics was conducted at one of the rubble mound structures within the walled settlement core. The structure was selected because there was high ceramic visibility. No measurable diagnostics were recovered in this collection, which yielded a total of 350 gm of body shards and unmeasurable rims (four bowls, seven jars, five unidentifiable). Black and brown plain ware shards dominated the assemblage (94 of 104 shards), with eight red plain ware shards, two burnished ware shards and one coarse ware shard. The high frequency of reduced, black and brown vessels is similar to that found in the Vijayanagara Urban Core.

Site Chronology

Because of the paucity of work conducted on historic, particularly medieval ceramics, in south India (particularly those before or after the Vijayanagara period), we lack a well defined ceramic chronology. However, detailed analyses have been conducted on Vijayanagara period ceramics and certain forms, particularly the shallow bowl form discussed above, do seem to be restricted to the Vijayanagara period. Other changes between Vijayanagara and post-Vijayanagara period sites include a decline in flange rims and a concomitant increase in straight rim forms, and changes in rim and vessel dimension. Drawing on all of these criteria, the ceramics from VMS-365, appear to fit firmly within the approximately two-century time span (i.e. 1350-1565) of the Vijayanagara capital. Other lines of evidence for dating VMS-365 to the Vijayanagara period include sculptural and architectural evidence. Much of the latter has already been touched upon above, and need only be summarized briefly here.

Sculptural evidence dating to the Vijayanagara period includes that large Hanuman image found within the recent shrine and the sculpted lintel fragment incorporated into the stairway to this structure. The sculpted columns located nearby have parallels in Vijayanagara constructions, but could also be post-Vijayanagara. A large number of stone blocks in the settlement area has square-based quarry marks that are quite distinct from modern quarrying traces produced by steel tools. Stones and columns in the nearby reservoir embankment, VMS-349, also have Vijayanagara quarry marks.

Several late nineteenth- and early twentieth-century maps of the region were examined in the India Office Library in London. The village site does not appear on any of the early maps and the settlement must have been abandoned at this time. Further, the presence of a wall enclosing the settlement core also supports the interpretation that this site was abandoned centuries ago. Contemporary villages in Bellary District are not walled. Walled communities were, however, common in the region until the mid-nineteenth century, when most were removed by command of British administrators (Francis 1904: 57), ostensibly to improve cleanliness and hygiene, but also, no doubt, to facilitate colonial control and limit local resistance. When the enclosure wall at Hospet was torn down, John Kelsall, the acting Subcollector for the region, wrote "the town was greatly improved in 1866 and 1867 by levelling the fort wall and filling up the ditch, formerly a receptacle for all kinds of rubbish" (Kelsall 1872: 18).

Taking all of these lines of evidence together, there is little doubt that VMS-365 can be assigned to the Vijayanagara period.

Discussion

The Vijayanagara region is justifiably known for its walled Urban Core with its dramatic and massive monumental temples, palaces, and administrative structures. However, as the research of the VMS is demonstrating, Vijayanagara period settlement in the region was in fact quite complex and varied. Occupants of the region included rural and urban dwellers, elites and non-elites. The site reported on here was a small and peripheral settlement during the Vijayanagara period. It was a small village, of at most a few hundred people, located roughly 6 km from the Urban Core and more than 2 km from a major Vijayanagara period road. The inhabitants were nonetheless an integral part of the Vijayanagara urban economy, members of the non-elite agricultural labourers and artisans without whom the imperial grandeur of Vijayanagara could not have been created or maintained. By examining both the small and large sites in the Metropolitan Region we can better understand the significance of Vijayanagara urbanism on the environment, population and social structures of South India.

Acknowledgements

I extend my profound gratitude to the Government of India, Karnataka Department of Archaeology and Museums and the American Institute of Indian Studies for sponsoring and supporting this research. The 1992 field season was supported by grants from the Smithsonian Institution (FR00627500), the National Geographic Society (4679-91) and the Wenner-Gren Foundation for Anthropological Research (Grant 5397). Analysis was supported by the National Endowment for the Humanities and the University of Wisconsin-Milwaukee. My thanks also to members of the 1992 VMS team.

Works Cited

Francis, W., 1904, *Madras District Gazetteer: Bellary District*, Government Press, Madras.

Kelsall, J., 1872, *Manual of the Bellary District*, Lawrence Asylum Press, Madras.

Means, B.K., 1991, A small settlement near the city of Vijayanagara. In, *Vijayanagara: Progress of Research, 1987-1988*, edited by D.V. Devaraj and C.S. Patil, pp. 85-94, Directorate of Archaeology and Museums, Mysore.

Morrison, K.D. and C.M. Sinopoli, 1992, Economic diversity and integration in a pre-colonial Indian empire. *World Archaeology*, 23: 335-52.

——, 1996, Archaeological Survey in the

Vijayanagara Metropolitan Region: 1990. In, *Vijayanagara: Progress of Research, 1988-1991*, edited by D.V. Devaraj and C.S. Patil, pp. 59-73, Directorate of Archaeology and Museums, Mysore.

Sinopoli, C.M., 1986, *Material Culture and Social Organization: A Study of Archaeological Ceramics from Vijayanagara, South India*, Ph.D. Dissertation, Museum of Anthropology, Department of Anthropology, University of Michigan, Ann Arbor.

——, 1993, *Pots and Palaces: The Earthenware Ceramics of the Noblemen's Quarter of Vijayanagara*, Manohar and American Institute of Indian Studies, New Delhi.

——, 1999, Levels of complexity: ceramic variability at Vijayanagara. In, *Pottery and People: A Dynamic Interaction*, edited by J. Skibo and G.M. Feinman, pp. 115-36, University of Utah Press, Salt Lake City.

Sinopoli, C.M. and K.D. Morrison, 1991, The Vijayanagara Metropolitan Survey: The 1988 Season. In, *Vijayanagara: Progress of Research, 1984-1987*, edited by C.S. Patil and D.V. Devaraj, pp. 55-69, Directorate of Archaeology and Museums, Mysore.

Table 1. Prehistoric Sites Documented

Vessel form	Number of shards	Frequency %
Unrestricted vessels		
Lamps	0	0
Shallow bowls	5	5.95
Other bowls	6	7.14
Restricted vessels		
Flange rim	43	51.19
Straight rim	23	27.38
Round rim	4	4.76
Other diagnostics		
(decorated sherds, water pipes, etc.)	3	3.57
Totals	84	

Table 2. Restricted Vessel Forms

Vessel form	Rim form			Total	%
	Straight	Flange	Round		
RV1 small serving	0	0	2	2	2.9
RV2 medium food preparation	6	16	0	22	31.4
RV3 large food preparation	1	3	0	4	5.7
RV4 small serving/storage	1	1	0	2	2.9
RV5 medium storage	5	21	0	26	37.1
RV6 large storage	10	2	2	14	20.0
Totals	23	43	4	70	

Table 3. Restricted Vessel Use-Class Frequences: VMS-365 and Urban Core

Use Class	VMS-365		Urban Core	
	#	%	#	%
RV1 small serving	2	2.9	711	8.0
RV2 medium food preparation	22	31.4	4049	45.4
RV3 large food preparation	4	5.7	373	4.2
RV4 small serving/storage	2	2.9	482	5.4
RV5 medium storage	26	37.1	2752	30.9
RV 6 large storage	14	20.0	552	6.2

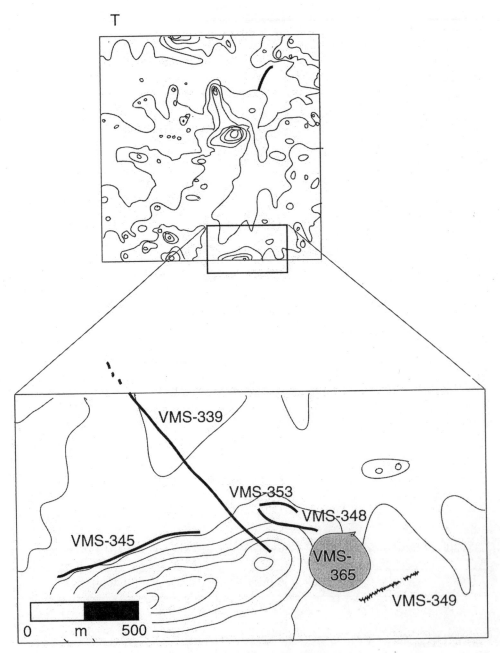

Figure 1. VMS-365 and associated sites.

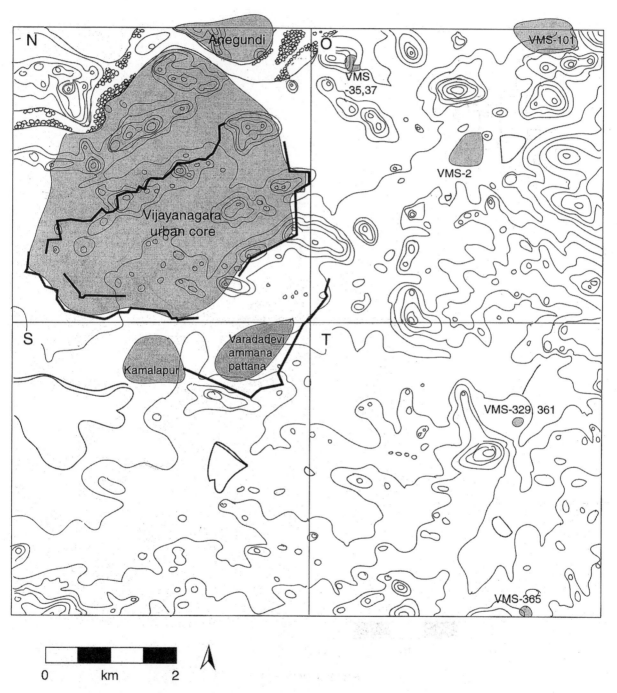

Figure 2. Distribution of settlement sites in the Vijayanagara Metropolitan Region.

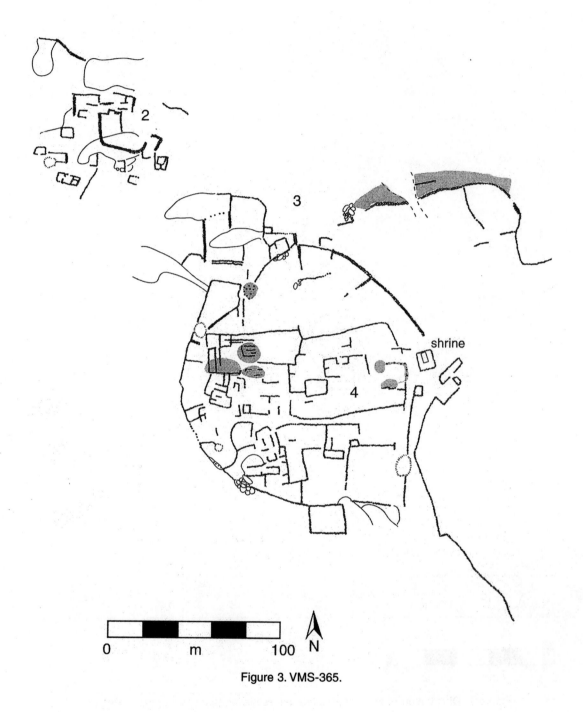

2

3

shrine

4

0   m   100   N

Figure 3. VMS-365.

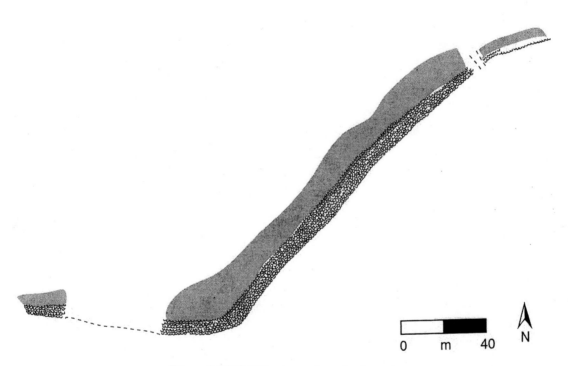

Figure 4. VMS-349, reservoir embankment.

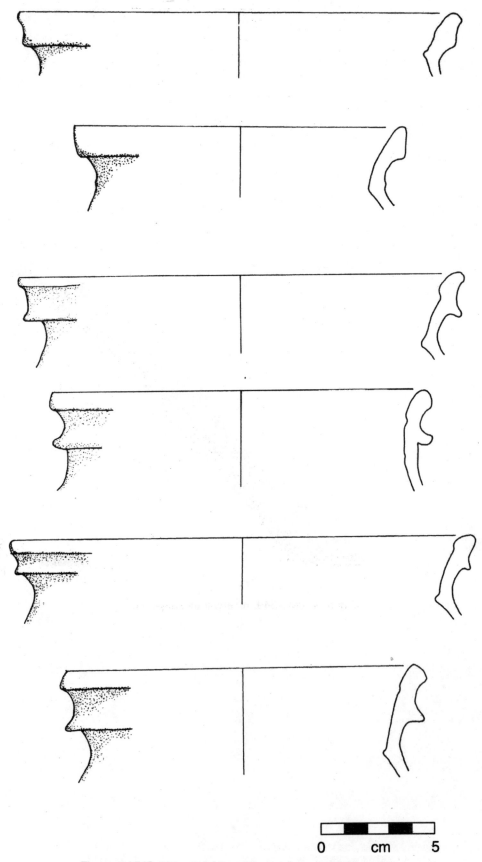

Figure 5. VMS-365, straight and flange rim restricted vessels.

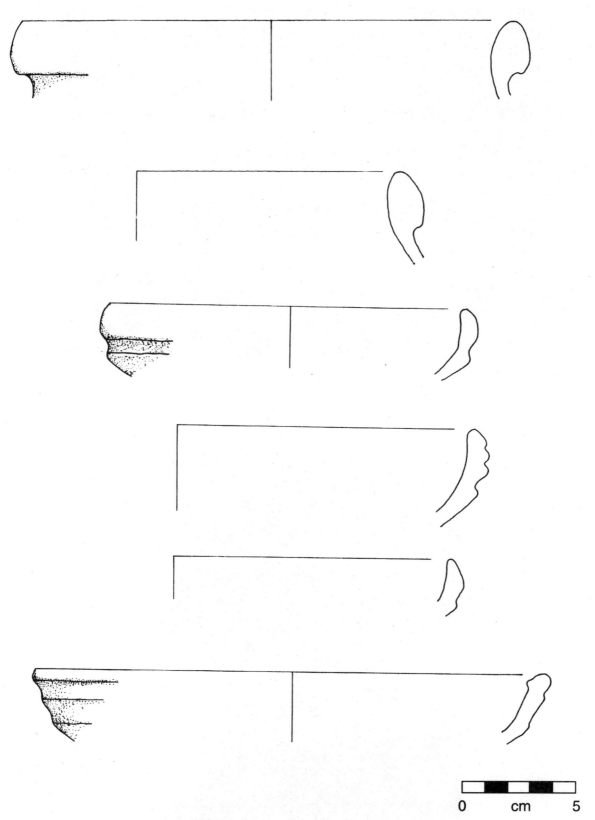

Figure 6. VMS-365, round rim restricted vessels and shallow bowls.

Plate 1. VMS-365, residential structure.

Plate 2. VMS-365, Hanuman image in modern shrine.

VMS-6: A FORTIFIED SETTLEMENT COMPLEX

Michael Dega and Robert P. Brubaker

Between the fourteenth and sixteenth centuries, the inhabitants of the Vijayanagara Metropolitan Region transformed the landscape into a complex network of settlements, fortifications, roads, agricultural features and ritual sites. Many of the features that have been documented by the Vijayanagara Metropolitan Survey (VMS) within the outlying areas of the Metropolitan Region have a clustered distribution suggestive of communities that were, in many ways, self-sufficient. Nonetheless, these communities were complexly embedded in the larger landscape of the imperial capital in an interdependent manner. Self-sustaining to varying degrees, communities in the outlying areas of the region contributed in a variety of ways to the core area of the imperial city. The population of the capital's centre depended on these hinterland areas for agricultural produce, craft and other domestic goods, and sources of labour to construct state works such as tanks, temples, fortifications and roads. All of these were necessary to the economic, political and military effectiveness of the empire (Sinopoli and Morrison 1991: 55).

Among the most important features constructed in outlying areas were fortifications or military outposts with associated living areas to support a military presence. Located in Block W, several kilometres to the southwest of the core area of Vijayanagara was one such settlement cluster, VMS-6 (Figure 1). Situated on and around a sinuous granite and basalt outcrop ridge on the west side of the north south road between Malapannagudi and Kariganuru, VMS-6 was a fortified complex consisting of several interdependent features varying in size, form and function (Figure 2).

The first of these was a fortified enclosure with five circular bastions located on the top of the outcrop ridge. Feature 2 consisted of the tumbled remains of a substantial walled settlement located at the base of the ridge immediately to the north and northeast of the fortified enclosure. Running from north to south along the east edge of the fort and settlement, Feature 3, a road wall, bounded the road between Malapannagudi and Kariganuru. Finally, Feature 4, a large stepped well, was located *c.* 50 m to the east of the road and settlement. First identified by Morrison during the initial phase of the VMS, a crew member mapped and documented the various components of VMS-6 during the 1994 field season. We describe and discuss each of its component features in the pages that follow.

Feature 1: The Fortified Enclosure

Constructed on the crest and upper northeast slopes of the outcrop ridge, the fortified enclosure of VMS-6 was somewhat irregular in plan; five stretches of wall of variable length were linked by five roughly circular bastions to enclose a roughly rectangular area of some 1,130 sq m that included several rooms along the interior of the north and east walls as well as a few additional rooms within the central area of the enclosure (Plate 1). The area incorporated within the enclosure walls varied significantly in terms of both elevation and character. The terrain in which the fort was situated descends generally from southwest to northeast with the western walls and bastions – particularly the southwest bastion – occupying the highest ground (the top of the southwest bastion attained an elevation some 12 m above

539

the top of the lowest bastion in the northeast corner). The western walls and bastions were situated on the crest of the ridge, the latter consisting of a series of jagged basalt outcrops. The southwest and west bastions were both situated on higher basalt boulder outcrops separated by an intervening lower (by 2 m or more) and somewhat flatter surface of similar boulders along the inside of the west wall. Immediately to the northeast and some 2 to 3 m below this lower boulder surface, the central portion of the enclosure consisted of a sloping earthen "terrace" dotted by scattered granite boulders. This terrace area included the somewhat ambiguous basal foundations of one to two rooms as well as several additional, more easily identifiable rooms abutting the western interior of the north wall. Midway along the north wall were the remains of what most probably constituted the only entry passage into the enclosure. Some 1 to 2.5 m lower than the sloping terrace, the northeast corner and eastern sides of the fortified enclosure consisted of an area of fairly level ground extending to the north and east walls. This area of artificial fill occupied an elevation *at most* only 80 cm below the top surface of the extant north and east walls. Consisting almost certainly of artificial fill retained by these walls, this surface was some 2 to 2.5 m higher than the ground surface at the exterior base of the enclosure walls. Along the interior of the east wall were the easily identifiable foundations of five-six contiguous rooms.

The Enclosure Walls

The exterior enclosure walls of Feature 1 were very similar with respect to construction, while differing in minor but interesting details. In all cases, the walls were double-faced with an inner core of mixed stone and earth fill, the latter containing frequent potshards and small pieces of iron slag. The stones used in constructing the wall faces were generally mostly medium to large-sized unmodified or split pieces of granite or basalt, with many small stones used for chinking. The wall stones were usually arranged in multiple sinuous, or more often irregular, courses. With some exceptions (described below), the walls averaged 1.3 to 1.4 m thick at the top surface and were

probably somewhat thicker at base. In all cases, the walls appeared to abut, rather than being bonded to, the bastions they adjoined. In no case did quarried stone blocks appear to have been used in construction.

With the exception of the very short stretch of wall linking the northwest and west bastions, the south enclosure wall was the shortest and least substantial. Beginning on the west side of the southeast bastion, this wall ascended the very steep slope of the basalt outcrop up toward the high southwest bastion. Composed of mixed basalt and granite stones and earth and stone fill, this wall was roughly 1.5 m wide. The wall survived to a maximum height of about 1 m (on the interior and exterior) and was almost certainly originally somewhat higher.

The east wall of the fortified enclosure extended from the southeast to northeast bastions and was in terms of absolute elevation (not height) the lowest wall of the enclosure. Viewed from the exterior, up to seven courses of the east wall were extant (*c.* 2.15 m) although in most places only five-six courses remained. As noted above, the artificially filled ground surface on the interior of the wall was considerably higher (*c.* 1.65 m) than the exterior ground surface. Interestingly, the northern and southern ends of the wall were constructed largely of distinct materials, the southern 4/7th of the wall consisting primarily of darker basalt stone and the northern 3/7th primarily of lighter coloured granite. Here there was a strong indication that the construction materials preferred were those close to hand, the darker basalt section being constructed of stones from the outcrops near the crest of the ridge and the lighter granite section of stone from the lower slopes (Plate 2).

Like the northern portion of the east wall, the north wall was composed primarily of granite rather than basalt stones, although a few of the latter were visible in the face of the wall. Extending from the northeast to the northwest bastions, the north wall followed the contour of the ridge, sloping gently upward to its western end. The north wall survived to a height of up to 2.4 m in places (up to nine courses of stone visible on the exterior). At its eastern end, the filled ground surface on the interior was *c.* 10 to 20 cm below the extant top surface of the wall. However, along more westerly portions of the wall, the interior ground surface was as much as 1.4 m below the top surface of the extant wall. Midway along the north wall was a breach that almost certainly constituted the main, and probably only, access into the fortified enclosure. Although the walls around the breech were badly tumbled, the passage appears to have been flanked by two three-sided rooms or alcoves the open sides of which faced the passage.

It is not entirely clear how the gate was approached from the settlement below, and it is possible that more than one route may have been used. Immediately outside the gate on the west side was a line of large boulders stretching northward to the edge of the steep northern slope. A jogging natural passage westward through these boulders opened out onto a relatively flat area at the base of the northwest bastion, thence sloping moderately northward down to an area just inside the western limits of the settlement. Immediately north of the gate, a narrow steep track defined by parallel rows of boulders led directly northward down the slope to the settlement. A third broader, shallower route led down among the boulders beneath the eastern portion of the north wall and beneath the northeast bastion. While it is unclear which, if any, of these routes was the primary entry route, each would have exposed those approaching the entry to the extended scrutiny of those manning the north wall and its bastions.

Bypassing the very short and badly preserved section of wall between the northwest and west bastions, the long western wall of Feature 1 differed in some interesting ways from the walls already described (Plate 3). Extending between the higher basalt outcrops on which the west and southwest bastions were located, the west wall ran along the western edge of the basalt ridge crest. Higher than the east and north walls both in terms of absolute elevation and height, the west wall survived to a height of 3.9 m on its exterior side. Viewed from the inside, the wall was somewhat shorter, rising *c.* 2.7 m above the relatively flat lower area of basalt outcrops between the west and southwest bastions. In contrast to the other enclosure walls, the western wall was constructed in two successive sections, one above the other. Viewed from the exterior, the lower 2.9 m of the wall consisted mostly of large, fairly regularly-coursed split or unmodified basalt stones. This lower section did not appear to include an earthen core, and *c.* three courses (1 m) of this lower wall section were visible from the interior. The upper portion of the wall consisted of five-six courses of small to medium, irregularly coursed, lighter colored granite stones that raised the wall another metre to its full height. Unlike the lower portion of the wall, the upper portion clearly contained considerable quantities of earthen fill (with potshards and small pieces of slag).

The Bastions

Like the enclosure walls, the five bastions of Feature 1 were all similar in broad terms with a few minor, though interesting, differences in detail. All roughly circular in shape, each of the bastions comprised an outer stone face with a largely earthen core. The double-faced "stone shell" of each was constructed of sinuous to irregular courses of medium to large sized, mixed granite and basalt split and unmodified stones with many small stones used for chinking. Although somewhat irregular in shape, the extant top surface of each bastion had a maximum diameter of *c.* 6.5 to 8 m. Each of the bastions appeared to be abutted rather than bonded to the adjoining walls. In each case, the earthen core of the bastions survived to a somewhat greater height than the surrounding masonry shell (*c.* 1 m higher), and the bastions farthest down the slopes of the ridge (the southeast and northeast) were badly tumbled on their exterior sides. These two bastions survived to a maximum height of *c.* 2.1 and 2.7 m, respectively. Constructed on the highest basalt projections on the crest of the outcrop ridge, the west and southwest bastions were actually the shortest in terms of absolute height (*c.* 1.8 and 1.3 m respectively). The northwest was the tallest and best preserved of the five bastions (Plate 4). This bastion survived to a maximum height of *c.* 6.1 m. Unlike the badly collapsed southeast and north-east bastions, the northwest bastion was constructed on a gentler slope and, in addition, had a broad projecting footing consisting of

three-four courses of large split and unmodified granite and basalt stones that also
incorporated a few natural boulders. Above
this footing, and set *c.* 20 cm in from its edge,
the upper portion of the bastion included
about nine additional courses of medium and
some large split and unmodified stones.

The Interior Rooms

The foundations of several small rooms were
situated within the bastioned enclosure walls
described above. Several such rooms were
located along the interior of the north wall,
several more along the interior of the east
wall and an undetermined number (one and
possibly two) on the higher ground in the
centre of the enclosure. Those rooms along
the north and east walls were arranged con-
tiguously, each sharing a wall with its nearest
neighbor. These rooms also made use of the
north or east enclosure walls as a fourth, outer
wall, the adjoining room walls being in all cases
abutted rather than bonded to the enclosure
walls. The construction of the interior rooms,
in contrast to that of the outer walls and
bastions, was comparatively insubstantial.
In several cases (notably along the east wall
and among the rooms at the centre of the
compound) only a single course of medium-
large unmodified or split stones *c.* 30 to 40 cm
thick indicated the line of the foundations.
Double-faced walls of similar stones, although
present in the construction of some of the
rooms along the east wall, were more common
in the rooms along the north wall and survived
to a greater height in the latter area.

Feature 2: The Walled Settlement

Extending northward from the slopes beneath
the fort and out onto the plain at the base of
the ridge, the VMS-6 settlement covered an
area of roughly 17,550 sq m when documented in 1994. Measuring *c.* 130 m wide
(north-south) x 135 m long (east-west) along
its maximal dimensions, the settlement was
almost certainly somewhat larger in the past
(Plate 5). Heavily mined for both fill and stone
by local inhabitants, the settlement appeared
at the time we documented it as an expanse
of rubble mounds and scattered cobbles, in

which it was nonetheless possible to frequently
detect stone alignments indicative of the
foundations of numerous and varied structures
(Plate 6). The impact of recent and ongoing
earth and stone removal activities was particularly apparent on the north and south-east
sides, where substantial borrow depressions
largely obscured the original margins of the
settlement. Field clearance activities and the
piling of fieldstones on the edge of areas of
mounded rubble produced a similar effect
along the western margins of the site.

Nevertheless, enough remained at the time
of documentation to suggest that the VMS-6
settlement may originally have been surrounded by an enclosure wall of some form,
as indicated by the foundations of a double-
faced wall of large cobbles and small boulders
traceable along the southwest, north and
northeast margins of the settlement. Probably
not as heavily constructed as the walls of
the fortification described earlier, the course
taken by this wall on the southwest edge of
the site suggests that the settlement was
completely enclosed within its circuit such that
access to the entryway of the fort could only
be gained by passing through the settlement
itself.

Evidence of what may have been the
primary, and possibly the only formally defined
entry way into the settlement was located along
its east side toward the northeast corner. Here,
the rectangular foundations of two platform-
like structures bounded by single-faced
boulder walls and packed with earth flanked
and defined a passage that would have would
have been wide enough to permit the passage
of oxcarts. Just within this entry passage, a
small flat expanse of exposed sheet-rock
showed marked evidence of wear almost certainly attributable to the passage of considerable traffic over a long period of time.
Evidence of another, larger single-faced rectangular foundation to the south of the more
southerly of the two platforms suggests that the
entry complex may actually have had two
passageways, one to either side of the central
platform. At the time we documented this
rapidly disappearing settlement, the more
northerly of these two probable entry passages
still appeared to be in use as an access point
into and through the settlement area, as

indicated by the presence of a cart and/or foot track that wended its way in a southwesterly direction among the grassed-over or partially grassed-over mounds of rubble that character-ized the heart of the settlement. Clearly in recent use, the settlement interior was tumbled enough that it was impossible to determine conclusively whether this track merely followed original routes of movement within, although this seems likely. Passing out the west side of the settlement area near the base of the ridge slope, this track way conti-nued westward along the base of the slope, bounded for some distance on the north by a line of large cobbles paralleling the slope base. Although there were some indications that the entry way on the east side of the settlement may have been complemented by a similar, albeit probably smaller, entryway on the west, architectural remains at the point where the track way departed the western edge of the settlement were insufficiently preserved to warrant a definitive conclusion in this regard (Figure 2).

At the time of documentation the interior of the settlement included the foundations of 40 to 50 more structures (recent activities of the kind already described have left only traces of what were probably numerous additional structures on the east and west edges of the site), a small circular bastion or storage facility and several platforms. Constructed of two rows of basalt and granite cobbles and boulders, the foundations of most of the structures were rectangular in form and appear to have been laid out in three roughly east-west rows separated by open areas or alleys. Presumably dwellings, most of the foundations in these rows seemed to conform to a rectangular, two-chamber configuration with a larger room measuring *c.* 8 m x 4 m, divided by a small rock wall from a second, smaller room to the south measuring *c.* 4 m x 4 m. Most of these two-chamber units were laid out with the long side of the rectangle running north south and the small running east-west. In most cases, adjacent units shared a common wall.

This dwelling configuration appears similar to that of many modern dwellings in nearby towns such as Kamalapur and Mallapannagudi, and may be an indication that the residential structures at VMS-6 were occupied by large extended families. In all likelihood, only the foundations of these dwelling units were constructed of stone. Early travellers to Vijaya-nagara such as Barbosa, Paes and Frederick noted that ordinary dwellings were usually thatched, single-storied and flat-roofed, with walls of packed earth (see Sewell 1992: 244, Purchas 1905: 97 and Dames 1989: 202). Significantly, no bricks, ceramic roof tiles, chunks of lime plaster or quarried granite blocks that might be associated with elite residences or public architecture were en-countered anywhere within the settlement or fort.

While the clustered rectangular foundations described above comprise most of the stru-ctural remains within the settlement, other foundations differing to varying degrees in form and possibly function were also noted. In a few locations, single or parallel alignments of boulders appear to have been positioned so as to define routes of movement within the settlement. Most prominent among such align-ments were the two parallel lines of boulders mentioned earlier that defined the straight but steep path leading up the ridge slope to the Feature 1 fortification.

Located approximately 50 m to the south-west of the east gateway were the double-faced foundation courses of what may have been a circular bastion *c.* 5 m in diameter constructed of medium-large unmodified and split cobbles. Situated on a small knoll roughly 3 m high, the bastion, if such it was, would have afforded wide views across all the rooms in the settle-ment, the entryways and paths through the settlement, the northern flank of the forti-fication, and the road running outside and to the east of the settlement. Given the relatively small diameter of this feature, it is also possible that these circular foundations were not the base of a bastion at all, but rather that of a circular storage facility. Seemingly a common feature of fortifications in south India, at least one example of such storage facilities has been documented in the Metropolitan Region within fort VMS-1060 located to the east of the capital on the heights bounding the north edge of the Daroji Valley. Unfortunately, poor preservation precludes a definitive con-clusion as regards the original function of the circular foundations in the VMS-6 settlement.

Some of the structural remains located on the slopes of the outcrop ridge to the north of the fort also differed from the foundations that occupy most of the low-lying areas of the settlement. Situated on the slopes to the west of the central path leading up to the fort entryway were the foundations of several structures bounded by single-faced walls consisting primarily of small boulders ranging from 0.5 to 0.75 m in diameter rather than the double-faced walls of smaller stones that comprised most of the residential structures in the settlement. Unlike the latter foundations, which were usually characterized by depressions in the centre, these single-faced boulder-defined foundations appeared to have been packed with earth and thus had more of a platform-like appearance. Also noted in this area was a cobble-lined pit *c.* 1.5 m deep and 1 m across that may have been used for storage. Somewhat smaller (*c.* 1 m deep and 50 cm in diametre), a second, similar pit was encountered on the slopes below the east wall of the fort.

Whether the platform-like character of the structures on the slope north of the fort indicates a different, possibly non-residential function, higher status dwellings, or simply a method of creating a level surface on, uneven ground, is impossible to say in the absence of additional data. However, it should be noted that other foundations on the slopes to the east of the fort entry way did conform more closely to the patterning characteristic of most of the foundations in the settlement. Additionally, several similar platform-like foundations were also noted on the level ground near the north margin of the settlement. Interestingly, two *naga* stones clearly in worship were noticed near this area in a room the foundations of which were partially obscured by the piling of stones from field clearance along the western margin of the settlement. These, together with a small modern shrine located on the summit of the outcrop ridge roughly 20 m south of the fort provided an indication that current use of the area did not focus solely on its value as a convenient source of stone and earth. Probably relatively recent, a small rock-cut well was noted in the heavily disturbed zone on the northern margins of the settlement.

Artefact Collections

For both the fort and adjacent settlement, surface artefacts were sampled through a combination of 37, 2 x 2-m judgement collection units and by diagnostic walkovers designed to cover site areas at 5-m intervals. Within the fort, thirteen judgement units were apportioned between the open central area and areas within the foundations of rooms along the north and east walls. In the much larger settlement area, the remaining 24 collection units were allocated using the 40-m grid established to map the site in order to ensure some coverage of all site areas and different kinds of structures. Following this procedure, 20 of these 24 collection units were placed within the foundations of rooms, and the remaining four units located in what were deemed to be open areas. As with these collection units, diagnostic walkovers of the large settlement area were based on the 40-m site grid in order to both facilitate uniform coverage and as a means of detecting potential differences in the frequency and kinds artefacts recovered from different parts of the settlement.

Whether in the fort or settlement, earthenware ceramics were by far the most frequently encountered artefacts both during the course of diagnostic walkovers and in the 2 x 2-m collection units. Collection units in the settlement alone, for example, produced a total of *c.* 2,000 Black, 240 Red and 700 Plain earthenware shards. Burnished and Polished vessels were not represented in any of the collections from the fort or settlement. Among the earthenware ceramics recovered from both areas, many were stylistically and compositionally consistent with Vijayanagara period ceramics (Sinopoli 1993). However, a significant proportion was likely of relatively recent date, and many of these shards had a metallic sheen on their exterior surfaces from the application of graphite. Comparison of the quantities of ceramics recovered from the 2 x 2 m units in the settlement suggests that ceramics were more common within structures than in the open areas outside of them. Having said this however, the relatively dense scatter of earthenware shards noted in the cleared field to the west of the settlement seems to lend credence to the idea that the settlement probably originally extended somewhat farther to the west.

Also recovered, albeit only infrequently and only from the settlement, were thick coarse-ware shards, presumably of relatively recent date. Other artefacts of interest recovered only in the settlement area included a few fragments of ceramic water pipe, an irregularly cylindrical steatite pencil, an oil lamp, an incense burner, a D-cell battery core, two pieces of glass, an iron ring *c.* 10 cm diametre, part of a coarse-ware stove base, and a granite block mortar *c.* 50 cm square with a central circular hole roughly 10 cm in diametre. A second, similar mortar was noted on the slope outside the east wall of the fort. Once again, no evidence of ceramic roof tiles or brick was seen in either the fort or settlement suggesting that the walls and roofs of residential structures were constructed primarily of earth and other, perishable, materials erected atop stone foundations. Considered together, the mix of Vijayanagara period and more recent artefacts just described leads us to suggest that the fort and settlement were established at some point during the Vijayanagara period (possibly during the sixteenth century) and that both survived for an undetermined period of time the demise of the imperial capital.

Associated with iron processing activities, two final classes of artefacts deserve special notice. First and far more frequent, were lumps of iron slag usually 1 to 4 cm in diametre, but occasionally far larger. Far less frequent were fifteen ceramic cylindrical mould or tuyeres fragments, all of which came from the settlement (Plate 7). Seemingly attesting to iron working activities at the site, we believe that the distribution of these materials within the settlement and additional evidence from the rubble core of the fort walls and bastions, indicate that both slag and mould fragments may have been brought into the site in fill at the time the settlement and fort were established. Although the scatter of slag within the settlement seemed to be somewhat heavier in the northwest quadrant, the results of the 2 x 2-m collection units and the diagnostic walkovers indicate that both slag and mould fragments were present over much of the area rather than being concentrated in any particular part of the settlement.

As noted earlier, quantities of both slag and earthenware shards were clearly also present in the earth and rubble fill of the fort walls and bastions. Faced with stone and thus better preserved than the predominantly earth walls of the settlement, we believe that the ceramic- and slag-bearing fill used for the core of the fort walls and bastions likely derived from the same source as the material used to construct the earthen walls of the settlement structures. Beyond the implication that the slag (as well as many of the ceramics) collected from the settlement likely eroded out of the earthen walls of the structures there, we further suspect that the use of similar slag- and ceramic-bearing fill for construction purposes in both the settlement and fort indicates that both were probably constructed at around the same time. Although we do not discount the possibility that iron processing activities were occurring at the site before and during the establishment and occupation of the fort and settlement, we think it also possible that the ceramic- and slag-bearing fill used in their construction were brought to the site from some other location nearby. It is thus interesting that when we documented the fort and settlement in 1994, this same fill was yet again clearly being appropriated for use elsewhere (Plate 6).

Feature 3: The Road Boundary Wall

Not much more than a rocky dirt track for much of its length, the modern road between the fortified Vijayanagara period town of Malapannagudi to the north and the new town of Kariganuru to the south runs along the east edge of the VMS-6 fort and settlement. Although the town of Kariganuru is recent, evidence at several points along the road suggest that much of this probably dates to the Vijayanagara period, if not before.

Further indications that the road is not recent are apparent along that stretch running adjacent to the fort and settlement of VMS-6. Here, the road is bounded on its east side by the intermittently preserved sections of a defining wall of dry laid stones that together extend for roughly 800 m. Presumably originally connected, these wall sections generally consisted of one to two single-faced courses of small to large, unmodified or split granite and basalt stones. Seemingly recent additions due perhaps to field clearance activities, some sections of the wall had one or two additional courses of smaller stones.

Artefacts

Pedestrian survey along the course of the road and bounding wall revealed a sparse to light scatter of earthenware ceramics. Most of these appeared to derive from the margins of the cotton fields to the east of the wall. In addition, an upright, albeit half-buried, hero stone was noted on the east side of the wall section running adjacent to the settlement (Plate 8). The visible portion of this stone featured a figure on horseback holding a raised sword. Spatters of white paint on the hero stone and adjacent stones indicated that the sculpture was currently in worship. Although it was not possible to determine conclusively whether the hero stone was displaced from its original location, such memorial stones are certainly consistent with a Vijayanagara period (or earlier) date.

Feature 4: The Stepped Well

A large Vijayanagara period stepped well situated on level ground in recently plowed fields some 40 m to the east of the road, Feature 4 presented something of a contrast to the badly tumbled and somewhat amorphous remains of the fort and settlement (Plate 9). Although partially collapsed on the northeast side and heavily overgrown with vegetation, this sizable keyhole-shaped well was constructed of quarried granite slabs rather than the unmodified and/or split stones that characterized the fort, the settlement and the road wall.

Oriented roughly west-northwest to east-southeast, the well consisted of a large, inwardly sloping, stepped central rectangular chamber, with a long, narrow, stepped entry passage extending westward from the middle of the west side. The stepped walls of this entry passage consisted of westward extensions of the west wall of the central chamber flanking a series of stone steps leading downward from the ground surface to the surface of the water within the well. Partially covered with fallen stone debris and vegetation, the individual stairs generally consisted of three to five rectangular slabs, with each successive step being *c.* 20 cm higher than the step below. Widest at ground surface, this entry passage narrowed gradually as the stairs descended toward the central well chamber.

Along the better-preserved sides of the well, fully 37 stepped courses of stone were visible from the ground surface to the surface of the water below. These alternated fairly consistently between courses of wider but thinner slabs, and intervening courses of higher, but narrower blocks of quarried stone. In most places, the faces of the courses constructed of thinner slabs projected very slightly past those of the thicker blocks forming the courses immediately below. In turn, courses constructed of thicker blocks were generally offset or stepped *c.* 10 cm from the edge of the thinner slab courses immediately below. Chinking stones were used with some frequency, and Vijayanagara period quarry marks were also common. Re-utilized column and lintel sections were also incorporated within the fabric of the well walls at several points.

At several locations, but most frequently along the east wall of the well, individual rectangular slabs projected horizontally 50 to 80 cm outward from the wall face at different heights in the wall. Such slabs were almost certainly intended to provide safe footings, thereby facilitating access to the well without using the entry stairs on the west side. Along the south wall of the well, additional access was provided by the construction of a three-sided, north-facing projecting platform built into the wall face roughly 5 m west of the southeast corner of the well. Roughly 2 sq m, the east, north and west walls of this platform consisted of sixteen courses of roughly square quarried blocks. Not stepped like the walls of the well, the walls of the platform presented sheer, nearly vertical faces extending from their foundations in the stepped south well wall to the ground surface. Running north-south, two long slabs were positioned along the east and west edges on the flat top surface of the platform. Extending northward over the edge of the platform, both of these parallel slabs had rectilinear notches cut in their north ends through which ropes could be run in order to facilitate the retrieval of water from the well by individuals positioned on top of the platform.

Situated amidst plowed fields, the precinct of the well was separated from the former by a low enclosure wall of stone conforming to the keyhole shape of the well and running 1 to 2 m outside the top surface of the well. Constructed of medium to large, single- or double-faced stones, this enclosure wall ranged from one to two courses in height on the north, south and east sides, to five courses on the west side opposite the well entrance passage. Abutting the enclosure wall were the remains of two rectangular structures. Situated north of the northwest corner of the central well chamber, the first of these structures consisted of a single-faced foundation wall of small to medium stones roughly 3 sq m. Located to the southwest of the central well chamber in the angle created by the chamber and the entry passage, the second structure comprised a low platform. Roughly 3.5 x 3.5 sq m, the walls of this platform were constructed of two to three heavily silted courses of small to medium cobbles.

Artefacts

With the exception of a few fragments of recent glass most probably from beer bottles, artefacts collected from the vicinity of the well consisted exclusively of earthenware ceramics, with no iron slag being noted. Mostly small, the shards were sparsely to moderately scattered along the west and east sides of the well, with moderate to heavy scatters along much of the north and east sides. These scatters were heaviest around the projecting platform near the southeast corner of the well and within and immediately around the square foundations north of the northwest corner.

Discussion

Described in the foregoing pages as including a fortification, a settlement, a road wall and a stepped well, the definition of VMS-6 was somewhat arbitrary, based on close geographic proximity and the sense that these features collectively formed something of a cluster or node in the surrounding landscape. Somewhat farther away, additional features almost certainly relevant to understanding VMS-6 could also have been included. Roughly 650 m to the west are the remains of a large Vijayanagara period reservoir embankment (VMS-1023). Some 530 m to the north and just east of the road are two agricultural terrace systems (VMS-373 and VMS-374), with a temple (VMS-375) situated across the road to the west. Several hundred metres to the northeast of VMS-6 is another small shrine (VMS-1001), and *c.* 350 m to the east, a series of erosion control walls (VMS-1000) bounding the margins of a deeply dissected drainage channel that ultimately empties into the Kamalapura reservoir (VMS-231). Finally, the nucleus of the VMS-6 complex – the fort and settlement – is wholly surrounded by agricultural fields today and almost certainly was so in the past. In effect, the very arbitrariness involved in grouping together the features we have designated as VMS-6 draws attention to the fact that these features, far from comprising a discrete cluster except in a spatial sense, were embedded in a much broader cultural landscape.

What inferences might we then draw about the place of VMS-6 within this landscape? Here we might begin by noting that the fort and adjacent settlement that together formed the nucleus of VMS-6 are not unique within the Metropolitan Region in terms of their basic configuration and general setting. In fact, the combination of elevated fort presiding over a settlement at slope base appears to be a common characteristic of intermediate-sized settlements in the region around the capital, a characteristic broadly duplicated at other Vijayanagara period fortification-cum-settlements such as Bukkasagara (VMS-655), Toranagallu (VMS-1077), Papinayakanahalli (VMS-1009), Ramasagara (VMS-1053) and probably elsewhere. In the case of VMS-6, the use of ceramic- and slag-bearing fill in the walls of both the fort and settlement suggests that both were constructed at about the same time, and the similarity of VMS-6 in setting and configuration to the complexes just mentioned might be an indication that the latter were established in similar fashion. Unlike VMS-6, which appears to have weathered the decline of Vijayanagara only to be abandoned during later times, each of these other fortification-cum-settlement complexes appears to have survived down to the present.

Another significant point of similarity between VMS-6 and these other complexes lies in their location along important Vijayanagara period routes of transport and communication. Whereas the communities of Bukkasagara and Ramasagara are located along the main northeast road leading from Vijayanagara to the fortified town of Kampli along the Tungabhadra River, VMS-6 appears to have been one (together with Papinayakanahalli and Toranagallu) of a series of fortified settlement complexes situated along the road leading toward the capital through the Daroji Valley on the south and southeast. The westernmost of the three, VMS-6 was founded at a strategic location near the point at which the Daroji Valley opens out into the broader Tungabhadra valley. Although other, as yet unidentified factors likely played a role, the commonalities of settlement configuration and setting outlined above lead us to suggest that VMS-6 and similar complexes were established at least in part to serve specialized functions beyond those generally characteristic of many settlements throughout the Metropolitan Region (e.g. see Sinopoli's discussion of VMS-365 in this volume).

To be certain, settlements located at outcrop margins are indeed common throughout the region, and for VMS-6 as much as other settlements, such settings were obviously useful in providing immediate access to plentiful supplies of stone for construction, as well as a means of reserving valuable arable lands for cultivation. In the case of VMS-6 and similar complexes, however, the choice of such outcrop margin settings clearly extended beyond such considerations, seemingly placing a premium on the synergistic strategic advantages associated with proximity to a major communication route and elevated terrain. In this regard, the value of the fort as a defensible feature was clearly enhanced by being situated

in a location where increased elevation made access difficult. Additionally, the ridge top location offered a superior vantage point from which to observe the surrounding area. Together with these advantages, the placement of complexes like VMS-6 along the major routes of movement into and through the Metropolitan Region made them ideal locations from which to monitor and exert some form of control over traffic moving along these routes, whatever that traffic might be. Thus, we suggest that concerns for security provided much of the impetus for the establishment of VMS-6 and other similar complexes. Indeed, together with linear defensive works such as VMS-370 situated on the margins of the Metropolitan Region (see Brubaker this volume), "settlement along the main roads to the city served as one of the first lines of defense against aggressors" (Sinopoli and Morrison 1991: 67). Such considerations take on added weight if we recall the somewhat anomalous location of Vijayanagara near the northern borders of the empire and its history of chronic warfare with the powerful neighbouring polities of the Deccan and Orissa.

Nonetheless, it would almost certainly be an error to portray VMS-6 and similar complexes solely as military camps devoted to garrison and security-related purposes – this at least for most of their inhabitants, most of the time. Although their very contiguity suggests that relationships between those in the fort and settlement were indeed close, the two precincts were certainly differentiated from each other in both spatial and architectural terms. Furthermore, the setting of the complex amidst agricultural fields and the numerous nearby agricultural features referred to earlier suggest that, aside most probably from a garrison of professional soldiers within the fort, most of the inhabitants of VMS-6 settlement were likely engaged in agricultural and other pursuits most of the time, although they likely would have assumed additional duties if the need arose. To draw a suggestive parallel, we suspect that the population of VMS-6 may not actually have been all that dissimilar in composition to that of most Vijayanagara armies, with their cores of professional soldiers, larger contingents of part-time combatants often serving on a seasonal basis, and sizeable groups of dependents and other camp followers.

Although some proportion of the agricultural production of VMS-6 and other similar complexes undoubtedly went to sustain the community and garrison, some of this production probably made its way down the road to supply the needs of the city's diverse urban population. Further, while we were unable to determine conclusively whether iron was being processed at the settlement itself, such activities almost certainly occurred somewhere nearby, and it seems highly probable that some of the resulting output of this – and probably other crafts – also helped to supply the needs of the Vijayanagara capital. Thus, although the establishment and growth of Vijayanagara – with its requirements for security as well as agricultural and other products – may well have supplied the original impetus for the establishment of fortified settlements like VMS-6, indications of functional diversity and the continuance of such settlements subsequent to the decline of the capital suggest that these were not so specialized that their survival was necessarily contingent upon that of the imperial centre.

Acknowledgements

We would like to thank the Government of India for granting us permission to work at Vijayanagara as crew members of the VMS, and also the Department of Archaeology and Museums of the Government of Karnataka for their sponsorship and support of this project. Special thanks are also due to Balasubramanyam and the late Dr C.S. Patil of the Directorate of Archaeology and Museums of Karnataka. Our visit to India as students would not have been possible without the assistance of Dr P.R. Mehendiratta and the American Institute of Indian Studies. We are most especially grateful to Drs Kathleen Morrison and Carla Sinopoli – the co-founders of the VMS – for their generosity in inviting us to participate in the 1994 field season. The 1994 field season was made possible by the Smithsonian Foreign Currency Program, the National Geographic Society (Sinopoli), and by additional support from the Social Science Research Institute, University of Hawai'i (Morrison). Fellow student crew members Lars Fogelin and Jennifer Lundal contributed greatly in our efforts to document VMS-6. Special thanks are due our driver, U.V. Srinivas, whose valuable services and extensive knowledge of local circumstances greatly facilitated the documentation of VMS-6. Finally, we are also grateful to the staff of the State Archaeology Camp for their considerable hospitality.

Works Cited

Dames, M.L., 1989, *The Book of Duarte Barbosa*, reprint, Asian Educational Services, New Delhi.

Purchas, S., editor, 1905, Extracts of Master Caesar Frederike his eighteene yeeres Indian Observations. In, *Hakluytus Posthumus or Purchas His Pilgrimes: Contayning a History of the World In Sea Voyages and Lande Travells by Englishmen and others*, pp. 88-142, James MacLehose and Sons, Glasgow.

Sewell, R., 1992, Narrative of Domingo Paes. In, *A Forgotten Empire (Vijayanagar)*, pp. 236-90, reprint, Asian Educational Services, New Delhi.

Sinopoli, C.M., 1993, *Pots and Palaces: The Earthenware Ceramics of the Nobleman's Quarter of Vijayanagara*, Manohar and American Institute of Indian Studies, New Delhi.

Sinopoli, C.M. and K.D. Morrison, 1991, The Vijayanagara Metropolitan Survey: The 1988 Season. In, *Vijayanagara: Progress of Research, 1987-1988*, edited by D.V. Devaraj and C.S. Patil, pp. 55-69, Directorate of Archaeology and Museums, Mysore.

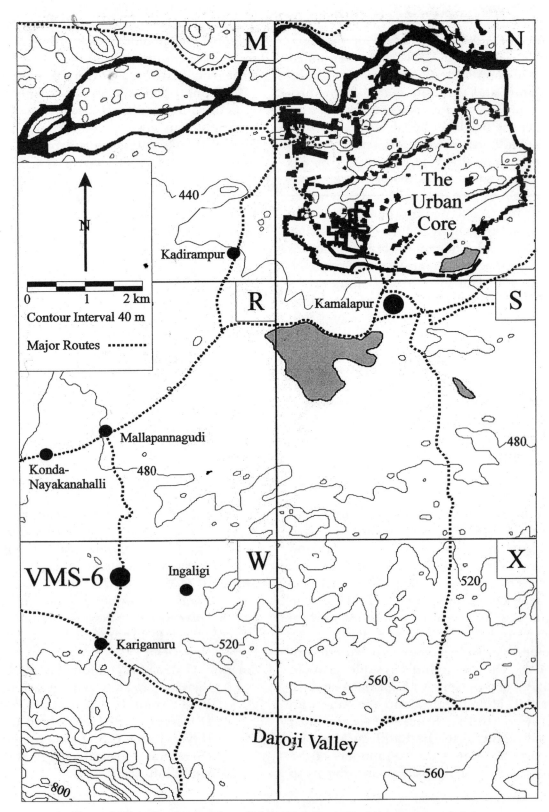

Figure 1. Map showing location of VMS-6 relative to the Vijayanagara capital.

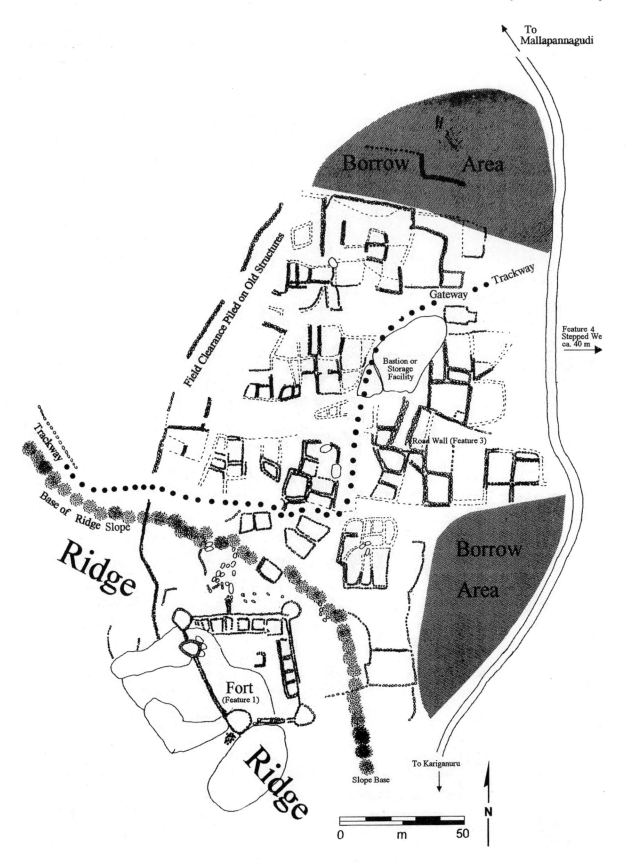

Figure 2. VMS-6, plan.

Plate 1. VMS-6, southwest view of fortified enclosure (Feature 1) from the road.

Plate 2. VMS-6, east wall of fortified enclosure (Feature 1).

Plate 3. VMS-6, southward view along west wall of Feature 1.

Plate 4. VMS-6, southward view of northwest bastion of Feature 1.

Plate 5. VMS-6, Feature 2 settlement as viewed from northeast bastion of Feature 1.

Plate 6. VMS-6, stone and earth fill being removed from Feature 2 settlement in 1994.

Plate 7. VMS-6, tuyeres fragments from Feature 2 settlement.

Plate 8. VMS-6, half buried hero stone near east edge of the road wall (Feature 3).

Plate 9. VMS-6, stepped well (Feature 4).

VMS-370: A FORTIFICATION WALL AND RESERVOIR EMBANKMENT

Robert P. Brubaker

During a history spanning several centuries, the Vijayanagara empire engaged in frequent warfare with rivals from different quarters. These conflicts involved threats to the imperial capital of Vijayanagara itself on more than one occasion. The importance attached to the defense and control of access to the imperial core area is reflected both in the fortified character of the imperial city and in the presence of fortifications throughout the Vijayanagara Metropolitan Region (Sinopoli and Morrison 1995).

Since its inception in 1988, the Vijayanagara Metropolitan Survey (VMS) has documented a number of features which clearly or potentially may have served functions related to the defence of, and/or control of and access to the Urban Core. These features have included fortification walls and watchtowers, as well as walled settlements and reservoir embankments (see Sinopoli and Morrison 1991, and Morrison and Sinopoli 1996). Some of the fortifications within the Metropolitan Region extend or otherwise make use of the defensive potential of the natural terrain features characteristic of the area around the city, such as steep outcrop ridges or narrow valleys. In this paper I describe one such structure, VMS-370, a substantial, multi-functional fortification wall restricting passage through a narrow valley to the southeast of the imperial capital.

Fortification Wall, VMS-370

Possibly the outermost among a series of fortifications controlling approaches to the city along a valley to the southeast, VMS-370 is located in Bellary District, approximately 11 km to the southeast of the walled Urban Core of the capital, in a relatively narrow, steep-sided east-west valley situated between the rugged outcrop ridges of the Bukkasagara and Billakallu Reserved Forests. West of the village of Nallapuram, this narrow valley broadens out somewhat into rolling topography providing a corridor to the Urban Core largely unimpeded by difficult natural terrain features. The wall itself is situated near the eastern end of the valley, roughly 2 to 2.5 km east of the modern village of Nallapuram. About 5 km east of the wall, the outcrop ridges encircling the Metropolitan Region quickly terminate and the land opens into an extensive plain.

Fortification VMS-370 is slightly less than 2 km in length, and traverses the valley along a somewhat sinuous north-south axis. The wall curves to the northeast as it incorporates the higher ground of a smaller, undulating outcrop ridge situated near the valley centre, and then resumes a northerly course toward the north end of the valley (Figure 1). At either end, the wall commences high upon the steep slopes of the outcrop ridges bounding the valley on the north and south, making circum-vention on foot difficult and probably impossible for equestrian traffic. Access through the wall is provided by two gateways situated at the base of the steep slopes at either end of the valley. Between the southern gateway and the outcrop ridges in the centre of the valley, the wall doubled as a reservoir embankment as indicated by a sluice channel located c. 20 m north of the southern gateway and a stepped stone western embankment face. Parallelling the wall for much of its length on its eastern side are large excavated ditches that probably served both to provide material for the construction of the wall and to slow the approach of potential attackers. I discuss these various characteristics of the wall in greater detail in the following sections.

Wall Structure

The curtain wall of VMS-370 is constructed of earth and largely unmodified medium and large granite or basalt cobbles, with an eastern facing of large, quarried granite blocks being provided along the entire length except for a section high on the slopes of the outcrop ridge at the northern end of the valley (Plate 1). Along its course, the wall varies in terms of height, width and construction. With the exception of the reservoir embankment, which is somewhat broader and was probably somewhat higher than other stretches because of its function, variability in height is likely due largely to differential preservation. While some sections (those traversing the central outcrop ridge of the valley, and the northern end of the wall on the steep outcrop slope) are well preserved and probably near their original height, other stretches are somewhat tumbled and may not be. This, for example, is the case on the steep slope at the southern end of the valley where the wall has largely collapsed. Additionally, the stretch running between the northern end of the central outcrop ridge and the northern end of the valley is bisected by the Tungabhadra High Level Canal, and very likely provided a convenient source of stone for the construction of the latter. Taking these differences in preservation into account, and considering the height of the better preserved sections, it seems probable that the wall, if not extended by other means, may have originally ranged from somewhere between 2 and 3 m in height, with the reservoir embankment being somewhat higher (3 to 3.5 m). While it is possible that a brick and earth superstructure topped the wall, increasing its height, no evidence of fired brick was noted along its course. This does not, of course, preclude the possibility that the height of the wall was significantly increased by the addition of a superstructure consisting entirely of packed earth (Carla Sinopoli, personal communication).

Differences in the width/thickness and construction of the wall appear to be strongly correlated with the nature of the topography through which it passes. Sections of the wall traversing steep outcrop slopes and ridge tops are somewhat narrower (generally between 3 and 4 m) than stretches running across low-lying ground (up to 5 m). Behind the eastern face of quarried granite blocks, these sections tend to be characterized by double-faced construction with two larger cobble faces being in-filled with smaller cobbles. The often wedge-shaped granite blocks of the eastern, outer wall face are separated from the first of the two cobble faces by fill consisting of a mix of small cobbles and earth. Thus, three faces are generally present along higher and steeper stretches of the wall. The wall is narrowest along the well-preserved section high on the slopes of the outcrop ridge at the northern end of the valley (*c.* 2.2 m). As noted above, this section lacks a quarried granite block eastern face and there is no evidence that one ever existed. Along this terminal section, then, the wall consists of only two basalt cobble faces filled with smaller cobbles (Plate 2).

In contrast to the higher-lying, narrower sections of the wall, sections of the wall at lower elevations (in low areas of the central ridge and between this ridge and the north end of the valley) are broader and differ somewhat in structure. Between the central ridge and the north end of the valley, the wall reaches a maximum width of 5 m, which tapers down to 4.5 m at the base of the northern slopes. Along this stretch three cobble faces filled with smaller cobbles are visible behind the quarried block eastern face at the southern end, while two faces are visible behind the eastern face nearer the base of the north ridge. Like more southerly sections, the area between the wedge-shaped blocks of the eastern granite face and the first cobble face is filled with a mixture of earth and cobbles. Aside from the reservoir embankment, the width of which (up to 15 m) was probably determined, at least in part, by functional considerations, it seems likely that the correlation between width, construction and topography may reflect a perceived need for stronger, more substantial walls along more accessible, low-lying stretches.

Complementing the relationship between

wall thickness and topography is a second relationship between variable local geology and the materials used to construct different stretches of the wall. Except for the basalt ridge at the north end of the valley, granite formations dominate much of the terrain traversed by VMS-370. Those sections of the wall crossing such granitic terrain are invariably faced on the eastern, outer side with quarried granite blocks. As already noted however, the northernmost section of the wall climbing the slopes of the basalt ridge at the north end of the valley lacks this outer granite facing and consists solely of two faces constructed of darker basalt cobbles with smaller cobbles of the same material used as fill. Almost certainly indicative of a desire to reduce construction costs wherever possible by minimizing the distances materials were transported, this patterning is also apparent to a lesser extent in the material chosen as fill for the core of the wall. Thus, earth usually provides the primary fill material for those sections of the wall traversing low-lying and less rocky terrain, while cobbles tend to predominate in the fill of those wall sections traversing more elevated and generally rockier terrain.

Exceptions to this patterning are apparent, however. Some of the higher sections of the wall (notably on the crest of one of the central outcrop ridges) include large amounts of earth fill in their construction despite the predominantly rocky character of the terrain, while some lower sections appear to have been filled primarily with stone cobbles despite the availability, in much closer proximity, of virtually unlimited quantities of earth suitable for use as fill. For example, cobbles predominate in the fill of the wall along that lengthy section traversing the flat valley floor between the central outcrop ridges and the basalt ridge at the north end of the valley even though these cobbles probably had to be transported some distance from rocky areas, and even though earth suitable for fill was available immediately at hand. In this context, the preference shown for the use of cobbles may plausibly reflect a desire to avoid damaging agriculturally valuable areas of the surrounding valley floor through the removal of earth for wall fill. By way of contrast, construction of the reservoir embankment at the south end of the valley clearly required enormous amounts of earth fill in order to minimize seepage through the embankment and, thus, stone could not be utilized to the same extent. In both cases, however, whatever earth was used for fill was probably taken from the excavated ditches in front of the wall whenever possible, in order to both minimize labour and potential adverse effects to valuable cultivable land.

Moving beyond the discussion of general characteristics, there are several features of specific interest along the course of the wall. For example, on the steep slopes near its southern end, evidence of stone faces perpendicular to the course of the wall suggest the possibility that the wall originally may have presented somewhat of a stepped appearance as it ascended the ridge slope. Evidence of Vijayanagara period quarrying activities is scattered along the course of the wall; quarry marks are located near the southern gateway, on the central outcrop ridges and high on the slopes of the outcrop ridge at the northern end of the valley. Finally, along a short section in this last area, the eastern, outer side of the cobble wall is somewhat higher than the west, suggesting the possibility that the wall may originally have had a parapet (Plate 2).

The Southern Gateway

Of the two gateways providing access through the wall, the southern is both more substantial and better preserved (Plate 3). This gateway is located at the base of the steep outcrop ridge forming the southern edge of the valley. Currently, the east-west road from Kamalapura passes through the gate, and it is very probable that a Vijayanagara period road did so as well (during the 1992 season VMS survey crews traced evidence of a broad avenue several kilometres to the west of Nallapuram [VMS-326; VMS-360]. This broad avenue runs south of and roughly parallel to the modern road; like its modern successor, it probably ran through the southern gate of VMS-370).

The southern gateway is composed of two platforms (each with 3 by 2 columns) flanking a central passage oriented west/northwest-north/southeast. The columns are surmounted by cubic brackets (the inner portions of those flanking the passage are angled) supporting cross beams and roof slabs. Quarry marks are visible upon several of the columns, cross beams and roof slabs. Although superficially homogeneous in appearance, it is possible that the eastern portion of the gateway (including the four easternmost columns and their supporting basements) may be a later addition to an original gateway with two roughly square platforms (each with 2 by 2 columns) on either side of the central passage. This more westerly portion of the gate is characterized by an *upana* surmounted by tripartite basements; the columns on either side of the passage rest upon the upper mouldings of the basements. In contrast, the basements of the more easterly portion of the gate rest upon separate sections of the *upana* and are somewhat lower, lacking the upper moulding characteristic of the tripartite basements to the west. In addition, the columns flanking the central passage at the eastern end are longer, resting upon separate column footings abutted to the eastern ends of the basements rather than surmounting the basements themselves. The arrangement of brackets and cross beams at the eastern end of the gateway also differs from that to the west; rather than presenting a face of uniform height, the cross beams on either side of the passage at the eastern end rest on top of the cross beam forming the lintel over the central passage (Carla Sinopoli, personal communication). Thus, the bays on either side of the central passage are higher than the passage itself. Finally, while the gateway as a whole nowhere meets the finest standards of Vijayanagara craftsmanship, its western portions are somewhat more refined in appearance.

Sculptures

Some 25 m to the southeast of the gateway, between the road to the north and the face of the slope to the south, are three sculptures resting on a small modern platform of sandy earth retained by a low wall of small-medium cobbles. The largest of these sculptures is a slab with the carved images of two figures, a male and female (possibly Rama and Sita). The larger, male image holds what appears to be a bow, while the smaller female image has hands pressed together in *anjali mudra*. The style of the images is somewhat colloquial, suggesting perhaps the work of a local artisan (Carla Sinopoli, personal communication). The two smaller sculptures consist simply of raised rings on smaller flat-faced cobbles. Next to these three sculptures is another cobble, also painted, with a (possibly pecked) flat front surface. It seems likely that the three sculptures and the accompanying cobble are displaced, quite possibly from the area of the nearby gate. White paint of fairly recent date on each of the sculptures provides an indication that these are currently in worship.

The Reservoir Embankment

From a point immediately to the north of the southern gateway to the base of the central outcrop ridge, the wall served an additional function as a reservoir embankment (Plate 4). Like many such embankments, this stretch becomes both wider and somewhat higher toward the centre, reaching a maximum width of 15 m and a height of *c.* 3 to 3.5 m. The western face of the embankment consists of up to seven stepped courses of medium-large cobbles near the centre, with fewer courses being present toward the north end. Like other reservoir embankments, earthen fill was heavily used in construction to prevent or slow seepage. A large breach currently disrupts the embankment some 25 m to the north of the southern gateway, revealing evidence of the stone sluice channel near the base. However, no evidence of a sluice gate remains.

The Excavated Ditches

At its eastern end the sluice channel described above opened into the southern end of a ditch proceeding northward in front of, and parallel to the east face of the wall. At its southern end, this ditch is *c.* 20 m wide and perhaps 2 m deep, becoming increasingly shallower and wider as it proceeds northward toward the base of the more southerly outcrop ridge in the centre of the valley. In addition to its function as a water channel, the location of the ditch probably provided a moat of sorts at times, and more generally served to make approach to the wall, and perhaps especially the gate, more difficult. This borrow ditch is undetectable by the time the wall reaches the first of the two central outcrop ridges. Roughly 20 m north of this point, however, another ditch begins, tracing its way eastward around the eastern base of the outcrops at the valley centre and veering northwest again to parallel the course of the wall as it crosses the flat northern half of the valley. This lengthier section of ditch is similar in proportions to the sections fronting the reservoir embankment. Like the latter, this section also becomes increasingly shallow as it proceeds northward, and is largely undetectable near the north end of the valley. It seems highly likely that the decrease in depth is due largely to subsequent silting rather than design. Taken together, the two sections of ditch most probably provided fill for the construction of the wall while at the same time augmenting its strength as a defensive feature.

The Northern Gateway

The northern gateway complements its southern counterpart, being located at the base of the steep outcrop ridge forming the north wall of the valley (Plate 5). Beyond this similarity, however, the northern gateway may have been very different. Although badly preserved, enough remains of the rectilinear basal course of the foundations on either side of the passage to indicate that this passage opened to the north and south rather than to the east and west. This north-south passage was made possible by setting the lines of the fortification walls to the north and south of the gate on either side of the passage. Thus, an individual passing northward out of the gate would begin with the fortification wall on their right hand side while within, and end outside the gate facing the slope of the outcrop ridge to the north with the eastern face of the fortification wall continuing on their left-hand side up the slope of the north ridge. While the northern gate may well have had columns surmounting platforms like its southern counterpart, no evidence of such columns was noted. Given the orientation of the passage, it seems possible that the gateway was designed to be inconspicuous when viewed from the east, suggesting that easily identifiable features such as basements and columns may not have been used.

Discussion

Limited reconnaissance in the immediate vicinity of the wall revealed no indications of occupational debris and few indications of habitation structures that might have served as quarters for troops stationed along the wall. Some foundations were noted on the north side of the modern road, roughly 150 m to the west of the wall. However, these rectangular foundations were small and could only have included a few rooms at best. It is certainly possible that the wall was manned only intermittently, or only by small numbers of individuals. Alternatively, it is equally likely that garrison forces or personnel responsible for collecting tolls could have been quartered in nearby villages such as Nallapuram 2 km to the west. Such an interpretation is certainly plausible given that the low-lying areas immediately adjacent to the wall on either side were very likely devoted to agricultural production.

Perhaps the most interesting and significant aspect of the fortification wall lies in its integration of defensive and water control functions within a single structure. While the presence of the sluice and ditch may have created a moat of sorts at certain times of the year, thus enhancing the defensive strength of the wall, the incorporation of an agricultural water control feature within a wall designed to control movement attests to the importance attached to the conservation of valuable agricultural land even in zones of military activity.

On another level, the integration of defensive and water control functions within the wall serves to blur distinctions between reservoir embankments as water catchment devices and as potentially defensible features. While many, if not most, reservoir embankments were probably designed with agricultural, rather than defensive considerations uppermost in mind, some embankments in particularly favorable locations, such as those spanning

Robert P. Brubaker

narrow valleys, probably presented serious impediments to movement during the monsoon season. Even during drier periods of the year, reservoir embankments may have served as valuable rallying points to stop or slow the advance of hostile forces seeking to penetrate the core area of the empire. During an era in which logistical considerations involving speed of movement were probably as important as military superiority in determining the outcome of campaigns, the value of reservoir embankments as obstacles to advance would most likely not have gone unrecognized.

Acknowledgements

I would like to thank the Government of India for granting me permission to work at Vijayanagara as a team member of the VMS, and also the Department of Archaeology and Museums of the Government of Karnataka for their sponsorship and support of this project. Special thanks are also due to Balasubramanyam and Dr C.S. Patil. My visit to India as a student would not have been possible without the assistance of Dr P.R. Mehendiratta and the American Institute of Indian studies and to them I am profoundly grateful. As part of the survey effort, the research upon which this paper is based was supported by grants from the Smithsonian Institution (FR00627500), the National Geographic Society (4679-91) and the Wenner-Gren Foundation for Anthropological Research (5397). I would also like to thank Shinu Abraham and Janice Bailey for their patient and invaluable assistance in documenting the site described above. Thanks are also due to U. Srinivas whose patience and skill behind the wheel made the work much easier. Finally, I would particularly like to thank my Advisor, Dr Carla Sinopoli for bringing me along for the 1992 field season.

Works Cited

Morrison, K.D. and C.M. Sinopoli, 1996, Archaeological Survey in the Vijayanagara Metropolitan Region: 1990. In, *Vijayanagara: Progress of Research, 1988-1991*, edited by D.V. Devaraj and C.S. Patil, pp. 59-73, Directorate of Archaeology and Museums, Mysore.

Sinopoli, C.M. and K.D. Morrison, 1991, The Vijayanagara Metropolitan Survey: The 1988 Season. In, *Vijayanagara: Progress of Research, 1987-1988*, edited by D.V. Devaraj and C.S. Patil, pp. 55-69, Directorate of Archaeology and Museums, Mysore.

——, 1995, Dimensions of Imperial Control: The Vijayanagara Capital. *American Anthropologist*, 97(1): 83-96.

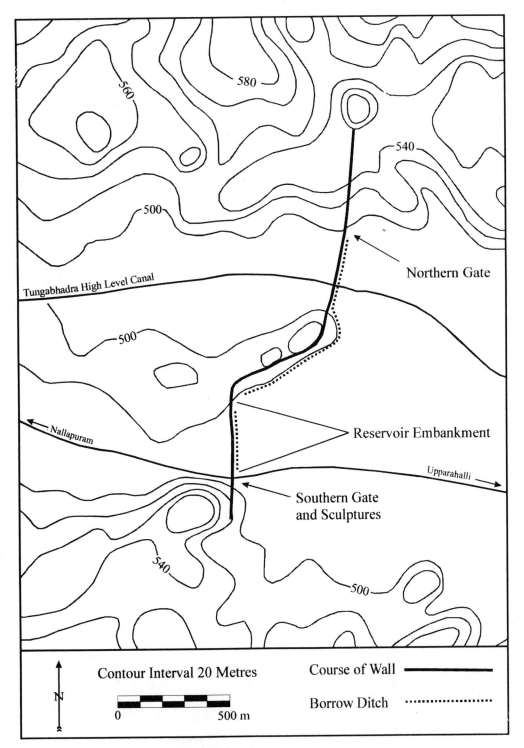

Figure 1. VMS-370, Site Map.

Plate 1. VMS-370, east quarried granite block face.

Plate 2. VMS-370, cobble wall without granite block, east facing at north end.

Plate 3. VMS-370, southern gateway.

Plate 4. VMS-370, overview of reservoir embankment and
south gateway from the south end.

Plate 5. VMS-370, overview of the remains of north gateway from near the north end.

VMS-440: A SMALL TEMPLE COMPLEX AND ASSOCIATED FEATURES

Jennifer Lundal Humayun

Through the efforts of the Vijayanagara Metropolitan Survey (VMS) directed by Drs Kathleen D. Morrison and Carla M. Sinopoli, a systematic archaeological survey has been conducted in the Vijayanagara hinterlands (Morrison and Sinopoli this volume). This survey has identified a variety of sites including water and land management features, temples, shrines and resource procurement areas. By examining the spatial distribution of these sites across the landscape, a more comprehensive understanding of the dynamics of the economic, political, civic and religious institutions within the Vijayanagara Urban Core will emerge. This paper examines a small temple complex (VMS-440) and associated sites (VMS-436, VMS-437, VMS-438, VMS-439 and VMS-441). Preliminary interpretations of the function, temporal affiliation and significance of these structures are offered.

The city of Vijayanagara contained monumental palaces, active bazaars and elaborate temples. These civic and ceremonial institutions supported a diverse socio-economic community. The city is situated in a region with sacred significance (Fritz 1986) and many modern and ancient temples and shrines occupy the city core and periphery. While temples primarily serve to provide a formal area for the worship of gods and/or goddesses, they also served as centres of learning, justice and commerce (Patil 1992: 20).

During the course of the VMS project, more than 75 temples and shrines have been recorded in the area surrounding Vijayanagara's Urban Core (for a detailed description and classificatory scheme for temples and shrines see Sinopoli 1993). This paper examines one such temple and associated structures, which were encountered during the 1994 field season. The main temple complex is located on the southeastern side of a long granite outcrop. Other structures include a water storage tank, a small shrine, three *mandapas*, a rock-cut *lingam* and two storage structures. Three sets of steps and several worn rock paths integrate these features. A long stone wall defines the site's northern and northwestern boundary. The Vijayanagara period Raya canal borders the site to the east and south.

VMS-440: Temple Complex

The temple complex is situated atop a 35 x 22 m platform and is accessible via two stair sequences (Figure 1; see also Figure 3, p. 470 and Plate 3, p. 437). One stair sequence begins by the Raya canal, 40 m southeast of the temple. Seven 1 to 3 m wide steps follow a gentle, east-west trending slope up from the Raya canal and pass between and outcrop and sheet-rock to the south and a low outcrop to the north. At the top of the steps, a footpath curves around the northern outcrop and emerges at the base of the temple's elevated platform. Where the footpath ends, several large boulders form a small terrace that stretches along the base of the platform's southern wall. This terrace may have served as an ancillary area that had less restricted access than the upper platform. The terrace area yielded the highest density of ceramics, suggesting that activities here were different than those elsewhere around the site.

Situated above the terrace on an artificially elevated platform, the temple complex is reached by means of a narrow, well defined stairway that connects the terrace with the platform's upper surface. The platform on which the temple was constructed abuts a natural granite outcrop to the northwest. A 1 to 3 m high retaining wall of unmodified and split boulders defines the platform's south-eastern side. A second 1 to 2 m high wall of irregularly placed, unmodified cobbles forms the platform's northeastern side. This platform serves as the substructure for the temple, a lamp-column and associated platform, and a 3 by 3 column *mandapa*.

The 4.5 x 4.5 m *mandapa* is located on the north edge of the platform between the natural outcrop and the northeastern retaining wall. The construction of the structure is simple (e.g. undressed columns and plain rectangular capitals). One of the roof beams is supported by the outcrop instead of a column. A 2.5 m square lamp-column platform is located 5 m southeast of the *mandapa*. The 2.8 m high lamp-column has tumbled, but is still adjacent to its platform. The *mandapa* and lamp-column platform are not oriented in the same direction as the main temple. Both the *mandapa* and lamp-column are oriented approximately north-south instead of the prevailing northeasterly-southwesterly align-ment for the majority of the site's structures. Despite the irregular orientation of the lamp column platform, it is predictably positioned directly in front of the temple's main entrance. Because of the irregular alignments of the *mandapa* and lamp column platform, I argue that these features represent a different construction episode than the temple's other structures.

Many architectural elements (e.g. capitals, column footings, fallen columns and ceiling slabs) are scattered within several metres of the *mandapa* and lamp-column. There is no indication of the original placement of the elements, but there is some evidence that at one time they were incorporated into a structure, rather than representing unused construction elements. Previous use is suggested by the plaster finish visible on a number of these displaced elements. Broken columns and dressed and detailed capitals appear with the greatest frequency along the platform's edge. It is possible that these

elements once formed a colonnade that en-compassed the *mandapa*, lamp platform and temple. Several of the displaced columns and capitals are embellished with a lotus motif. Interestingly, the lotus design is not seen on any of the site's intact elements.

The main temple is positioned on a slightly raised (10 to 20 cm) platform atop the main platform. Like the latter, this low platform extends out from the natural outcrop, creating a level surface. A pecked column footing at the south-east corner of this low temple plat-form suggests that columns once formed an even more enclosed space around the temple.

The temple itself consists of four increasingly restricted spaces (from northeast to south-west), with the most secluded of the chambers positioned inside a cavity in the granite outcrop (Figure 2). The outermost of the four spaces is an open *mandapa* defined by simple, crude-ly dressed square columns topped with cruciform capitals. The columns form a row along the front of the temple. Two of the *mandapa's* three remaining columns still have heavy plaster on their surfaces. Long roof beams connect the two southernmost columns. The roof beams, along with the presence of seven plastered slabs immediately to the east of the *mandapa*, suggest that this section of the temple was once roofed.

A low doorway connects the open outer *mandapa* with an inner 4 by 4 column walled antechamber. The doorway is designed simply, with a bevelled edge around the door-jamb and a single square medallion centred above the doorway. Sockets can be seen on the interior side of the lintel, indicating that a door once separated the antechamber from the outer porch and platform area. Partially preserved cobble and rubble walls enclose the antechamber, even along the outcrop forming the northwestern side of the temple. Plaster is still visible on the interior side of many of these wall segments.

The southwestern wall of the antechamber has a doorway leading into the inner sanctuary. This door is flanked to the right (northwest) by a three-quarter height, rammed earth wall, and to the left (southeast) by a low platform. The low retaining wall that defines the plat-form extends for approximately 2 m to a plain square column that marks the southern corner of the antechamber. A small 20 cm wide x 30 cm high window has been built into the southwestern wall that connects the south wall of the antechamber with the natural rock overhang. A small enclosure formed by the platform, wall segment, and slight natural rock overhang, creates a niche that may have served as a small subsidiary shrine adjacent to the doorway leading to the sanctuary.

The antechamber's four inner columns and capitals differ from those that support the outer walls. The outer columns have plain, temporally ubiquitous undecorated columns and cruciform capitals. The four inner columns each have a single octagonal inset band. Additionally, the inner columns are topped with capitals consisting of three discs that increase in size as they ascend to the ceiling. The uppermost disc may be carved separately, but heavy plaster obscures any perceptible gap between the elements. Since disc-shaped capitals are associated with early Vijayanagara period construction throughout the Urban Core (Fritz, Michell and Nagaraja Rao 1984: 90), the disc-shaped capitals at VMS-440 help to establish an early Vijayanagara period construction date for this section of the temple. Above the disc-topped columns are heavily plastered, cruciform capitals, some with traces of red paint still remaining. Although the temple is not currently in worship, the plaster and paint are probably the result of post-Vijayanagara maintenance activities.

A large granite image base and carved Nandi are situated in the centre of the antechamber and flanked by the four decorated columns. The Nandi image also faces southwest, toward the second doorway of the temple. Nandi is finely carved and detailed, but since the image is almost as large as the base itself, it is unlikely that these elements were the original image and/or image base. The spout of the image base faces the doorway; an unusual orientation that suggests the base has either been shifted or was moved to this location after the temple's initial abandonment.

Most of the roof over the antechamber remains intact, but some collapse on the southern portion has exposed a multi-layer roof construction. The roof is supported by beams that stretch between the columns. Roofing

slabs are placed closely between these beams and covered with a thick layer of plaster. A layer of Vijayanagara type cement overlays the plaster surface, followed by several courses of bricks. The bricks are then covered with another layer of cement (10 to 25 cm). It appears that at one time the roof covered the entire antechamber.

The doorway to the innermost sanctuary is only slightly more elaborate than the temple's outer door. Like the outer door, the door-jamb and lintel are decorated with an incised square arch and bevelled border, but the inner doorway also has covered vessels carved into the lower portion of each door-jamb. The door restricts access into a natural rock chamber that forms the inner sanctuary. Although some modifications to the space have been made, the natural form of the rock chamber determines the fundamental shape of the rooms. Five roughly dressed square columns support irregularly aligned ceiling slabs and rubble and earth walls that have been built against the northern side of the room. The southern side of the chamber is unmodified and consists of an enormous boulder leaning against the outcrop.

The entrance marking the innermost sanctuary is defined by a partial rammed earth wall forming a narrow opening to the restricted area. Two packed earth steps lead into the irregularly shaped rock cavity that forms the sanctuary. Two large (0.9 x 1.3 m and 0.9 x 1.5 m) granite image bases appear to be randomly placed inside the sanctuary and probably do not represent the original placement. There are no images associated with these bases. Rubble walls are built over several of the larger gaps between the boulders, creating a dim enclosure. Some light enters the sanctuary through a narrow natural opening between the two boulders that form the southern wall. The small opening leads to a 2 by 2 column *mandapa* that connects the sanctuary with another large boulder immediately to the south. This construction creates a completely enclosed space around the temple's innermost sanctuary.

One of the most striking features of the temple is a 1.5 m high *shikhara* that has been built atop the outcrop that forms the sanctuary. The plastered *shikhara* incorporates four, successively smaller square tiers topped by a modified dome. The first tier is unadorned and serves as a base for the *shikhara*. The second tier has detailed plasterwork figures; the southern panel is decorated with two peacocks, the east panel displays two *hamsa* (geese). The third and fourth tiers are plain except for oval medallions in the centre and half medallions at the corners. The northern side of the *shikhara* has collapsed, obliterating any other images but exposing a rubble and cement construction fill. Although the *shikhara's* square shape is similar to those of other early Vijayanagara temples in the Urban Core (Fritz, Michell and Nagaraja Rao 1984: 56), C.S. Patil interpreted it as a later addition to the complex (personal communication). Patil's assessment is based on the *shikhara's* excellent preservation and the stone cobble construction fill. Based on the diverse architectural styles, multiple construction platforms and variable orientations of structures, VMS-440 probably expanded accretionally with building phases occur-ring during early as well as late Vijayanagara periods and possibly beyond.

VMS-439: Tank and Associated Structures

Like many temples, VMS-440 has an associated water tank (VMS-439). Other site elements of VMS-439 include a stairway, terrace, wall, pecked *lingam* and two small structures of indeterminate function (Figure 3).

The 5 x 6-m tank is located on a southeast sloping sheet-rock surface 5 m west of the temple complex. The tank is accessed from the temple platform by an 8-m long granite block stairway. The top of the stairway is adjacent to a slightly raised earthen terrace that defines the tank's southeastern side. This terrace augments a natural depression in the sheet-rock and serves to increase the tank's water catchment and storage capabilities. Siltation has obscured most of the tank's bottom, but quarry marks are visible on exposed sections suggesting that quarrying was done to enlarge the natural depression. Slightly stepped, medium to large split and unmodified stones have been used to construct the tank walls that reach a maximum height of 1.9 m on the eastern side. The only water source for the tank seems to be from runoff, although it is possible that water was transported to the tank from the Raya canal. The presence of an outlet spout at the southeast corner of the tank shows a concern about overflow.

A small *lingam* is situated 4 m south of the tank's southwest corner. This is one of the few features that provide information about the nature of worship that occurred at the site. The *lingam* measures 15 cm in diametre and 5-cm high, and is pecked directly into the sheet-rock. A square base and drainage spout are etched into the rock surface around the *lingam*.

A footpath is visible in the sheet-rock near the *lingam* and water tank. Considerable traffic has polished the rough granite surface along this route. The narrow footpath links the main temple complex with the sites farther to the southeast. Situated just north of the footpath and southeast of the tank is a 3 x 3 m platform formed by a single course of large slabs. A 3-m long wall extends north from the platform's northeast corner toward a natural crevasse in the outcrop which has been modified to form an 8-m long, 1- x 3 to 2-m wide enclosure. Five courses of small blocks form a wall on the south side of the enclosure. The wall helps support five granite slabs that create a partial roof over the space. Several disturbed slabs with Vijayanagara type quarry marks rest on the floor of the enclosure suggesting that at one time more of the structure was roofed.

VMS-438: Temple and Associated Structure

A small temple on a low platform and an associated storage structure (VMS-438) are located approximately 100 m east of the temple tank. A single course of variable sized stones defines the edges of a 17 x 15 m platform upon which the site's structures are located. The stone coursing on the eastern side of the platform is placed to create a step for accessing the platform. A displaced image base lies against the northern wall of the platform. The original location of the image base is not apparent, but since there is no image base in the temple's inner sanctuary it is possible that it is close to its original position.

The temple is oriented northeast, like VMS-

440, and consists of a 4 by 3 column *mandapa* and a 2 by 2 column sanctuary. The *mandapa* is built with square columns that still show Vijaya-nagara type quarry marks on their roughly dressed surfaces. Rubble walls connect some of the columns, but they seem to be recent additions. Cruciform capitals top the 1.4-m high columns and serve as a foundation for the long ceiling beams. The ceiling beams extend 20 cm beyond the *mandapa's* eastern side, probably to support eaves. Ceiling slabs, some with traces of plaster, enclose the *mandapa*. A displaced chlorite image base lies inside the *mandapa*. One side of the image base, presumably the front, has an attractively carved Nandi image; the opposite side has a drainage channel.

A low unadorned doorway provides entrance to the inner sanctuary. Several coats of plaster and white paint cover the two slabs and lintel that form the doorway. The sanctuary walls are formed by granite slabs that have been placed horizontally between the corner columns. Additional granite slabs and blocks have been used to construct a ceiling of rotated square design. Above this rises a low brick and plaster *shikhara*.

Located several metres northeast of the temple's platform is a small structure of unknown use. The structure consists of three walls formed by five courses (2 m) of irregularly shaped granite slabs and rocks, and an "entrance" that is partially blocked by several large boulders. The semi-obstructed entrance is located on the south side of the structure and oriented toward the temple and platform. The enclosed space, which measures approximately 1 x 3 m, may have been used for storage.

VMS-347: *Mandapa*/**Storage Structure**

Another small structure is located southwest of the main temple complex. This structure is heavily disturbed by termite activity, making it impossible to determine whether it served as a *mandapa*, a storage structure or even a small shrine. The structure's four rectangular columns (0.2 x 0.4 m in section) broaden toward the top. Some Vijayanagara quarry marks are still visible on the 1.6 m high, crudely dressed columns. Although large termite

mounds obscure most of the structure, some wall segments are still visible between the columns, revealing a small and medium stone, double-faced construction.

VMS-441: *Mandapa*

This site consists of a 3 by 2 column *mandapa* (VMS-441) positioned on a high earthen platform located 80 m northeast of the "main" temple complex. Like VMS-440 and VMS-439, a platform has been built to create a level construction surface against the outcrop. The northern side of the platform is almost level with the slope, but the south side has been elevated approximately 3 m. The platform's retaining walls are constructed of split slabs that are positioned in a slightly stepped pattern. Some chinking stones fill the largest gaps. A second lower platform (0.2 m) sits atop the larger one, forming a base for the north-eastern oriented *mandapa*. The natural orientation of the outcrop seems to have affected the alignment of this (and other) structures.

The *mandapa* is accessed from the eastern side by a stairway flanked with balustrades. The balustrades are constructed with medium to large unmodified stones. The only artefacts collected at this site were six ceramic shards found at the base of the stairs. It is possible that erosion washed these and other artefacts and soil off the platform surface.

The *mandapa's* irregularly shaped columns still have Vijayanagara quarry marks visible on them. They are topped by cruciform capitals and joined by notched ceiling beams. Two bevel-edged columns are placed against the interior sides of the two central columns forming a simple doorway for the *mandapa*. A repair episode for a cracked roof beam is evidenced by a short column topped with a capital and three unmodified stones which have been piled to support both parts of the broken ceiling beam and prevent it from collapsing. The repair episode obviously postdates the initial construction phase and probably would have required the cooperation of several individuals. Quarried blocks of one to three courses high have been erected to form partial walls on the southern, western and northern sides of the *mandapa*.

VMS-436: Wall, Shrine and Inscription

The remains of a 500-m long wall runs atop the ridge of the outcrop northeast of the site. The wall begins approximately 150 m to the northeast of VMS-440 and extends northeast for approximately 190 m along the ridge before turning almost due east to follow another lower ridge for an additional 250 m. The wall is double-faced along its entire length, but varies in height, width and construction materials.

The southwestern wall segment traverses a large granite sheet-rock ridge. Unmodified granite stones, split granite stones, and a few quarried granite slabs constitute the construction materials. Rubble fill is frequently used between the two faces. The wall loses elevation as it moves northeast crossing a low drainage area 100 m from the wall's southwestern end. The wall is less clearly defined around the drainage. Although many of the larger boulders remain intact, smaller rubble is strewn about the sheet-rock. The wall continues past the drainage for another 50 m, gaining elevation until it reaches a low, gabbro boulder ridge. At the gabbro ridge, the wall turns east for approximately 250 m before it begins to lose definition as it reaches the end of the gabbro dyke. This segment of the wall is constructed with unmodified, medium-sized gabbro boulders and some earthen fill. The width of the wall segment remains fairly consistent at around 1.8 m.

Where the gabbro dyke ends, medium- and large-sized boulders appear to form a crude wall, but whether or not this represents human modification is not evident. There is little need for a boundary or defensive wall here since the Raya canal doubles around, forming a small isolated peninsula of land. A small, heavily silted shrine is situated 10 m from the canal, beneath a southeasterly facing overhang. A low wall demarcates the area around the shrine and may account for much of the siltation within it. Only the top portions of two sculpted images and the pointed hat of a third are visible above the layer of soil deposition. Despite the remote location and heavy siltation, the shrine is currently in worship as evidenced by recently applied plaster and red paint.

An eight-line inscription has been etched into the sloping sheet-rock surface in front of the shrine. The text is slightly worn and covers an area of 2 x 0.6 m. Based on the appearance of the script, C.S. Patil believes the inscription postdates the Vijayanagara period (personal communication).

Discussion

Although the scope of this analysis leaves many questions unanswered, it is possible to interpret the sites of VMS-440, VMS-437, VMS-438, VMS-439 and VMS-441 as constituting a single temple site complex. The wall segment VMS-436 is associated with the temple complex but probably correlates with other, more ephemeral, Vijayanagara period sites as well. Access to the temple complex was restricted by the natural outcrop and the construction of the wall and Raya canal. The positioning of the temple complex, in a location with limited, or tightly restricted access is also observed at other Vijayanagara temple sites in the Vijayanagara Metropolitan Region. During the Vijayanagara period, the temple complex's remote location probably served to maintain the distinction between sacred and secular space.

Today, the sites remain isolated from modern transportation routes. This location may explain, in part, why there is no indication that efforts are being made to maintain the site for religious purposes. Since vegetation has overgrown much of the area in and around the site's structures, it is doubtful that the complex is occupied in any capacity. It is possible that portions of the site once served as a residence for individuals who had religious duties or were responsible for the maintenance of the temple complex. The low density of artefacts is inadequate for analysis but suggests that if the site was occupied, the number of residents was minimal.

Temples and temple complexes are common features on the landscape surrounding the ancient capital of Vijayanagara. This brief description of one such religious site, by itself, provides little insight into the religious, political or social life of the inhabitants of the

Metropolitan Region. When compared and contrasted with other such temple sites around the Urban Core, a greater knowledge of the Metropolitan Region will develop. The efforts of the VMS have provided some of the information necessary to better understand the institutions and individuals that occupied this region.

Acknowledgements

Drs Kathleen D. Morrison and Carla M. Sinopoli, Directors of the VMS, deserve my special thanks for their guidance and encouragement. Special thanks to the Karnataka Department of Archaeology and Museums and especially to the late Dr C.S. Patil. I am grateful for the efforts of Robert Brubaker, Michael Dega, Lars Fogelin, Kathleen Morrison and Carla Sinopoli who all prepared sections of the initial site reports and maps. I would also like to acknowledge S.B. Darsana from Deccan College who assisted with site mapping and artefact collection. Lars Fogelin was particularly generous with his time and patience during the more detailed mapping of the site.

Works Cited

Fritz, J.M., G. Michell and M.S. Nagaraja Rao, 1984, *Where Kings and Gods Meet: The Royal Centre at Vijayanagara, India,* University of Arizona Press, Tucson.

Fritz, J.M., 1986, Vijayanagara: Authority and Meaning of a South Indian Capital. *American Anthropologist,* 88: 44-55.

Patil, C.S., 1992, *Temples of Raichur and Bellary Districts,* Directorate of Archaeology and Museums, Mysore.

Sinopoli, C.M., 1993, Defining a Sacred Landscape: Temple Architecture and Divine Images in the Vijayanagara Suburbs. In, *South Asian Archaeology 1991,* edited by A.J. Gail and G.J.R. Mevissan, pp. 625-35, Franz Steiner Verlag, Stuttgart.

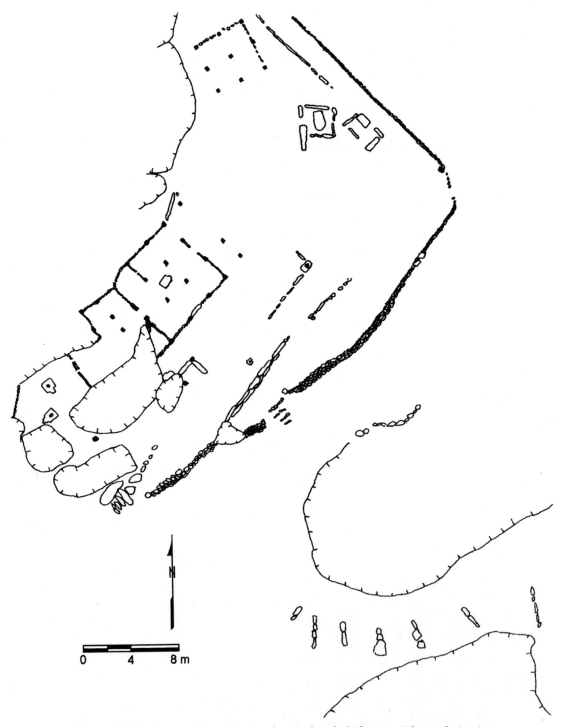

Figure 1. VMS-440, temple complex and associated platforms, stairs and structures.

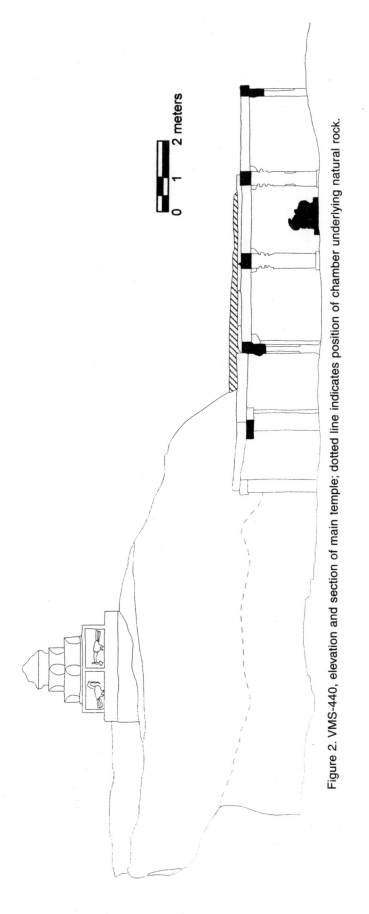

Figure 2. VMS-440, elevation and section of main temple; dotted line indicates position of chamber underlying natural rock.

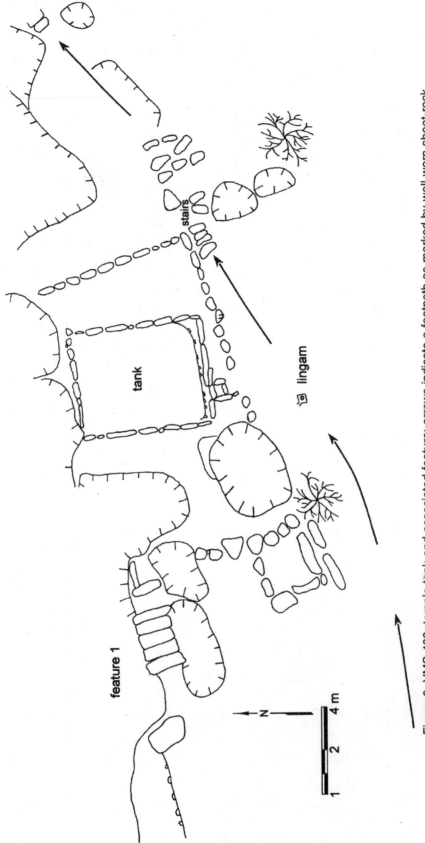

Figure 3. VMS-439, temple tank and associated feature; arrows indicate a footpath as marked by well worn sheet-rock.

BRICKMAKING IN MALAPANNAGUDI: ETHNOARCHAEOLOGICAL RESEARCH AND ARCHAEOLOGICAL IMPLICATIONS

Lars Fogelin

In the fields south of the town of Malapannagudi are found the smoking furnaces of active brickyards. Located only 5 km from the city of Hospet, Malapannagudi supplies the bricks for its expansion. In the fifteenth and sixteenth centuries Malapannagudi was a suburb of another large city, Vijayanagara. Within this abandoned city are the remains of massive temples with brick superstructures. While much of the brick production in Malapannagudi can be seen as thoroughly modern, some of the smaller operations still follow techniques which may serve as analogues for Vijayanagara brick production. For three days in July 1994 I conducted ethnoarchaeological research in the brickyards as part of the Vijayanagara Metropolitan Survey (VMS) (Sinopoli and Morrison 1991, 1992 and 1995; see also papers in this volume). The primary goals of the investigation were to determine the imprint that brickmaking would leave on the archaeological record and to predict the likely foci of historic brickmaking. In the process of collecting this information, I also realized that this research could be used to address the resource constraints that would have affected brickmaking in the past. I approached this project with the belief that bricks were common building materials of little value. I now believe the opposite. Resource competition, particularly in regard to agriculture, made brick a relatively costly building material, used only where weight was a significant concern.

Ethnoarchaeology of Brickmaking

In 1994 the brickyards at Malapannagudi were located immediately south of the town. The brickyards themselves covered only a few acres each, but left a trail of barren land as they worked across the landscape turning topsoil into brick. Most of the operations worked at a large scale, with as many as 30 employees. Scattered between the more intensive brickyards were smaller operations. Prior to firing, there is little difference in the methods, rates or resources used for brick production between the more intensive and less intensive brickmaking operations. The difference lies in the fuel employed to fire the bricks. In the larger operations, coal is used. The higher temperatures allow for larger, stronger bricks. The smaller scale brickyards fire smaller bricks using only rice husks. It is these operations on which I focused my research. Clearly the use of coal significantly post-dates the Vijayanagara period and limits its use as an analogue. What follows is a detailed description of the stages of production of rice-husk fired bricks from the excavation of the soil through their firing in a custom-built kiln.

Step 1: Soil Excavation

At the end of each workday, the soil is softened for the following day's work by pooling water on the ground surface and allowing it to soak into the soil overnight. These pools are generally 2 cm deep and cover roughly one square metre. The amount of soil softened is determined by the amount of soil needed for the following days work. The next morning the soil is excavated to the depth of approximately 4 ft (122 cm). This is both part of the lease arrangement the brickmakers have with the landholder and usually the depth at which the soil is no longer suitable for brickmaking.

The brickmakers describe the deeper soil as too "sticky" for use in making bricks. In the morning the soil is removed with shovels and placed in a location suitable for mixing dirt, water and rice chaff. This is usually done in a previously excavated pit near the area in which the finished bricks will be dried.

Step 2: Mixing Ingredients

Water is mixed into the soil until it is "sticky". The amount of water needed varies, based upon the judgement of the brickmaker. After the water has been added, the brickmakers add rice husk. Although the actual amount of rice husk added to the mixture is also based on the judgement of the brickmaker, on average eight tins of husk are needed for every 1,000 bricks. Each tin holds 17 litres of husks, for a total of 136 litres of husk per 1,000 bricks. The mud and rice husks are mixed using a shovel.

Step 3: Forming the Bricks

Before the bricks are made, an area is cleared for drying the freshly made bricks. This area is cleared and smoothed of debris. A light dusting of ash is thrown over the surface to prevent the drying bricks from sticking to the surface. Ample quantities of ash are available from the remains of previously fired furnaces. Once the drying area is fully prepared, the mixture of rice husk and mud is brought to the work area and the process of making the bricks begins. If the mixture has dried, water is added to make it "loose". Brickmakers report that "looser" mud goes into the mould faster.

Bricks are formed individually in moulds. The mould is a simple, rectangular tin box with a makers mark soldered into the bottom with wire. Only the top of the mould is open. The dimensions of the moulds are 9″ x 4″ x 3″ (23 x 10 x 7.5 cm). This results in a bricks with dimensions of 8″ x 3″ x 2″ (20 x 7.5 x 5 cm) after drying and firing. To form the brick the mould is first moistened with a splash of water prior to throwing in the mud mixture. The surface of the mud is then smoothed with the top of the mould, and the entire mould is inverted to remove the newly shaped brick. Bricks are laid out together with the makers mark facing upward on the previously prepared drying area. Every half hour the workers throw ash over the surface of the newly made bricks to prevent them from cracking in the sun as they dry. Each worker can make between 800 and 1,000 bricks in a day. Roughly ten people are employed by the rice-husk brickmaker. The total output is 8,000 to 10,000 sun-dried bricks per day.

The most important tool in the process of brickmaking is the mould. These are owned by the head brickmaker, who also is the leaseholder for the land on which the bricks are made. Each brickmaker has one or more maker's marks that are unique to his operation. The operator brickyard was using three different makers marks during the time I observed his operations. The maker's marks are used to identify who made an individual bricks for payment after delivery.

Step 4: Drying Bricks

The bricks are dried for three days. During this time the bricks shrink to approximately 87 percent of their original volume. This shrinkage accounts for almost all of the shrinkage that occurs from the mould to the finished fired brick. After this time the bricks are stacked in piles of ten to be counted by the employer. Any bricks that crack in the drying process are not counted. Workers are paid Rs. 70 for every 1,000 bricks they make. Once a sufficient number of bricks have dried, the head brickmaker begins constructing the kiln to fire them.

Step 5: Furnace Construction (Figures 1-2)

A key element of the rice-husk furnace is that it is constructed of unfired bricks themselves. No permanent kilns are employed and all of the bricks used in the furnace are later sold. The owner of the brickyard makes the furnace himself. He considers furnace construction to be the most difficult part of the process and does not trust any of his workers to do it. Each furnace fires between 20,000 and 30,000 bricks at a time. The first step consists of stacking the sun-dried bricks in rows. The lowest levels of bricks are arranged to allow the flow of air through the base of the furnace. Each row is between 15 and 20 ft (5 and 6.5 m) long, with the spacing between rows equal the width of one brick. The rows are roughly 5 ft (1.8 m) tall. The total number of rows is variable, but typically is enough to make the area of stacked bricks roughly square. While stacking the bricks the owner makes periodic connections between the rows in order to solidify the construction.

Once the interior rows have been constructed, an exterior wall of previously fired bricks is constructed surrounding the interior rows of unfired bricks. A space of approximately 1 ft (30 cm) is left between the wall and the rows. The width of this wall is equal to the length of a single brick. The exterior wall extends 6″ (15 cm) higher than the interior rows. Once the entire wall has been completed, it is covered in a mixture of rice husk and mud. Once dry, this covering acts to seal the gaps between bricks. On the upwind side of the furnace small holes are formed in the base of the exterior wall at approximately 5 ft (1.6 m) intervals. These holes allow air into the bottom of the furnace to aid in the burning of the rice husk. Bricks can be placed in front of this hole to adjust the amount of air entering the furnace while it is being fired. A small ridge of dirt is placed roughly 6″ (15 cm) in front of these air holes to prevent water from seeping into the furnace.

Once the furnace has been completed, rice husk is poured in through the top filling the bottom 2 to 3 ft (0.65 to 1.0 m). The rice husk is burned, leaving ash. Another 2 or 3 ft of husk is added and burned again. This process is continued until the rice husks have been burned all the way to the top of the furnace. When the furnace has been filled to the top, prior to the final burning, the surface is covered in clay, and windbreaks are made from either bricks, or banana fronds. The purpose of all of these precautions is to keep the rice husk from blowing out of the furnace during firing. It takes the owner two days to build the furnace working alone.

In the dry season it takes eight or nine days to fire an entire furnace of bricks. In the wet season this time can increase to fifteen days, with a corresponding increase in the quantity of rice husk needed. In the dry season it takes seven to eight bags of rice husk to fire 1,000

bricks. Each bag contains roughly 75 litres of rice husk. Once the furnace has cooled, all the bricks, including those from the outside wall, are removed and sold. A small number of bricks is retained for constructing the exterior walls of future furnaces.

Land and Resource Use

The resources used for brickmaking are water, soil, and rice husk. Since all of these materials are purchased, the operator of the brickyard was able to provide a detailed description of the total resources used in production. The production of 1,000 bricks requires 55 gallons of water, 700 litres of rice husk and approximately 2 cubic metres (cu m) of soil. Given this information, a daily production of 10,000 bricks requires 550 gallons of water, 7,000 litres of rice husk and 20 cu m of soil. These resource needs have direct implications on the locations of brick production.

The owners of both the coal and rice-husk fired brickyards stated that the most important factor in choosing areas for brick production is the availability of water. Only with prompting did they discuss the preferred soils. Both brickmakers stated that while "red soils" are preferred over "black soils", there is no lack of the "red soils" in the area. Surprisingly, it is the "black soils" that have the higher clay content. All of the brickmakers I have talked with try to avoid soils which they describe as "sticky". The "red soils" used in Malapannagudi have a fairly high sand content (60% sand, 10% silt, 30% clay). In contrast, the "black soils" have more clay (33% sand, 20% silt, and 50% clay). Rice husks are the final resource used in brickmaking. The operator of the brickyard did not consider the cost of rice husk to be important in his business despite the large quantity used. While important for brick production, rice husks are cheap, plentiful and easily transported to the brickyard.

Table 1. Resources used for 1,000 bricks

	1,000 Bricks (1 worker, 1 day)
Water	55 gallons
Rice Husk	700 litres
Soil	2 cubic metres

One final aspect of modern brick production bears directly upon the issues of past brick production. Brickmaking removes the topsoil from the land on which it is conducted. In the six years of production at Malapannagudi over 17 acres of topsoil have been lost. Unfortunately, this area includes both rice-husk, fired brick production and more intensive coal fired production. For this reason, it is not possible to generate a rate of land use for rice-husk brick production over the longer term. Rates of resource use can only be postulated through the details of lease arrangements and the rates of brick production discussed earlier.

The rice-husk fired brickyard has a six year lease on two acres of land, though the owner believes it will only take four years to remove all of the topsoil from the parcel. With ten people producing roughly 10,000 bricks a day, it would take roughly 400 consecutive days of work to remove all of the topsoil. Given 200 workdays per year, this corresponds to roughly two years of work. Since the owner of the brickyard expected to complete the plot in roughly four years, this suggests that either production occurs less than 200 days a year, or that less people work on average than I observed. The latter explanation seems likely since my observations occurred near the end of the dry season when the operator was stockpiling bricks for the monsoon.

The area of past brick production north of the Malapannagudi brickyards is heavily eroded and barren. In the six years since production ceased in the oldest areas no significant soil formation has occurred. This land is now completely unsuitable for agriculture, though buffaloes wallow in some of the water filled depressions. The locations of sugarcane fields immediately adjacent to this area confirm that without brick production this land could have been agriculturally productive. Thus, the cost of brickmaking is not limited to the price of the resources used in their production, but also the displacement of other activities, particularly agriculture. As will be discussed at greater length below, this has important implications in the role of brickmaking during the Vijayanagara period.

The Archaeological Signature of Brickmaking

Vijayanagara period bricks are smaller and flatter than modern bricks, measuring 8 ¾″ x 4 ¾″ x 1 ³/₈″ (19.5 x 11.5 x 3.5 cm). For this reason it is not difficult to differentiate between modern and historic bricks. The more difficult problem is finding historic brick production and differentiating brick production areas from historic construction sites. The abandoned areas of the brickyards at Malapannagudi provide an opportunity to document the waste produced and the potential archaeological signature of brick production. As a final phase of my research at Malapannagudi I observed these remains with the goal of predicting the archaeological signature of historic brickmaking. If modern rice-husk fired brick production is a suitable analog for historic brickmaking, several features can be used to identify the locations of this production.

Many bricks are cracked during firing and dismantling the furnace. At the Malapannagudi brickyard these bricks are thrown into piles surrounding the work area. These piles of broken brick could be found in the archaeological record. This is the only archaeological imprint of brickmaking that has a reasonable chance of being visible on the modern landscape surface. Unfortunately, similar piles can also be expected at building sites.

The most distinctive aspect of brickmaking is the furnace. Unfortunately, the furnace is dismantled after firing. However, within the abandoned portions of the Malapannagudi brickyard are the remains of the lowest levels of these furnaces. It appears that many of the lowest bricks become fused to the ground, making it difficult to remove them after firing. In other cases the heat of the furnace hardens the ground on which the bricks were fired, leaving an indelible impression of the furnace. In both cases, bricks leave a pattern that shows the distinctive rows and encircling wall of a rice-husk fired furnace. The only potential problem with this imprint is that the encircling wall could easily be mistaken for a foundation of a building without the presence of the imprint of the interior rows.

One final signature of brickmaking is the presence of large quantities of burnt and unburned rice husk. In the abandoned brickyards of Malapannagudi the soils are mottled with a combination of both. These mottled soils extend several metres beyond the furnaces. Together, the imprint of the furnace and charred remains of rice husks can be used to identify brickmaking in the archaeological record. Despite relatively clear indicators for brick production, no brickyards have been identified in either the Vijayanagara Research Project or VMS. The reasons for this absence constitute the final portion of this paper.

Archaeological Implications of Brickmaking

As reported by the brickmakers in Malapannagudi, the availability of water is the primary factor in the location of brick production. This is not a factor that is likely to have been different in historic brick production. Water is heavy and difficult to transport. Without diesel pumps, it is reasonable to assume that historic brickmaking occurred near rivers, irrigation canals, or next to reservoirs. The intensive use of these same areas today for agriculture partially explains why the VMS has found no brick production areas. Modern agricultural fields would have destroyed what surface evidence may have existed for brick production. The importance of land with access to water for brick production also suggests an interesting conflict with agriculture during the Vijayanagara period.

Morrison (1995) has shown that agriculture in the area surrounding Vijayanagara was greatly intensified during the occupation of Vijayanagara. Among the most intensively utilized areas were those with access to water. The importance of wet agriculture is shown in the large amount of labour used to construct and maintain irrigation canals and seasonal reservoirs. Brickmaking would have been in direct competition with agriculture for land with access to water. Furthermore, the process of brickmaking removes all of the topsoil from this land, limiting the agricultural potential for a significant period of time after brickmaking ceased. The only alternative to this would be to transport soil from less critical areas to

brickmaking facilities near the water. It is not possible to predict which option would have been used without a much clearer idea of the relative importance of bricks and agriculture in Vijayanagara. However, in either case, the relative cost of brick production would have been higher than it is today.

In addition to the competing land claims of bricks and agriculture, several other land uses also would have been in conflict with brickmaking. Like agricultural land, settlements must have access to water. Historical documents also cite large numbers of horses and elephants at Vijayanagara. These animals would have needed pasture land with access to water. In the driest periods of the year, potential pasture may have been increasingly restricted to the lands near the canals, rivers and reservoirs. Given all of these competing demands for land, the relative costs of bricks would include the displacement of other important economic activities.

While no historic brickyards have been identified in either the core of Vijayanagara or the Metropolitan Area, hundreds of structures using brick have been identified. Given the rates of production and land use of modern brickyards near Malapannagudi, it is possible to predict the scale of production needed to make the bricks for individual monuments, and for architectural structures as a whole within the Urban Core of Vijayanagara. The Vijayanagara Research Project, directed by John M. Fritz and George Michell, has documented architectural features in the Urban Core of Vijayanagara (Michell 1990, Fritz, Michell and Nagaraja Rao 1984 and Fritz 1985; see also papers in this volume). When combined with other studies on some of the large temple complexes, a picture of the quantity of brick in Vijayanagara emerges.

For the most part, brick is restricted to the superstructures of temples, shrines, and gateways. The use of brick in these situations was determined by the need for lighter building material for higher construction. Once built, the brick superstructures were covered in ornamental plaster. While brick was extensively used, it would not have been visible. In addition to bricks used in superstructures, brick was also used as fill in the enclosing walls of a few large temple complexes. For example, the Vitthala temple complex has brick in the super-structures of its shrines and gateways and a core of brick throughout the length of its enclosure wall. I have estimated the total volume of brick used in the construction of the Vitthala temple complex at 4,000 cu m (based upon architectural plans in Filliozat and Filliozat 1988). Fully half of this brick is in the core of the enclosure walls. A ten-person brickmaking operation using rice-husk furnaces produces between 8,000 and 10,000 finished bricks a day. This translates into between 14 and 17.5 cu m of finished brick a day. Given the higher rate, ten people could have made all of the bricks in 230 days. In this time the topsoil of slightly more than an acre of land (1.14 ha) would be made barren. This contrasts with the seven decades it took to build the temple complex before its abandonment after the collapse of Vijayanagara in 1565. Clearly, brickmaking was only a minor aspect of the overall construction process.

While the total brick production of Vitthala temple is interesting, it was not a typical structure in Vijayanagara. *The Architectural Inventory of the Urban Core* provides the most complete published sample of architecture available for Vijayanagara (Michell 1990). George Michell and his team have described and drawn almost all of the architectural features of the Urban Core. Using this information I have attempted to estimate the total quantity of brick present in the architecture of the Urban Core. This in turn can be used to estimate the scale of production of brick more generally. It should be noted at the outset that this sample does not constitute the total quantity of brick within the city or within the larger metropolitan area. The Vijayanagara Research Project recorded all of the architectural remains within the Urban Core of Vijayanagara, an area of roughly 22 sq km within the city walls. Outside these walls are several large temples and numerous smaller ones. With the exception Vitthala temple discussed above, these have not been analysed.

Within the Urban Core are 181 structures that either have, or can be assumed to have had, bricks as part of their construction. Within the Urban Core bricks are only found in the superstructures of temples. The largest of these buildings recorded in the *Architectural*

Inventory are the Raghunatha and Virupaksha temples. Unlike Vitthala temple, Raghunatha temple does not have a core of bricks within its enclosure wall. The total volume of bricks used in the construction of this temple is 1,200 cu m. However, when averaged with the 2,000 cu m of bricks in Vitthala temple (excluding enclosure walls), large temple complexes average roughly 1,600 cu m of brick in their construction.

A total of six smaller enclosed temples are found in the Urban Core. Their super-structures are typically much smaller than those of large enclosed temple complexes. The quantity of brick is correspondingly less. These small enclosed temples average only 312 cu m of brick in their construction. Smaller still are unenclosed temples associated with four by four columned antechambers. The total quantity of brick in these temples averages only 43 cu m. However, over 73 of these temples have been found in the Urban Core. In the smallest category are shrines and temples with columned antechambers smaller than four by four. While the most common within the Urban Core with 101 features, the brick superstructures of these buildings contain only 2.5 cu m of brick.

When added together, the total quantity of bricks within the Urban Core is about 8,500 cu m. This represents roughly 485 days of brick production by ten brickmakers. In this time only 2 acres of soil would have been depleted. Given 200 work days a year, it would have taken only two years to produce all of the bricks found in the Urban Core. Given this, it is evident that brick production at Vijayanagara was extremely limited. In the competing demands between brick production and agricultural production, bricks came in second. For the most part, the value of bricks did not exceed the value of the agricultural land destroyed by their production. Therefore, those few bricks that are present in the temple architecture can be assumed to have had a relatively high value. This point is reinforced by missing brick superstructures on many of the temples described in the *Architectural Inventory*. It is impossible to say if these brick superstructures were dismantled and reused in historic or modern periods. However, the potential for recycling brick between older and newer temples in Vijayanagara should be considered. If recycling were common, the total output of brick would be even lower than the previous estimate. Far from being a common building material, bricks should be viewed as a precious commodity, used only in specific architectural contexts.

Conclusion

The scarcity of bricks in Vijayanagara reinforces the conclusions of Morrison (1995) that agricultural intensification was a major priority in the Vijayanagara Metropolitan Region. Given competing demands between brick production and agriculture, brickmaking was substantially limited. The relation between brick production and other land uses are less clear, but would have also played an important part in the determination of the value of bricks in Vijayanagara. It seems that areas that could be used for wet agriculture around Vijayanagara, were. Brick production and many other land uses were secondary to agricultural production.

Through investigation of modern brickmaking this ethnoarchaeological study has proposed critical differences between modern and historic brick use. With the advent of diesel pumps, bricks have become a relatively cheap construction material in Karnataka. This is shown in the extensive use of brick in domestic architecture in Hospet. Historically, the importance of agriculture and other land uses limited brick production, increasing the relative value of bricks. As a result, bricks were used only in situations in which other building material would be impractical. The value of bricks in Vijayanagara is best shown in the scale of production in comparison to the population of the city itself. It would have taken ten people only two or three years to produce almost all of the bricks found in a city of several hundred thousand people.

Acknowledgements

I thank Carla M. Sinopoli and Kathleen D. Morrison for the opportunity to work at Vijayanagara and to conduct the research that has led to this paper. U.V. Srinivas also provided important assistance. Finally, I thank the owners and workers of the Malapannagudi brickyards. The 1994 research at Vijayanagara was sponsored by the National Geographic Society (Grant 5170-94), the Smithsonian Institution (Grant FR99B404), and the American Institute of Indian Studies. This work was also supported by the Karnataka Directorate of Archaeology and Museums and the Government of India. A previous version of this paper was presented at the 24th Annual Conference on South Asia (20-22 October 1995: Madison, Wisconsin).

Works Cited

Filliozat, P.-S. and V. Filliozat, 1988, *Hampi-Vijayanagar: The Temple of Vithala*, Sitaram Bhartia Institute of Scientific Research, New Delhi.

Fritz, J.M., 1985, Report of Research 1980-1984. In, *Vijayanagara: Progress of Research, 1983-1984*, edited by M.S. Nagaraja Rao, pp. 69-95, Directorate of Archaeology and Museums, Mysore.

Fritz, J.M., G. Michell and M.S. Nagaraja Rao, 1984, *Where Kings and Gods Meet: The Royal Centre at Vijayanagara, India*, University of Arizona Press, Tucson.

Michell, G., 1990, V*ijayanagara: The Architectural Inventory of the Urban Core*, 2 volumes, Directorate of Archaeology and Museums, Mysore.

Morrison, K.D., 1995, *Fields of Victory: Vijayanagara and the Course of Intensification*, Contributions of the University of California Archaeological Research Facility No. 53, Berkeley.

Sinopoli, C.M. and K.D. Morrison, 1991, The Vijayanagara Metropolitan Survey: The 1988 Season. In, *Vijayanagara: Progress of Research, 1987-1988*, edited by D.V. Devaraj and C.S. Patil, pp. 55-69, Directorate of Archaeology and Museums, Mysore.

——, 1992, The Vijayanagara Metropolitan Survey. *Research and Exploration*, 8: 237-39.

——, 1995, Dimensions of Imperial Control: The Vijayanagara Capital. *American Anthropologist*, 97: 83-96.

Table 2. Brick Production and Land Depletion by Ten Brickmakers

Days of Production (10 workers)	Volume of Fired Brick Produced	Area of Topsoil Depleted
1 200 (Dry season production) 365 (Year round production)	17.5 m³ 3500 m³ 6387.5 m³	20 m² 1 acre 1.8 acres

Table 3. Structures with Brick in the Vijayanagara Urban Core (from Michell 1990)

	Number of Structures	Average Volume of Brick per Structure (m³)	Total Volume (m³)
Large Temple Complexes Enclosed Temples Unenclosed Temples Small Temples	2 6 73 101	1600 312 43 2.5	3200 1872 3139 252.5
		Total:	8463.5

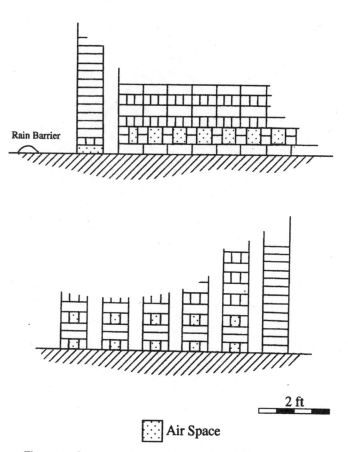

Figure 1. Cross-sections of rice-husk fired brick furnace.

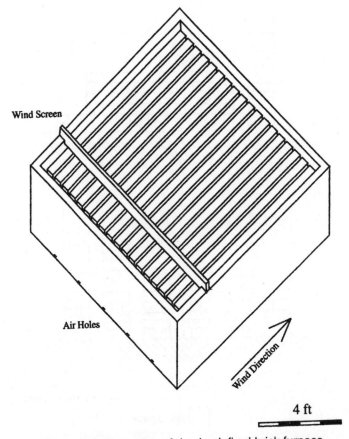

Figure 2. Oblique view of rice-husk fired brick furnace.

POLLEN ANALYSIS FROM THE KAMALAPURA KERE

Kathleen D. Morrison

The sedimentary record of Vijayanagara reservoirs constitutes a potentially important source of information on past agriculture and landuse in the area in and around the city of Vijayanagara. In any region, the vegetation record is an artefact of both ecological and human forces, but the Vijayanagara vegetation record, in particular, must be viewed as the record of a transformed landscape, the consequence of years of human manipulation of the environment. In this paper I will present some preliminary findings of an analysis of fossil pollen from the sediments of the Kamalapura *kere*, a large reservoir or tank located to the southwest of the city of Vijayanagara. In the pollen record from the Kamalapura core, it is possible to view the rather dramatic impact of patterns of agricultural land use on the regional vegetation and on the more local history of the Kamalapura *kere* itself.

Pollen Analysis: Basis

Pollen analysis, the study of "fossil" (that is, non-contemporary, although the material is not truly fossilized) pollen for the purposes of environmental reconstruction, is one way of detecting and analysing past agriculture. Environment, in this sense, may include factors such as soil, temperature and rainfall as well as the activities of human beings. Human impact on vegetation is variable at different scales, and diverse agricultural strategies might be expected to shape local and regional vegetation in fairly complex ways.

Pollen grains, the "microscopic single-celled (multinucleate) gametophyte generation produced by vascular plants that are responsible for the exchange of genetic information during plant reproductive processes" (Bryant and Holloway 1983: 194), consist of two layers. The inner, or iintine, is composed mostly of cellulose (Moore and Webb 1978: 31), and is not particularly resistant to decay. The outer layer, or exine, is composed of cellulose, hemicellulose, lignin, pectic substances, and sporopollenin (Bryant and Holloway 1983: 194). The sporopollenin is highly resistant to decay. Identification of pollen and spores rests on the observation that each family or genus (and sometimes species) produces a morphologically distinctive product, with a specifiable size range, number and arrangement of pores and apertures, and exine characteristics.

Understanding Pollen

Pollen produced by plants in a region continuously accumulates in soils, lakes, bogs and other bodies of water, creating a temporally stratified record of vegetation. The methodological bases for interpretation of fossil pollen profiles consist of bodies of information drawn from the operation of contemporary processes in plant biology and ecology, hydrology and sedimentology. Differential pollen production, dispersal and preservation, as well as specificity of identification, sampling, and even forms of data presentation all affect the nature of the relationship between observed pollen distributions and past vegetation (Morrison 1992).

The ecological interpretation of pollen profiles ultimately depends on studies of contemporary vegetation dynamics, and on studies of the relationships between contemporary vegetation and pollen in specific environments.

Unfortunately, there are few analyses of contemporary pollen spectra and their relationship to vegetation in South India, apart from some studies from the Ghat forests (e.g. Blasco and Thanikaimoni 1974) and none at all for dry interior Karnataka. Thus, only very general statements about vegetation can be made on the basis of the pollen record from the Kamalapura *kere*.

The results of pollen analyses are commonly presented as percentage diagrams, with taxa values calculated as a proportion of the number of terrestrial pollen grains. However, absolute pollen diagrams, which employ pollen concentration values (calculated with reference to some known volume of a "marker" species such as Lycopodium or Eucalyptus added to the sample), also display significant information. Minor vegetation changes may be discernible only with absolute diagrams, since the values of a dominant species in a percentage diagram may mask trends in rarer species. For this reason, both percentage and absolute diagrams of grouped taxa from the Kamalapura core are provided.

Pollen Analysis from the Vijayanagara Region

Pollen analyses were made from an 57-cm long core extracted from the sediments of the Kamalapura *kere*. The Kamalapura *kere* (VMS-231) is a large reservoir which contains water year-round. Water is retained by a masonry-faced earthen dam nearly 2 km long (Figure 1). Approximately 1,700 m of the embankment appear to belong to the Vijayanagara period reservoir; recent additions in concrete have extended the embankment on either end. Three sluices date to the Vijayanagara period.

The Kamalapura *kere* is one of the few reservoirs in the Vijayanagara Metropolitan Region which is not solely dependent on runoff from seasonal or semi-permanent water sources. instead, its holdings are supplemented by the Raya canal, which itself is supplied by an *anicut* from the Tungabhadra River. Thus, the Kamalapura *kere* contains a much more certain water supply than other reservoirs in the region. In addition to water from the Raya canal, the Kamalapura *kere* was also supplied by seasonal runoff and the overflow from several Vijayanagara period reservoirs upstream. This constancy of water supply has

important implications not only for agricultural production, but also for pollen preservation. Pollen grains are more likely to be preserved where conditions are either uniformly wet or dry; pollen degrades rapidly under conditions of alternate wetting and drying. Samples taken from the fill of several seasonal reservoirs in Block O (see Sinopoli and Morrison 1991), for example, did not contain any pollen.

The Kamalapura reservoir was probably constructed in the early Vijayanagara period (Morrison 1992; an inscription of 1518 also appears to refer to the Kamalapura *kere*; Gopal 1990: 180), giving this body of water the potential to provide information on the entire span of Vijayanagara, Colonial and Post-Independence vegetational history.

The Raya canal *anicut* was submerged by the Tungabhadra reservoir (Kotraiah 1959), and the flow through the canal is now regulated by the irrigation authorities at the Tungabhadra dam. Because of the submergence of the Raya *anicut*, it is not possible to study it in detail or to assess its reliability.

It is assumed that the Raya, like other Vijayanagara canals, provided a fairly secure, year-round flow of water. The date of the Raya canal is not entirely clear. Davison-Jenkins (1988: 97) argues that the *anicut* and canal mentioned by Nuniz in his recap of Vijayanagara history is the Raya canal, dating it to the fifteenth century. However, this argument is unconvincing. Even if Nuniz' account is treated as a simple, factual historical account, he mentions a canal which was "brought inside the city" (Sewell 1992: 301), a description which matches the route of the Turtha (Hiriya *kaluve*; Filliozat and Filliozat 1988: 11) and not the Raya canal. It may be that the Raya canal and the reservoir are contemporaneous, but the occurrence of an inscription from Penukonda (Gopal 1990: 42) referring to the construction of a canal in order to supplement a reservoir's supply should indicate that this contemporeneity cannot be assumed.

Vegetation

The Vijayanagara region is characterized by vegetation of the xeric Albizia amara Acacia series. The slopes of the Sandur Hills support vegetation of the Hardwickia Anogeissus series, while the hilltops contain plants of the

Anogeissus-Terrninalia-Tectona series (Gaussen et al. 1966). The vegetation in the area has, however, been greatly modified by human activity and cultivated species today constitute a significant proportion of the regional flora (Singh 1988). The Kamalapura *kere* receives input from a wide catchment area, particularly since the water of the Raya canal is ultimately derived from the Tungabhadra River. The runoff catchment of the Kamalapura *kere* is also large. Overflow from the smaller reservoirs VMS-241 and VMS-242 upstream was channeled into the Kamalapura *kere*, the watershed of these reservoirs included the Sandur Hills. Thus, the pollen source area for the Kamalapura reservoir is likely to have been quite large, including all three of the vegetation series found in the region, and the pollen record from this reservoir ought to provide a large-scale, regional record of past vegetation.

Sampling Programme

Three sediment cores were extracted from the Kamalapura *kere*, only one of these (1KP) is discussed here. The reservoir was cored in early June 1990, at the height of the dry season. In spite of this and despite several years of drought in northern Karnataka, the water level was only slightly below the average, perhaps 1 m less, judging from water staining on the masonry embankment. The reservoir was not very deep, ranging from less than one metre at its marshy edges, to the deepest area near the sluice, where the water depth was about 4 m. Water depths and core locations are indicated in Figure 1. All cores were taken from a raft, using a modified version of the "UNAM" core developed by Roger Byrne of the University of California, Berkeley. The core used on the Kamalapura sediments was constructed under the direction of Dr Phadke at the Department of Instrumentation Science, University of Poona, and was christened "UNAM Dho". (Core descriptions and pollen processing procedures can be found in Morrison 1992.)

Core Chronology

The stratigraphy of the core provides a broad framework for chronological assessment. The reservoir was probably constructed early in the fourteenth century, and the recovered core almost certainly did not reach the original land surface (or the base surface, since the reservoir was likely to have been excavated into the original soil), so that the basal levels are thought to post-date the early fourteenth century, but perhaps not by much. The Kamalapura reservoir is still in operation, so that the uppermost levels date to the twentieth century. Thus, if there are no gaps in the core – and none could be discerned stratigraphically through visual inspection or by X-ray of the core – the pollen record should extend from approximately the fourteenth to the twentieth centuries. The lowest portions are suggested to date to the Vijayanagara period, and the higher portions to the Colonial and Post-Independence periods. It cannot be assumed that the length of core represented by each century is of equivalent length, since that would require that the sedimentation rate of the reservoir be constant through time. This assumption cannot be supported, and in fact, the archaeological and historical evidence suggests, quite to the contrary, that erosion was more of a problem at some times than at others, as differential grain sizes of the sediment also suggest.

In addition to stratigraphy, the presence of plants introduced into India from other parts of the world provides an additional temporal control. New World plants provide a fairly precise marker of time, since they all post-date AD 1500. Afemanthera, a New World weed, appears in the core at 28 cm. Thus, the portion of the core above 28 cm should date to the sixteenth century or later. Casuarina was introduced into India in the 1780s (Tissot, personal communication 1992); it appears first at 18 cm, and occurs consistently in the upper portions of the core. Thus, if there are no gaps in the sequence, the portion of the core between 18 and 0 cm should represent the eighteenth, nineteenth and twentieth centuries. As noted, a constant sedimentation rate cannot be assumed, so this sequence cannot be retrodicted.

Vegetation Groups: Identification

The identification of pollen grains and spores from 1KP was facilitated by use of the excellent pollen reference collection of the French Institute, Pondicherry, India. Much of the pollen from the Kamalapura core could only be identified to family, although some genus and species-level identifications were possible. Families characterized by a single form of vegetation such as herbs, shrubs, or trees are grouped together in Figures 2 and 3. A few families are quite variable in form; these were not included in the overall groupings. The most serious difficulty is presented by the grasses, which dominate the pollen assemblage. The most important agricultural crops of the Vijayanagara period: rice, sorghum, millets, and possibly sugarcane, are all grasses, and in Bellary and Raichur Districts alone, 97 species in 63 genera of non-cultivated Gramineae were reported by N.P. Singh (1988). Most of these occur in disturbed zones such as cleared areas and cultivated fields, and as weeds around habitations and along roads. The great diversity of grasses defies precise ecological cate-gorization, however. General trends can be discerned in both the proportion of grasses to other types of vegetation and in the absolute amount of grass pollen deposited in the reservoir through time (see below).

Vegetation Groups: Results

The overall results of the Kamalapura pollen core are presented in Figure 2, which indicates relative abundance of taxa, and Figure 3, indicating pollen concentrations. It can be seen that grasses dominate the assemblage, followed by herbs and trees. The category of cultivated species refers to non-grass cultigens. On the far right of the diagram are species introduced into India from the New World. Figure 3 indicates a decline in overall pollen concentration in the middle portion of the core, between approximately 28 and 14 cm. This decline can be seen quite clearly in the grass curve (Gramineae), the dominant pollen type, but it is a general feature of this portion of the core. The declining concentration of pollen in the core could have been caused by an increased sedimentation rate at this time. At the 24 cm level, the core contains almost no pollen, and counts from this level were not included in the diagram. There is no visually apparent stratigraphic break at this level. There are several possible explanations for this lack

of pollen. One may be that the reservoir actually dried out during this period, and the consequent wetting and drying destroyed pollen in sediments near the surface. Alternately, the low pollen concentration could be seen as an extreme example of the low concentrations in nearby levels.

What can be seen in the grass curve is a marked peak near the base of the core which rises to a very high proportion of the total assemblage, approximately 90 per cent. This peak undergoes a long and sustained decline, until it reaches a minimum at about 40 cm. Following this low point, grasses rebound somewhat between 40 and 28 cm, after which they again undergo a slow and sustained decline. Because of the composite nature of the grass curve, it is difficult to interpret this pattern. It is tempting to suggest that the dramatic increase in grass pollen between 56 and 52 cm is a consequence of agricultural intensification, caused by the expansion of cultivated fields and the concomitant growth of both weeds and crops, and by the clearing of non-grass vegetation. Figure 3 indicates, however, that grass was dominant in the pollen record from the very beginning of the sequence, and in fact, the relative increase of grass at 52 cm is largely a product of a relative decrease in unidentified grains. However, these unknown types are quite unlikely to be grasses, which are easily identified. Thus, the proportional rise in grass pollen actually relates to a decrease in other taxa. The preponderance of grass at the base of the core is significant. At no other level does the relative or absolute abundance of grass pollen reach the levels it attains near the base. It is not possible to assess the proportion of vegetation types directly from the proportion of pollen types, but it is very striking that the contemporary landscape – deforested, overgrazed, virtually denuded of natural vegetation and covered by agricultural fields – does not create as strong a grass signal.

The basal grass maximum declines between 52 and 40 cm, with only a slight rebound at 42 cm. This decline is evident in both relative and absolute pollen counts, and represents a change in environment conducive to grass growth. The cause of that change is open to interpretation; it may represent a decrease in cultivated grasses, or in open habitats favoured by wild grasses, some combination of factors. Between 14 cm and the top of the core, grass pollen increases in absolute terms, but continues to decrease as a percentage, largely due to the increase in Compositae (see Morrison 1992 for more details).

Herbaceous plants exhibit a very clear pattern of growth in the upper portion of the core. Proportionally, they experience two growth peaks, at approximately 10 and 28 cm. The initial peak actually seems to reflect the striking decline in numbers of grass pollen grains deposited, however, and the concentration of herbaceous plants in the core is very consistent before the upper 10 cm, with only a slight increase between 48 and 44 cm.

Shrubs constitute only a very small proportion of the pollen record, and in several levels no shrub pollen at all was counted. For this reason, it is difficult to assign much significance to the distribution of shrub pollen. There are three periods during which shrubs appear in the record. The first two of these correspond with periods of increase in arboreal pollen, and it is probable that both trees and shrubs were responding to similar conditions at these times. Both the tree and shrub curves exhibit a decline between approximately 52 and 44 cm, during the period of most significant change in the grass curve. The loss of trees and shrubs is not precisely aligned with a growth in grass pollen, although there is a slight increase in herbaceous plants. At the base of the core, grasses already dominate the record and trees and shrubs are already undergoing a precipitous decline. The proportion of trees and shrubs remains low until about 40 cm, when it begins to increase. This pattern may indicate pressure on the woody vegetation in the study area from the beginning of the record, followed by a period of more open vegetation, with a later (and limited) regeneration of trees and shrubs.

The curve representing cultivated plants does not include any cultigens belonging to the family Gramineae. Only pollen grains which could be securely identified to genus, and which are known to have been cultivated (that is, they do not occur naturally in the area and are cultivated today) are included in this category.

Grasses and Aquatic Plants

Figure 4 indicates the concentration of three taxa of aquatic plants in the core, which exhibit a very striking pattern. There is a well-defined peak in aquatic vegetation (with a slight decline at 40 cm) between about 44 and 32 cm. The rapid growth in aquatic plants corresponds with a decline in grasses, and begins somewhat before the period in which trees and shrubs begin to reappear in the record. Normal maintenance of reservoirs includes cleaning out aquatic plants, so that the rapid growth in aquatic vegetation almost certainly indicates a period during which the reservoir was not well maintained. By the time trees and shrubs began to regenerate, the reservoir had become choked with aquatic vegetation. The rapid decline in the concentration of pollen of aquatic plants (at about 28 cm) occurs at the same time as the first introduced species appear in the record, and shortly before the possible drying out of the reservoir at the 24-cm level. Thus, the postulated drying out period follows the beginning of renewed maintenance of the reservoir. Because the Kamalapura *kere* is supplied by both seasonal runoff and the river fed Raya canal, virtually the only way the reservoir could dry out (seasonally) would be to block, divert, or otherwise stop the flow from the canal. Today, canals are periodically blocked in order to clean out silt and vegetation. Perhaps the potential drying out actually represents maintenance of the reservoir, including the removal of aquatic plants.

Most of the aquatic plants are represented by plants belonging to just three families: Typhaceae, Cyperaceae and Potomagetonaceae. Typha angustata is an aquatic or marshy-habitat herb which grows in shallow water around the edges of reservoirs and other bodies of water. Similarly, the five genera of Cyperaceae that are found in the study area grow in shallow water. In contrast, Potomageton nodosus, although it also grows in shallow water, can grow partially or almost completely submerged, so that it has the potential to invade more of a reservoir than simply its edges. The strong pattern in aquatic plants is created almost entirely by Potomageton, with some contribution by Cyperaceae.

Typha concentrations are remarkably consistent throughout the core, with a slight increase near the top and a decrease in the lowest levels.

The strong pattern exhibited by the aquatic plant concentrations in the core also raises questions about the pattern of the grass curve. Below 48 cm, there appears to be no relationship between the concentration of Gramineae and of aquatic plants in the core. During the period of maximum aquatic plant growth, however, smaller peaks in the grass curve co-occur with those of aquatic plants. It is not possible to discount the possibility that some of the grasses making up the overall curve may be aquatic species, and in the areas where grass pollen patterns echo those of aquatic plants, the possibility is even stronger. If this were the case, then the pattern of non-aquatic grass decline above 52 cm would be even more marked.

Non-Gramineae Cultivated Plants

The combined pattern of non-grass cultivated plants shows little significant patterning through time except for a slight increase in the upper levels of the core. However, some interesting patterns do emerge when this composite curve is separated into its component species (Morrison 1992). *Arenga pinnata* (gomuti palm) and *Jasminum auriculatum* (jasmine) are very rare in the sample. More common are *Cocos nucifera* (coconut) and *Ricinus communis* (castor oil plant). *Cocos* is an important cash crop on the area today, and this dominance is reflected in the larger amounts of coconut pollen between 10 cm and the top of the core. *Cocos* has its second highest concentration at the base of the core, but it quickly declines in importance before reaching a small peak between 44 and 40 cm. This pattern may simply be a product of the small sample size of coconut pollen at the base of the core, but it is at least qualitatively interesting as it indicates the production of coconuts in the Vijayanagara period (also noted in historical sources). Whether or not the apparent decline in *Cocos* in the lower third of the core is a "real" phenomenon or just a sampling fluctuation, it is apparent that overall, the earlier record of coconuts indicates that they were of lesser importance than in the later record. The more recent focus on *Cocos* production occurs at the time of the first New World species and during the period in which it was suggested that renewed maintenance of the reservoir was taking place. *Ricinus* may originally have been a native of Africa, as are many other Indian cultigens, although some botanists feel that *Ricinus* may be indigenous to India (see discussion in Narain 1974). The distribution of *Ricinus*, which may be grown as either a dry or an irrigated crop, is strikingly different from that of *Cocos*, occurring neither in the earliest nor in the latest portions of the core. The context of *Ricinus* cultivation thus appears to have been quite different from that of coconut cultivation.

Discussion

Only a very general discussion of the Kamalapura pollen record could be presented here. Interpretation of the pollen analysis from the Kamalapura core is hampered by the imprecision of dates from the core and by the lack of detailed studies relating modern vegetation dynamics in dry interior south India to the pollen record. Nevertheless, several strong patterns have emerged from the pollen analysis. These patterns include very high values for grass pollen at the very beginning of the record and a concurrent sharp decrease in the pollen of trees and shrubs. The quantities of tree and shrub pollen were reduced significantly in what is suggested to be the Middle or Late Vijayanagara period, only to undergo a rebound, probably at the end of the Vijayanagara period. In the post-Vijayanagara period, the reservoir became choked with aquatic vegetation. About the time the reservoir was cleared of swampy vegetation, the first introduced New World species appear in the record, and the concentrations of pollen also decreased, possibly as a result of increased erosion (associated with renewed clearance of vegetation?). At 24 cm, the reservoir may have dried out completely for a time.

Toward the top of the record, probably the later Colonial or the Post-Independence periods, agricultural production seems to be of renewed importance, but this agricultural landscape appears different form the

Vijayanagara period landscape in several important respects. First of all, the grass-dominated Vijayanagara record is not duplicated in the record of modern, commercial agriculture. Instead, herbaceous plants appear much more important, and specifically, Compositae come to constitute a significant proportion of the pollen flora. Coconut pollen also appears in greater quantities. While coconuts did appear in the Vijayanagara period record, their numerical importance in more recent sediments is striking, and is consistent with their current value as commercial crops. Thus, the impression of Vijayanagara agriculture is one of a pattern of land use that was already intensive from the beginning of the pollen record. Grasses did increase proportionally at the beginning of the record, but the concentration of grass pollen at the base of the core was consistently high.

Pollen analysis of Vijayanagara area sediments is still at a preliminary stage, and significant problems of chronology and interpretation remain to be addressed. Future research will include analyses of the pollen and charcoal records from additional cores and from additional sampling locations in order to place the record from this single Kamalapura core in context.

Acknowledgements

Thanks are due to the Government of India and the Archaeological Survey of India for granting research permission, and to the American Institute of Indian Studies (AIIS) for their invaluable assistance in facilitating this research. I extend thanks to Dr P. Mehendiratta and the entire Delhi office of the AIIS as well as to M. Bhandare of the Pune office. In addition, I would like to acknowledge the ongoing assistance and hospitality of the Karnataka Department of Archaeology and Museums (KDAM). Research funding was provided by the American Institute of Indian Studies, the National Geographic Society, and the Wenner-Gren Foundation. My pollen collection and analysis were facilitated through the generous cooperation of the Deccan College Postgraduate and Research Institute (Deemed University), Poona University, and the French Institute, Pondicherry. Additional advice was given by local irrigation authorities. U. Srinivas and the staff of the KDAM archaeological camp were instrumental in constructing the raft. Iranna was our invaluable assistant in the coring effort, and Mark Lycett my fearless coring partner.

Works Cited

Blasco, F. and G. Thanikaimoni, 1974, Late Quaternary Vegetational History of Southern Region. In, *Aspects and Appraisal of Indian Palaeobotany*, edited by K.R. Surange, R.N. Lakhanpal and D.C. Bharadwaj, pp. 632-43, Birbal Sahni Institute of Paleobotany, Lucknow.

Bryant, V.M. and R.C. Holloway, 1983, The Role of Palynology in Archaeology. In, *Advances in Archaeological Method and Theory*, vol. 6, edited by M.B. Schiffer, pp. 191-224, Academic Press, New York.

Davison-Jenkins, D.J., 1988, The Irrigation and Water Supply Systems of the City of Vijayanagara, Ph.D. Dissertation, Department of Oriental Studies, University of Cambridge, Cambridge.

Filliozat, P.S. and V. Filliozat, 1988, *Hampi-Vijayanagar: The Temple of Vithala*, Sitaram Bhartia Institute of Scientific Research, New Delhi.

Gaussen, H., P. Legris, L. Labroue, V.M. Meter-Homji and M. Viart, 1966, Carte Inernationale Du Tapis Vegetal, Notice de la Feuille: Mysore. *Extrait ties Travaux de la Section Scientifique et Technique de l'Institut Français de Pondicherry*, Hors Serie 7.

Gopal, B.H., 1990, *Vijayanagara Inscriptions*, vol. 3, Directorate of Archaeology and Museums, Mysore.

Kotraiah, C.T.M., 1959, Ancient Anicuts on the River Tungabhadra. *Indian Journal of Power and River Valley Development*, Tungabhadra Project Number 1: 49-53.

Moore, P.D. and J.A. Webb, 1978, *An Illustrated Guide to Pollen Analysis*, Wiley, New York.

Morrison, K.D., 1992, Transforming the Agricultural Landscape: Intensification of Production at Vijayanagara, India, Ph.D. Dissertation, University Microfilms International, Ann Arbor.

Morrison, K.D. and C.M. Sinopoli, 1996, Archaeological Survey in the Vijayanagara Metropolitan Region: 1990. In, *Vijayanagara: Progress of Research, 1988-1991*, edited by D.V. Devaraj and C.S. Patil, pp. 59-73, Directorate of Archaeology and Museums, Mysore.

Narian, A., 1974, Castor. In, *Evolutionary Studies in World Crops: Diversity and Change in the Indian Subcontinent*, edited by I.

Hutchinson, Cambridge University Press, Cambridge.

Sewell, R., 1992, *A Forgotten Empire Vijayanagar: A Contribution to the History of India*, reprint, Asian Educational Services, New Delhi.

Singh, N.P., 1988, *The Flora of Eastern Karnataka*, Mittal, New Delhi.

Sinopoli, C.M. and K.D. Morrison, 1991, The Vijayanagara Metropolitan Survey: The 1988 Season. In, *Vijayanagara: Progress of Research, 1987-1988*, edited by D.V. Devaraj and C.S. Patil, pp. 55-69, Directorate of Archaeology and Museums, Mysore.

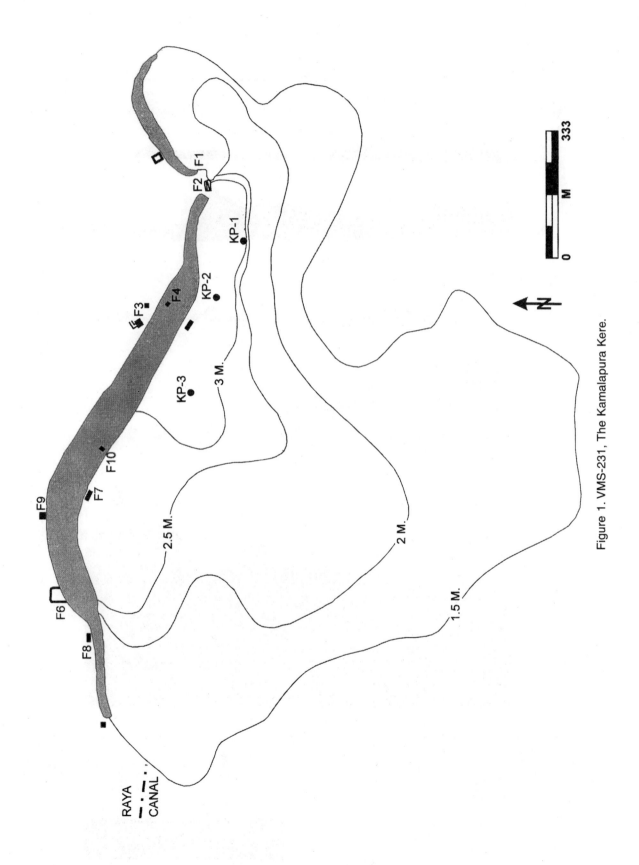

Figure 1. VMS-231, The Kamalapura Kere.

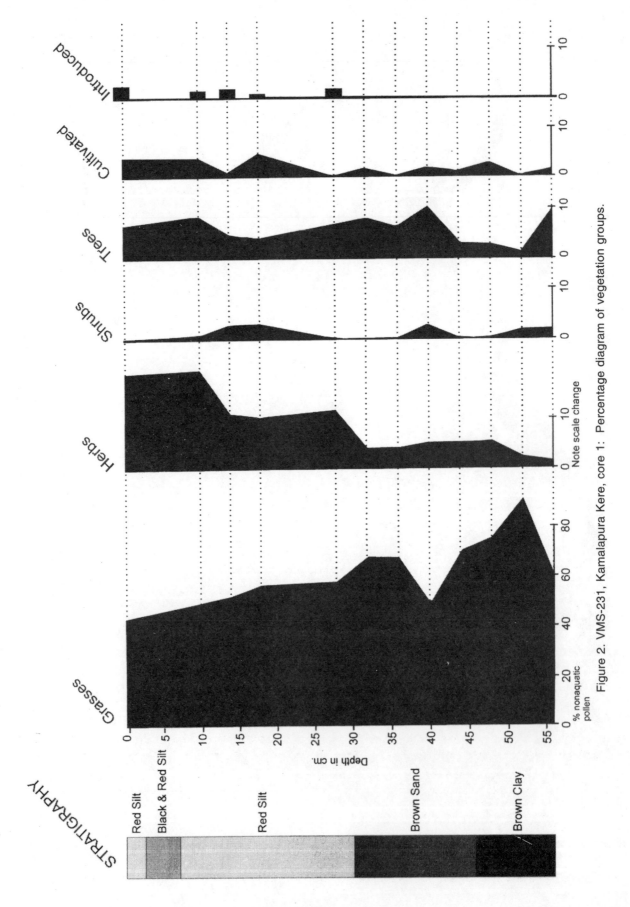

Figure 2. VMS-231, Kamalapura Kere, core 1: Percentage diagram of vegetation groups.

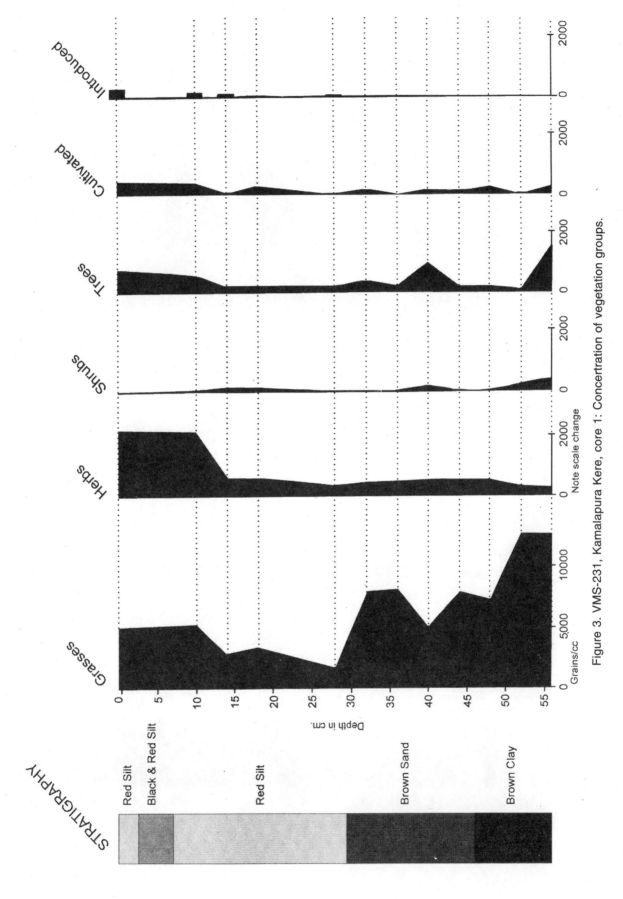

Figure 3. VMS-231, Kamalapura Kere, core 1: Concentration of vegetation groups.

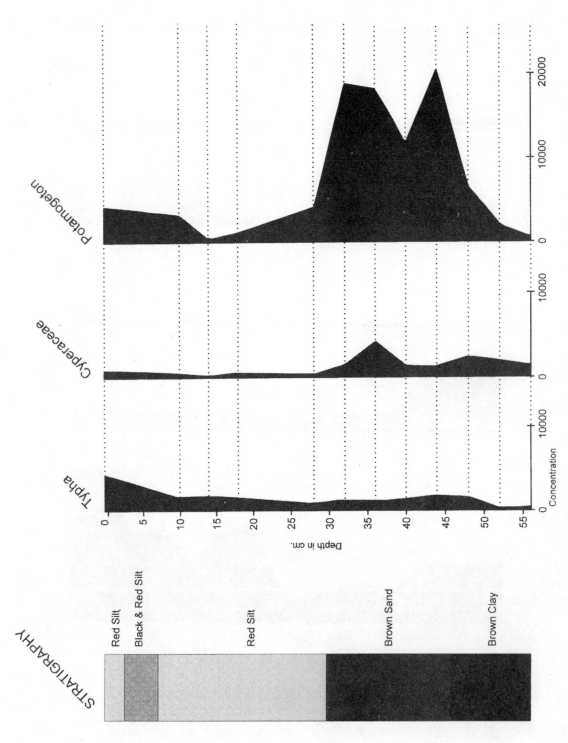

Figure 4. VMS-231, Kamalapura Kere, core 1: Concentration of aquatic plants.

VIJAYANAGARA METROPOLITAN SURVEY BIBLIOGRAPHY

Monographs and Articles

Brubaker, Robert P.

2000   The infrastructure of imperial security at a pre-colonial south Indian capital: Recent research at Vijayanagara. In, *South Asian Archaeology 1997*, edited by M. Taddei and G. de Marco, pp. 1471-88, Instituto Italiano per l'Africa e l'Oriente, Rome.

2005   VMS-370: A Fortification Wall and Reservoir Embankment in the Vijayanagara Metropolitan Region. See this volume.

2004   *Corner Stones of Control: The Infrastructure of Imperial Security at Vijayanagara, South India*, University Microfilms, Ann Arbor.

Dega, Michael F. and Robert P. Brubaker

2005   VMS-6: A Fortified Settlement Complex in the Vijayanagara Metropolitan Region. See this volume.

Fogelin, Lars

2005   Brickmaking in Malapannagudi: Ethnoarchaeological Research and Archaeological Implications in the Vijayanagara Metropolitan Region. See this volume.

Gogte, V.D., Kathleen D. Morrison and Mark T. Lycett

In preparation: Early Historic Metallurgy at VMS-110: A Specialized Iron Production Site. In, *Recent Research on the Archaeology and Bioarchaeology of South India*, edited by V.V. Rami Reddy and K.D. Morrison, Munshiram Manoharlal, New Delhi.

Humayun, Jennifer Lundal

2005   VMS-440 A Small Temple Complex and Associated Features. See this volume

Humayun, Jennifer Lundal and V.D. Gogte

In preparation: Spatial Analysis of Early Historic Iron-Working Debris at VMS-110, in *Recent Research on the Archaeology and Bioarchaeology of South India*, edited by V. Rami Reddy and K.D. Morrison, Munshiram Manoharlal, New Delhi.

Lycett, Mark T.

1991   Chipped stone tools of the Vijayanagara Metropolitan Region. In, *Vijayanagara: Progress of Research, 1987-1988*, edited by D.V. Devaraj and C.S. Patil, pp. 85-94, Directorate of Archaeology and Museums, Mysore.

1995   Non-architectural sites of the Vijayanagara Metropolitan Region: Searching for patterns in ambiguous categories. In, *South Asian Archaeology 1993*, edited by A. Parpola and P. Koskikallio, pp. 413-24, Academiae Scientarium Fennica, Series B, vol. 271, Helsinki.

Lycett, Mark T. and Kathleen D. Morrison

In preparation: Scales and Monumentalities: The Production of an Iron Age Landscape in North Interior Karnataka. In, *Recent Research on the Archaeology and Bioarchaeology of South India*, edited by V.V. Rami Reddy and K.D. Morrison, Munshiram Manoharlal, New Delhi.

Lycett, Mark T, Kathleen D. Morrison and V.D. Gogte

In preparation: Early Historic Iron Production in Northern Karnataka: Technology, Organization, and Change. In, *Recent Research on the Archaeology and Bioarchaeology of South India*, edited by V.V. Rami Reddy and K.D. Morrison, Munshiram Manoharlal, New Delhi.

Means, Bernard K.

1991 A small settlement near the city of Vijayanagara. In, *Vijayanagara: Progress of Research, 1987-88*, edited by D.V. Devaraj and C.S. Patil, pp. 154-64, Directorate of Archaeology and Museums, Mysore.

Monahan, Belinda

In preparation: South Indian Subsistence Practices and Exchange Patterns: Fauna from VMS-110. In, *Recent Research on the Archaeology and Bioarchaeology of South India*, edited by V.V. Rami Reddy and K.D. Morrison, Munshiram Manoharlal, New Delhi.

Morrison, Kathleen D.

1991a The Vijayanagara Metropolitan Survey: Preliminary investigations. In, *Vijayanagara: Progress of Research, 1984-1987*, edited by D.V. Devaraj and C.S. Patil, pp. 136-41, Directorate of Archaeology and Museums, Mysore.

1991b Small-scale agricultural features: Three Vijayanagara embankments. In, *Vijayanagara: Progress of Research, 1987-1988*, edited by D.V. Devaraj and C.S. Patil, pp. 81-84, Directorate of Archaeology and Museums, Mysore.

1992 *Transforming the Agricultural Landscape: Intensification of Production at Vijayanagara, India*, Ph.D. dissertation, Department of Anthropology, University of California at Berkeley, University Microfilms, Ann Arbor.

1993 Supplying the city: The role of reservoirs in an Indian agricultural landscape. *Asian Perspectives*, 32: 133-52.

1994 Monitoring regional fire history through size-specific analysis of microscopic charcoal: The last 600 years in south India. *Journal of Archaeological Science*, 21: 675-85.

1995a (2000) *Fields of Victory: Vijayanagara and the course of Intensification*, Contributions to the Archaeological Research Facility, University of California, No. 52, Berkeley. Reprinted 2000, Munshiram Manoharlal, Delhi.

1995b Agricultural Intensification and Vijayanagara: An Overview. In, *Sri Nagabhinandanam (Dr. M.S. Nagaraja Rao Festschrift)*, edited by L.K. Srinivasan and S. Nagaraju, pp. 145-56, Dr. M.S. Nagaraja Rao Felicitation Committee, Bangalore.

1995c Investigating regional land use patterns: Pollen, charcoal, and archaeological analyses in precolonial south India. In, *South Asian Archaeology 1993*, edited by A. Parpola and P. Koskikallio, pp. 539-49, Academiae Scientarium Fennica, Series B, Vol. 271, Helsinki.

1997a Agriculture at the Edges: Archaeology and History in the Vijayanagara Hinterland. In, *South Asian Archaeology 1995*, edited by R. and B. Allchin, Oxford and IBH, New Delhi, pp. 783-91.

1997b Commerce and Culture in South Asia: Perspectives from Archaeology and History, *Annual Review of Anthropology*, 26: 87-108.

2000 Naturalizing Disaster: From Drought to Famine in South India. In, *Environmental Disruptions and the Archaeology of Human Response*, edited by G. Bawden and R. Reycraft, pp. 21-33, Anthropology Papers of the Maxwell Museum of Anthropology, Albuquerque.

2001a Coercion, Resistance, and Hierarchy: Local Processes and Imperial Strategies in the Vijayanagara Empire. In, *Empires: Perspectives from Archaeology and History*, edited by S.E. Alcock, T.N. D'Altroy, K.D. Morrison and C.M. Sinopoli, pp. 252-78, Cambridge University Press, Cambridge.

2001b Patterns of Transportation Outside the City of Vijayanagara: Some Archaeological Evidence of Roadways. In, *Professor A.V. Narasimha Murthy Felicitation Volume*, edited by D.V. Devaraj, R. Gopal, et al., Mysore.

2002a General Introduction: Historicizing Adaptation, Adapting to History. In, *Forager-Traders in South and Southeast Asia: Long-Term Histories*, edited by K.D. Morrison and L.L. Junker, Cambridge University Press, Cambridge.

2002b Introduction: South Asia. In, *Forager-Traders in South and Southeast Asia: Long-Term Histories*, edited by K.D. Morrison and L.L. Junker, Cambridge University Press, Cambridge.

2002c Pepper in the Hills: Upland-Lowland Exchange and the Intensification of the Spice Trade. In, *Forager-Traders in South and Southeast Asia: Long-Term Histories*, edited by K.D. Morrison and L.L. Junker, Cambridge University Press, Cambridge.

2005 Pollen Analysis from the Kamalapuram Kere. See this volume.

In press: Rethinking Intensification: Power Relations and Scales of Analysis in Precolonial South India. In, *Rethinking Intensification*, edited by T. Thurston and C. Fisher, Plenum Press, New York.

In preparation: *Oceans of Dharma: Landscape, Power, and Place in South India.*

Morrison, Kathleen D. and Peter G. Johansen

In preparation: Recent Excavations at Ingaligi (VMS-110): General Introduction. In, *Recent Research on the Archaeology and Bioarchaeology of South India*, edited by V.V. Rami Reddy and K.D. Morrison, Munshiram Manoharlal, New Delhi.

Morrison, Kathleen D. and Mark T. Lycett

1994 Centralized power, centralized authority? Ideological claims and archaeological patterns. *Asian Perspectives*, 32(2): 312-53.

1997 Inscriptions as Artifacts: Precolonial South India and the Analysis of Texts. *Journal of Archaeological Method and Theory*, 3(3-4): 215-37.

Morrison, Kathleen D. and Carla M. Sinopoli

1992 Economic diversity and integration in a pre-colonial Indian empire. *World Archaeology*, 23/3: 335-52.

1996 Archaeological Survey in the Vijayanagara Metropolitan Region: 1990. In, *Vijayanagara: Progress of Research, 1988-1991*, edited by D.V. Devaraj and C.S. Patil, pp. 59-73, Directorate of Archaeology and Museums, Mysore.

2005a Production and Landscape in the Vijayanagara Metropolitan Region: Contributions of the VMS. See this volume.

2005b The Vijayanagara Metropolitan Survey: Overview of the 1994 Survey Season. See this volume.

2005c The Vijayanagara Metropolitan Survey: Overview of the 1996 Survey Season. See this volume.

Rami Reddy V.V. and Kathleen D. Morrison, editors

In preparation: *Recent Research on the Archaeology and Bioarchaeology of South India*, Munshiram Manoharlal, New Delhi.

Sinopoli, Carla M.

1991 A Vijayanagara period road system: VMS 42-47, VMS 50. In, *Vijayanagara: Progress of Research, 1987-1988*, edited by D.V. Devaraj and C.S. Patil, pp. 70-80, Directorate of Archaeology and Museums, Mysore.

1993 Defining a sacred landscape: Temple architecture and divine images in the Vjayanagara suburbs. In, *South Asian Archaeology 1991*, edited by A.J. Gail and G.J.R. Mevissen, pp. 625-35, Franz Steiner Verlag, Stuttgart.

1994 Political choices and economic strategies in the Vijayanagara empire. In, *The Economic Anthropology of the State*, edited by E.M. Brumfiel. Monographs in Economic Anthropology No. 11: 223-43.

1995 Learning about the past through archaeological ceramics: An example from Vijayanagara, India. In, *Research Frontiers in Anthropology*, edited by C.R. Ember, M. Ember, and P.N. Peregrine, pp. 1-24, Prentice-Hall, Inc., Englewood Cliffs, NJ.

1996a An early Vijayanagara temple complex in the Vijayanagara Metropolitan Region. In, *Sri Nagabhinandanam: Dr. M.S. Nagaraja Rao Festschrift*, edited by L.K. Srinivasan and S. Nagaraju, Dr. M.S. Nagaraja Rao Felicitation Committee, Mysore.

1996b The archaeology of empire: A view from South Asia. *Bulletin of the American School of Oriental Research*, No. 299/300 (1995): 3-11.

1997 Nucleated settlements in the Vijayanagara Metropolitan Region. In, *South Asian Archaeology 1995*, edited by R. and B. Allchin, pp. 475-87, Oxford and IBH, New Delhi.

1998 Identity and social action among craft producers of the Vijayanagara period. In, *Craft and Social Identity*, edited by C.L. Costin and R.P. Wright, pp. 161-72, Archaeological Papers of the American Anthropological Association, No. 8, Washington, D.C.

1999 Levels of complexity: Ceramic variability at Vijayanagara. In, *Pots and People: A Dynamic Interaction*, edited by J.M. Skibo and G.M. Feinman, pp. 115-36, University of Utah Press, Salt Lake City.

2000 From the Lion Throne: political and social dynamics of the Vijayanagara empire. *Journal of the Economic and Social History of the Orient*, 43(3): 364-98.

2003a Echoes of empire: Vijayanagara and historical memory, Vijayanagara as historical memory. In, *Archaeologies of Memory*, edited by R.M. Van Dyke and S.E. Alcock, Blackwell Publishers, Massachusetts.

2003b *The Political Economy of Craft Production: Crafting Empire in South India, AD 1350-1650*, Cambridge University Press, Cambridge.

2005 VMS-365: A Walled Settlement Site. See this volume.

In press a: Scalar images of the imperial capital of Vijayanagara. To appear in *Forgotten Cities*, edited by R.P. Wright.

In press b: Site formation processes in the Vijayanagara Metropolitan Region. To appear in *Site Formation Processes and Indian Archaeology*, edited by K. Paddayya and V.N. Misra, Deccan College, Pune, India.

Sinopoli, Carla M., Peter G. Johansen and Kathleen D. Morrison

In press: Changing cultural landscapes of the Tungabhadra Valley, South India. To appear in *States and the Landscape*, edited by S.E. Falconer and C.L. Redman, University of Arizona Press, Tucson.

Sinopoli, Carla M. and Kathleen D. Morrison

1991 The Vijayanagara Metropolitan Survey: The 1988 season. In, *Vijayanagara: Progress of Research, 1987-1988*, edited by D.V. Devaraj and C.S. Patil, pp. 55-69, Directorate of Archaeology and Museums, Mysore.

1992 Archaeological Survey at Vijayanagara. *Research and Exploration*, 8(2): 237-39.

1995 Dimensions of imperial control: The Vijayanagara capital. *American Anthropologist*, 97: 83-96.

1996 Archaeological Survey in the Vijayanagara Metropolitan Region: 1990. In, *Vijayanagara: Progress of Research, 1988-1991*, edited by D.V. Devaraj and C.S. Patil, pp. 59-73, Directorate of Archaeology and Museums, Mysore.

2001 The Vijayanagara Metropolitan Survey Project. In, *New Light on Hampi*, edited by J.M. Fritz and G.A. Michell, pp. 100-11, Marg Publications, Bombay.

2005a The Vijayanagara Metropolitan Survey: Overview of the 1992 Survey Season. See this volume.

2005b The Vijayanagara Metropolitan Survey: Overview of the 1997 Survey Season. See this volume.

2005c Reports of the Vijayanagara Metropolitan Survey: Introduction. See this volume.

In press a: Land Use and Settlement in the Vijayanagara Metropolitan Region: Results of the Vijayanagara Metropolitan Survey. In, *Recent Advances in Vijayanagara Studies: An Anthology*, edited by S. Srinivasan, New Era, Madras.

In press b: The regional landscapes of the imperial city of Vijayanagara: Report on the Vijayanagara Metropolitan Survey project. In, *South Asian Archaeology 1999*, edited by K.R. van Kooij and E.M. Raven, Egbert Forsten Publishing, Groningen.

In press c: *The Vijayanagara Metropolitan Survey: Preliminary Monograph*, vol. 1, University of Michigan, Museum of Anthropology Monograph Series.

Trautmann, Thomas and Carla M. Sinopoli

2002 In the beginning was the word: Excavating the relations between history and archaeology in South Asia. *Journal of the Economic and Social History of the Orient*, 45(4): 492-523.

Conference Papers

Brubaker, Robert P.

1995 *Fortifications in the Environs of Pre-Colonial Vijayanagara and the Infrastructure of Imperial Control.* Paper presented at the 24th Annual Conference on South Asia, Madison, Wisconsin, 22 October.

1997 *The Infrastructure of Imperial Control at a Pre-colonial South Indian Capital: Recent Research at Vijayanagara.* Paper presented at the 14th International Conference of the European Association of South Asian Archaeologists, Rome, Italy, 7 July.

1998 *Charting the Evolution of a Pre-colonial Indian Capital: Archaeology, Epigraphy, Travel Literature and the Development of Imperial Vijayanagara.* Paper presented at the 63rd Annual Meeting of the Society for American Archaeology, Seattle, Washington, 27 March.

2001 *Internal and External Frontiers of the Vijayanagara Empire.* Paper presented at the 66th Annual Meeting of the Society for American Archaeology, New Orleans, Louisiana, 19 April.

2003 *Peer Polity Borderlands: A South Asian Example.* Paper presented at the 68th Annual Meeting of the Society for American Archaeology, Milwaukee, Wisconsin, 13 April.

Fogelin, Lars

1995 *Brickmaking in Malapanagudi.* Paper presented at the 24th Annual Conference on South Asia, Madison, Wisconsin, 22 October.

Lundal, Jennifer and Kathleen D. Morrison

1995 *Contemporary Pollen Spectra and their Relevance for Vijayanagara Land Use.* Paper presented at the 24th Annual Conference on South Asia, Madison, Wisconsin, 22 October.

Lycett, Mark T.

1993 *Nonarchitectural Sites of the Vijayanagara Metropolitan Region.* Paper presented at the 12th International Conference of the European Association of South Asian Archaeologists, Helsinki, Finland.

Lycett, Mark T. and Kathleen D. Morrison

1998 *Scales and Monumentalities: The Production of an Iron Age Landscape in North Interior Karnataka.* Paper presented in "South Asian Archaeology," at the 97th Annual Meeting of the American Anthropological Association, Philadelphia, Pennsylvania, 1-3 December.

Morrison, Kathleen D.

1989   *Urban Agricultural Production in South India: Agricultural intensification at Vijayanagara.* Paper presented at the 54th Annual Meetings of the Society for American Archaeology, Atlanta, Georgia.

1991   *Supplying the City: The role of reservoir irrigation in an Indian urban landscape.* Paper presented at the 56th Annual Meetings of the Society for American Archaeology, New Orleans, Louisiana.

1992   *Charting the Path of Change: Intensification and expansion in Indian agriculture.* Paper presented at the 57th Annual Meetings of the Society for American Archaeology, Pittsburgh, Pennsylvania.

1993   *Microscopic Charcoal and Land Use: Lake sediments and regional burning.* Paper presented at the 58th Annual Meetings of the Society for American Archaeology, St. Louis, Missouri.

1993   *Settlement and Land Use in the Regional Archaeological Record.* Paper presented at the 12th International Conference of European Association of South Asian Archaeologists, Helsinki, Finland.

1993   *Centralized Power, Centralized Authority? Ideological claims and archaeological patterns.* Paper presented at the 92nd Annual Meeting of the American Anthropological Association.

1994   *Transportation and Movement: Vijayanagara roads and routes.* Paper presented at World Archaeological Congress III, New Delhi, India.

1995   *Patterns of Vijayanagara Land Use: Implications for regional models.* Paper presented at the 24th Annual Conference on South Asia, Madison, Wisconsin, 20 October.

1995   *Agriculture at the Edges: Archaeology and history in the Vijayanagara hinterland.* Paper presented at the 13th International Conference of the European Association for South Asian Archaeology, Cambridge, England, 3-7 July.

1996   *Long-Term History, Anthropogenesis, and Change: Archaeology asanthropology.* Presidential session, "The Place of Archaeology in Anthropology." Paper presented at the 95th Annual Meeting of the American Anthropological Association, San Francisco, California, 20-24 November.

1997   *Coercion, Resistance, and Hierarchy: Local Processes and Imperial Strategies in 14th to 16th Century South India,* Wenner-Gren International Symposium No. 122, "Imperial Designs: Comparative Dynamics of Early Empires," Mijas, Spain, 24 October-1 November.

1997   *Taxpayer Revolts of the 15th Century: Drought, Famine, and the Archaeology of Human Response in South India.* In, "Natural Disaster and the Archaeology of Human Response." Paper presented at the 60th Annual Meetings of the Society for American Archaeology, Nashville, Tennessee, 3-6 April.

1999   *Rethinking the Course of Intensification: Scale and Power.* In, "Intensification of Production." Paper presented at the 62nd Annual Meeting of the Society for American Archaeology, Chicago, Illinois, 25-28 March.

2001   *Changing Contexts of the Pepper Trade: Long-Distance Exchange, Local Politics, and the Transformation of Southwest India.* In, "The Middle East and the Indian Ocean: Connections and Patterns," Middle East Studies Association, San Francisco, California, November.

Morrison, Kathleen D. and Mark T. Lycett

1989   *Persistent lithics: Post-Iron age Chipped Stone Technology in South India.* Paper presented at the 18th Annual Conference on South Asia, Madison, Wisconsin.

1996   *Inscriptions as Artifacts: Precolonial South India and the Analysis of Texts.* In, "New Approaches to Combining the Archaeological and Historical Records: Current Research in the New and Old Worlds." Paper presented at the 59th Annual

Meetings of the Society for American Archaeology, New Orleans, Louisiana, 10-14 April.

Sinopoli, Carla M.

1989   *The political Economy of a South Indian Empire.* Paper presented at the 54th Annual Meetings of the Society for American Archaeology, Atlanta, Georgia.

1989   *The Vijayanagara Metropolitan Survey 1988-89.* Paper presented at the 18th Annual Conference on South Asia, Madison, Wisconsin.

1991   *Political Structure and Economic Strategies at the Imperial Capital of Vijayanagara,* South India. Invited Paper presented at "The Economic Anthropology of the State," Society for Economic Anthropology, Bloomington, Indiana.

1991   *Sacred Architecture in the Vijayanagara Suburbs: Some preliminary observations.* Paper presented at the 11th International Conference of the Association for South Asian Archaeologists in Western Europe, Berlin, Germany.

1992   *Vijayanagara Polity and Economy: The view from the capital.* Paper presented in "Looking for India, 1492," Southern Asian Institute, Columbia University, New York.

1993   *Merchants and Mercenaries: The Portuguese at Vijayanagara, India.* Paper presented at Society for Historical Archaeology Meetings, Kansas City, Missouri.

1994   *Movement and Distribution of Craft Producers and Products at the Vijayanagara Imperial Capital.* Paper presented in "Trade and contact in the Vijayanagara Empire," World Archaeology Congress, New Delhi, India.

1995   *Craft and Social Identity in Precolonial South India.* Paper presented in "Craft and Social Identity," 94th Annual Meeting of the American Anthropological Association, Washington, D.C.

1995   *Urban Survey at a Precolonial Indian Imperial Capital.* Paper presented at the University of Michigan-Universidade de Brasilia Archaeological Conference in Brazil, Brasilia.

1995   *Scale and Variability: Challenges in the archaeology of empire.* Paper presented at the University of Michigan-Universidade de Brasilia Archaeological Conference in Brazil, Brasilia.

1995   *Imperial Control at Vijayanagara.* Paper presented at the University of Michigan-Universidade de Sao Paulo, Archaeological Conference in Brazil, Sao Paulo.

1995   *Nucleated Settlements in the Vijayanagara Metropolitan Region.* Paper presented at the 13th Biannual Meeting of the Association of South Asian Archaeologists in Europe, Cambridge, England.

1996   *Levels of Complexity: Assessing sources of ceramic variability at Vijayanagara.* Paper presented at "Pottery and People," invited symposium, Illinois State University, Normal, Illinois.

1996   *Ceramic Use and Ritual Practices in Hindu India: Historic and archaeological evidence,* Asian Ceramics: Functions and Forms, Field Museum and Asian Ceramics Research Organization, Chicago, Illinois.

1997   *Imperial Designs: Comparative dynamics of early empires,* with S.E. Alcock, T.N. D'Altroy, and K.D. Morrison. Paper presented at Wenner Gren Foundation for Anthropological Research: International Symposia Program, #122: "Imperial Designs: Comparative Dynamics of Early Empires."

1997   *On the Edge of Empire: Form and substance in the Satavahana dynasty.* Paper presented at Wenner Gren Foundation for Anthropological Research: International Symposia Program, #122: "Imperial Designs: Comparative Dynamics of Early Empires."

1998   *The Imperial City of Vijayanagara: Symbolizing power in a dynamic political landscape.* Paper presented at "Forgotten Cities," organized by Rita Wright. New York, University and Asia Society, New York.

1999   *Site Formation Processes in the Vijayanagara Metropolitan Region.* Paper presented at conference on "Site Formation Processes and Indian Archaeology," organized by Drs K. Paddayya and V.N. Misra, Deccan College, Pune, India, December.

1999   *Conceiving Imperial Designs.* Paper presented at Wenner Gren International Symposium Program, #125: "Anthropology at the End of the Century," Baja, California Sur, Mexico, October.

1999   *The Regional Landscapes of the Imperial City of Vijayanagara: Report on the Vijayanagara Metropolitan Survey project.* Paper presented at the 15th Biennial Conference of the Association of South Asian Archaeologists in Europe, Leiden, Netherlands, July.

2000   *Representing Vijayanagara: Contradiction, competition, and conflicting messages of imperial authority.* Paper presented at the Conference of "Theoretical Archaeology Group," Oxford, England, December.

2000   *Echoes of Empire: Vijayanagara and historical memory, Vijayanagara as historical memory.* In, "Archaeologies of Memory: Case Studies, Comparative Perspectives," Society for American Archaeology, Philadelphia, Pennsylvania, April.

Sinopoli, Carla M. and Kathleen D. Morrison

1995   *Recent Archaeological Research at Vijayanagara.* Paper presented at the 24th Annual Conference on South Asia, Madison, Wisconsin, 20 October.

1999   *The Regional Landscapes of the Imperial City of Vijayanagara: Report on the Vijayanagara Metropolitan Survey Project.* Paper presented at the Conference of the European Association of South Asian Archaeologists, Leiden, Netherlands, July.

A STUDY OF THE BRIDGE AT VITTHALAPURA

A STUDY OF THE BRIDGE AT VITTHALAPURA (NBs and NBx)

John M. Fritz

The stone bridge at Vijayanagara is well known. Its sinuous form and engineering boldness have attracted photographers, artists and writers of guidebooks as well as scholars.[1] Almost certainly built during while the city was occupied, the bridge is located northwest of the Vitthala temple complex. The bridge consists of two parts that link the opposite banks of the Tungabhadra River by means of an intermediate island (Figure 1). The island, bounded by the north and south branches of the river, provides this connection at its east end, below an important fifteenth-century temple. The longer segment to the south (NBx) spans the river where the south branch emerges from a rocky gorge, turns and widens to the northeast. The gorge is south-southwest of the bridge. Today this part of the bridge is represented by an array of high pylons that extend in a long sinuous line across water, silt and sheet-rock in the river bed. The standing elements of the bridge are even more impressive when one realizes that the river in flood has carried away almost all their stone superstructure. The shorter northern part (NBs) crosses the small north channel of the river, before it rejoins the main channel.

Most visitors to Hampi see the longer segment of the bridge from the south bank of the river. Yet, the southern termination of this segment, a short distance west of the Vitthala complex, is not preserved. Only the occasional pilgrim to Pampa-Sarovar or to present-day *ashrams* on the north side of the river are likely to see its better preserved north end. During our drawing of the Chandramauleshvara temple in this area early in 1992, members of the Vijayanagara Research Project documented the north end of NBx and its relation to the embankments on which the temple sits. In subsequent seasons we examined the form and construction of standing and collapsed elements in the riverbed, as well as the collapsed remains of NBs. Emphasizing the better-preserved north end of NBx, the following article reports our observations about the construction of the embankments and of the pylons that supported the bridge, and also the present condition of the remaining bridge elements. It concludes with consideration of dating, longevity and a comparison with similar structures.

The Upper Embankment
(Figures 1-3, Plates 1-3)

The Chandramauleshvara temple (NBx/1; see Michell and Wagoner 2001: I, 11-12) is sited on a spacious terrace that, in turn, rises above a broad lower terrace (see Table 1). The upper terrace is retained by a wall composed of two offset basements of massive undressed granite blocks on top of which is further offset a basement of large dressed slabs. In plan this embankment is broadly U-shaped, with a long wall to the east and shorter walls to the north and south; the last two walls abut boulders of an outcrop to the west. Its east side is aligned a few degrees to the east of north, and its north and south sides are approximately perpendicular to it.

At present the aggregate height of the three offset stages is about 445 cm. The lower two basements, an elaboration of the standard simple tripartite basement, are similar in several details. Each is plane and consists of a horizontal top made up of blocks rectangular in transverse section and laid end-to-end, forming a broad shelf. At least three intermediate courses occur consisting of blocks, approximately square to slightly rectangular in transverse section, laid alternately parallel and perpendicular to the face of the wall. Unlike tripartite basements, the long parallel blocks are placed on their broad rather than on their narrow sides. The "soldier" or perpendicular blocks extend back into the fill of the embankment and now, sometimes forward past the plane of the parallel blocks.[2] The soldier blocks anchor the basement into the embankment. In those few cases where the length of these blocks can be observed, they are longer than the offset between the faces of lower and higher stages. If deep foundation courses underpin each basement, the soldier courses would interlock with these buried blocks in some manner that cannot be directly observed. However, even if basements do not have deep foundations, the soldier courses would still provide some support. While exceptions occur, the perpendicular blocks tend to be positioned above each other in alternative courses, with those in one course being set halfway between those in the adjacent courses. All blocks are undressed except for occasional slight shaping of margins. Lines of sectioned quarry holes are seen frequently along the edges.

The base of the lowest basement is buried in alluvium; its foundations cannot be seen. The visible structure consists of a broad horizontal top course and three horizontal courses. The second basement is set behind the vertical plane of the first from 85 cm to more than 115 cm. While the faces of the top and fourth course of the lowest basement appear to be in the same plane, those of the intermediate courses may have been recessed. The face of the parallel blocks of the second course from the bottom is recessed *c.* 5 to 10 cm, and that of the third course, *c.* 15 to 20 cm from this plane. However, the faces of several soldier blocks project forward almost to the plane of the top course; erosion and slumping may have distorted the configuration of either or both types of blocks in these courses.[3]

The top and three lower courses of the intermediate basement appear to rest on a foundation course that sits, in turn, on rubble at a level somewhat below the top of the lowest

basement.[4] While the base of the intermediate basement does not seem to rest on the top of the lower basement, the top of this basement, which forms a shelf some 100 to 125 cm wide, does extend under the upper structure.[5] The upper course of the second stage has slumped backward at places and here the terrace surface is broken.

The third basement has a simple tripartite scheme, consisting of slabs with opposed upper and lower bevelled mouldings. The intermediate vertical course is recessed some 24 to 33 cm. The lowest bevelled element rests on a foundation course, which projects 15 to 17 cm. Each slab is dressed on its outer face. The top of the upper slab is dressed only along its juncture with the outer face; the top is undressed and shows no sign of wear. Presumably, foundation slabs are only dressed on their upper face along the juncture with the front face. The slabs of the bevelled courses are long and the joints generally are not aligned with those in the inset course. There are no sockets visible on the exposed surface of the upper course or on slabs displaced from the ruined southeast corner of the embankment.

A possible fourth stage of construction is indicated by one to two courses of triangular blocks that rest on the upper course of the third stage.[6] These blocks are set back some 27 cm from the front of this stage. They form a continuous vertical face, but are set on end or on their side so that no flat surface exists on their top. No interior (second) face is seen. They may have extended along all of the east retaining wall, but they have fallen, along with the lower stages, at the northeast corner and along the north wall. These blocks may have formed part of a vanished compound wall around the temple complex.

The lowest basement is preserved at the north-east corner of the embankment. But while the east face of the intermediate structure has collapsed here, remnants are preserved of the north face. Two courses rest on top of the lowest basement, their north faces set back only about 5 cm from the face of the block on which they lay. These courses continue about 5 m to the west where much of the upper basement of the north wall has collapsed, burying the lower stages. A stairway of irregular blocks gives entry to the upper terrace and breaks the line of basements. At the west end of the north wall, the slumped upper basement extends upward from the west side of the stairway to a basement of a Vijayanagara period *mandapa* on the upper terrace. This, in turn, rests on boulders.

The south half of the east wall, the southeast corner, and much of the south wall of the upper embankment have been broken apart by the river. Slabs and blocks lie scattered at angles to the south and east of the Chandramauleshvara temple below their original position. While much of the remaining embankment is in place, some of the constituent fill has been eroded, and elements are slumped or often lie askew. However, the west end of the south wall, while partly disarticulated, is still preserved. Here the upper basement rests on long blocks that sit on boulders; that is, the lowest two basements do not extend this far west.

A stairway on the south side of the upper embankment may have lead from the lower to the upper terrace. Several features support this possibility. First, the angled moulding in the top course of the upper basement stops at a block near the end of the last slab. The front and east faces of the block are well dressed. Such changes in the form of mouldings generally indicate that they end at the block. The east face may have formed one side of a passage or may have even abutted a gateway. Second, a number of undressed pillars, capital blocks and roof slabs lie here to the east and northeast. Third, two segments of a (*prakara?*) wall are preserved immediately above (north) of the fallen pillars. Each segment consists of two parallel layers of dressed slabs set on edge. These remains are too fragmentary and disorganized to reconstruct the layout of the possible entry structure.

The Lower Embankment
(Figures 1 and 4, Plates 4-7)

The lower embankment consists of two sections. The main embankment is a single-faced wall of long granite blocks that occurs to the south and east of the Chandramauleshvara temple. The north end of the southern bridge (NBx) abuts the middle of its east leg. The second section occurs to the north of the

temple and is made up of offset rows of boulders. The south end of the northern bridge (NXs) abuts the middle of this construction. The two sections do not appear to meet.

The terrace east of the upper embankment – i.e. between it and the top of the lower embankment – is wide, flat and has few features. There is the remnant of a wall about 7 m west of the east face of the lower embankment. It is first seen at a point about 16 m north of the south face of the embankment and continues for about 15.5 m (with a 4-m gap) to the north as a double-faced wall ca 86 cm wide. It continues northward at first as a single-(east) faced wall (probably continuing the remains of the double-faced wall) and then, just northwest of the end of the bridge, as an alignment of small blocks and rubble, with gaps, to a point almost opposite the northeast corner of the upper embankment. The purpose of this wall is unknown. It may have separated the public road associated with the bridge from more private space below the upper embankment.

East of the southeast corner of the temple, and a few metres in front of the projected line of the upper embankment occurs alignments of blocks and rubble that may be the remains of a structure. The west side of the feature is marked by the east and north face of a block wall about 7 m long. A small section of double-faced wall, 144 cm wide, occurs 268 cm to the east of the north end. The west face stops at a single-faced wall 134 cm south of the north end of the west wall. The east face continues southward for several metres. A block oriented east-west abuts the north end of the west wall. Two rectangular and two long triangular blocks oriented north-south (the latter similar to those in the lower embankment) extend 7 m to the east. This feature may have been the foundations for a structure; the use of blocks like those from the lower embankment suggests reuse of elements and, thus, a construction date more recent than that of the bridge.

The South and East Embankment

A slightly sloping wall, L-shaped in plan, forms the face of this section of the lower embankment, rising just above the river. The north end of the east wall of the lower embankment is buried in alluvium. Nine courses of granite blocks are visible in a gully east of the northeast corner of the upper embankment, and from here the wall extends continuously to the south and joins the south side, which extends westward away from the river.[7]

At the bridge, the bottom of the east wall rests on a rise of sheet-rock that gradually slopes down to the river bed. Here the wall is 418 cm high and includes ten courses. At the southeast corner of the embankment wall the south face is 424 cm or ten courses high above a small boulder, while the north face extends down an additional five courses (128 cm) to bedrock. Thus, the full height of the corner is about 550 cm. The base of the south wall here rests on a low rise of sheet rock that is higher in elevation than that at the bridge. The height of the south wall at the staircase (see below) is 375 cm (nine courses).

A Vijayanagara period staircase links the riverbed to the lower terrace. It is approximately on axis with the stairways and south entrance of the temple. During flood it leads to the water's edge.[8] (The embankment is entirely submerged during periods of high water.) It abuts the south embankment and projects outward at an angle to the wall. The sixteen risers (one or two more would have carried the steps to the top of the wall) consist of stacked long blocks laid parallel to the face of the wall. The third tread from the bottom is 388 cm long. Long horizontal blocks that form the sides of the staircase are laid perpendicular to and mostly abut the north sides of the risers. Few cases of interlocking coursing are seen.

The wall of the lower embankment contains elements quite different from those of the higher walls. Large blocks, square to rectangular in elevation, triangular (some are rectangular) in plan, and rectangular in longitudinal section are pegged into fill. No evidence for anchor pegs at the base of the wall or for iron clamps is seen. Each higher course is set back from the lower by about 5 cm giving the wall a rearward slant. The wedge-shaped blocks form courses that are continuous and do not pinch out. However, because of variation in elevation of the river bed and in the height of constituent blocks, the courses are somewhat sinuous. Overall, the courses in

this embankment incline downhill to the southeast corner.

Blocks in lower courses are somewhat larger than those in higher courses. Representative blocks at the top of the wall measure 55 x 39 x 154 cm and 34 x 35 x 123 cm.[9] Blocks in the east wall along the river are similar in size from those above the south embankment wall. While most of the surface of the blocks is left undressed, it has often been tooled along the edges of the outer face where it abuts other blocks. Such tooling is particularly prominent on lower courses at the southeast corner.

The southeast corner, like other such constructions at the site, is made up blocks larger than those in the rest of the wall. The long axes of these blocks extend north or west in alternative courses. Each block parallel to the face of the wall is positioned between at least three perpendicular blocks above and below.

The North Embankment
(Figure 1, Plate 19)

This section consists of a sloping bank that is faced by rows of small boulders and a few blocks each set back behind the one below so as to create small terraces. The stones in the lower courses are smaller than those used in upper courses. Erosion and human and animal traffic have displaced the boulders in some areas. Here the embankment stretches for several 10s of metres up and downstream from the end of the bridge, stabilizing the bank on which the upper embankment is set. This type of construction is seen elsewhere at Vijayanagara, facing the back slopes of fortification walls and also the sides of *bunds* and canals.[10]

The Bridge: Southern Section (NBx)
(Figure 4, Plate 10)

Our observations of the bridge indicate that it has the following configuration: It consists of more than 117 pylons, each composed of three granite pillars on which are laid two layers of blocks and beams. These elements are held together both by their dead weight and also by stone pegs set into sockets. Occasionally, metal clamps add strength. Each pillar is set into sockets excavated into sheet-rock in the river bed. The pillar bases are also supported by stone boxes packed with rubble, horizontal stone braces and cobble pavements between these boxes, and sometimes also by angled stone braces. While the top of the super-structure was approximately horizontal in longitudinal section, the topography of the riverbed varied; the length of the pillars was adjusted accordingly to create a level upper surface. Presumably, a roadway founded on wooded beams that spanned the gaps between pylons was built on top.

The Pylons
(Figures 4, 5 and 7, Plates 7-9 and 11)

We have documented the remains of 117 pylons, numbered here from north to south. The best evidence for the structure of the bridge is found at its north end. Pylon 1 is located from 110 to 135 cm from the base of the retaining wall of the lower embankment. Only this pylon preserves the entire super-structure that supported the roadway. The base of this pylon consists of three granite pillars (layer A), square in section and undressed. Above this is a superstructure of stone elements in four layers. The first layer (B) consists of crude rectilinear capital blocks that rest on the pillars while the second layer (C) comprises two beams that rest on these blocks and abut over the central pillar. Set on these beams is a second layer of blocks (D) followed by a layer of longer beams (E). The cumulative height of the pylon elements at this point is more than 385 cm.[11] The combined length of the top beams is 670 cm. While the bottoms of the pillars are not visible, pre-sumably they are seated in square sockets cut into bedrock. Such pillar sockets are visible on exposed bedrock to the south.

The system of assembly of these elements can be inferred from the elements fallen from pylons further to the south. Stone pegs and, in a few cases, metal clamps held the elements of each pylon together. The top of each pillar in layer A is dressed to form a shallow concave basin. Presumably, this ensured that the outer edges of the pillar formed a level surface that could support the capital block. A cubical anchor hole occurs in the centre of this basin, and a basalt peg placed here also fits into a corresponding hole in the bottom of the

superimposed block in layer B. The blocks on the outer pillars have a second hole in the middle of the top of the block and this seats a peg that fits into a hole centred near the underside of the beam above in layer C. (In several cases, the top or bottom of a beam at one or both ends is trimmed to seat blocks and perhaps to maintain a level upper surface. We did not determine whether these beams were in layer C or E.) The top of this beam, the top and bottom of the next layer of capital blocks (D) and the undersides of the top beams (layer E) also have holes to seat pegs. However, over the central pillar the lower capital block in layer B supports the juncture of two beams in layer C. The tops of these blocks have two anchor holes that correspond to holes in the underside of the superimposed beam. These beams also have two holes in their top faces that match holes in the underside of the upper capital block in layer D. Finally, a pair of holes in the top of this block matches those at the abutting ends of the top beams in layer E. There are no holes in the tops of the beams of this layer. The abutting ends of beams in layer C (or E?) may also be secured by metal clamps.

From this description it is possible to deter-mine the position in the superstructure of many of these elements based on the number of anchor holes. Capital blocks with a single hole on top and bottom were positioned above the outermost pillars in layers B or D. Those with a single hole on one face and two holes on the other face were above the central pillar in layer B; those with two holes on each face were above the same pillar in layer D. Beams with pairs of holes on opposite faces formed layer C while those with holes only on one face made up layer E.

Basalt pegs can still be seen in the tops of a few standing pillars, for example on Pylon 12 and several north of Pylon 100 as well as in the tops of fallen pillars. In two fallen examples, a peg projects 5 cm from an anchor hole in a block and 4 cm from a beam. But displaced pegs were not observed in the rubble around the bases of pylons. However, a great deal of basalt stone working debris was noticed amid this rubble and even packed between pillars and socket walls. Some of it may have been produced during the manufacture of pegs. (For other sources of this material, see below.)

We measured anchor holes in the tops of four fallen pillars (see Table 22). Their dimensions were (length x width x depth): 8 x 7.5 x 7.5 cm, 8.5 x 8 x 6.5 cm, 6 x 5 x 7 cm and 8 x 7 cm (this example contained the base of a basalt peg). The range of values is consistent with sockets documented elsewhere at the site (see Table 11 and article by Fritz on a rock-cut feature in this volume).

We noted evidence for the use of metal clamps when we documented the attributes of fallen beams (see below). The seating for clamps consists of a small anchor hole on the upper face of the beam several centimetres from the end and a small channel leading from the hole to the edge (see Table 2).[12] We suggest that during construction, beams were closely abutted, holes cut into upper surface on either side of the juncture and connected by a channel. A metal bar (almost certainly of iron) was pounded into the holes and channel. We identified a clamp seating in four out of ten documented beans; one of these had a pair of seatings. From all holes, a channel extended to the edge of these beams. Comparing the measurements of the sockets for anchor pegs and clamps, we observe that the former are considerably larger both in plan and in depth while the latter are proportionately deeper. The distance of the clamp holes from the edge of the beam is variable (compare description above with Table 2; see also Table 11).

Approximately 47 per cent of the pillars in the 117 pylons observed still stand complete based on counts of upstream and downstream elements (53 upstream and 57 downstream pillars; see Table 19). An additional 17 per cent are preserved only in part, ranging in size from basal fragments lodged in pillar sockets to shafts snapped off at half their height (23 upstream and 16 downstream). Some 29 per cent of these pillars are entirely absent (34 upstream and 35 downstream) and in 7 per cent of cases no observation can be made (7 upstream and 9 downstream).

Pillars in a given pylon are roughly aligned so that their north and south sides are lined up. However, we observed that some pillars are turned approximately 45 degrees to this plane. This was not documented systematically but was observed in eight cases, most of which were located upstream (Pylons 51-53, 61, 62, 67, 90 and 93). This deviation probably was intended, so that the apex of the pillar rather than its face bore the brunt of the flood.

Pillar height varies considerably, presumably depending on the depth of the river bed (see Tables 3 and 20). At the extreme, downstream pillars vary from 215 cm to an impressive 648 cm high. Their average height is greater than upstream pillars perhaps because the riverbed slopes downstream (464 cm vs. 438 cm). While the range of horizontal dimensions is considerable, their averages vary little either within or between types of pillar location (range between type averages is 50.3 to 53.1 cm). No systematic variation is seen; for example, the longitudinal dimension is not always longer than the transverse. In some cases pillar bases appear to have been trimmed to fit sockets (see Table 22).

The dimensions and other attributes of seventeen fallen capital blocks were recorded (see Tables 4 and 24). They are not square in plan; average length is about 2.5 times longer than width; average width is 1.3 times greater than height.

All blocks have at least one anchor hole in the upper or lower face. We observed three blocks with two holes in each face, one with two holes in one and one in the opposite face, five with single holes in each face, and two with a hole in only one face. One face could not be observed for five blocks. The distribution can be compared to the expected frequency of blocks if the system described above was followed: in each pylon, one block would have a pair of holes in the upper and lower faces; another block would have double and single holes; four blocks would have single holes on opposing faces; no blocks would have only one anchor hole. The difference between this "expected" pattern and that observed might be attributed to (in order of likelihood) the inadequate sample of observed blocks, the divergences from the expected in practice, and/or the erroneous inclusion of beams (broken or not).

The location of each hole in the face of a block was also noted according to a simple ordinal scale: that is, 1 designates a point at the outer edge of the face, 5, at the centre, 3, halfway between 1 and 5, etc. (see Schematic diagram on p. 630 and Table 5). In faces having single holes, we would expect it to be located in the centre; in fact, fifteen out of seventeen observed cases were at or close to this point. In faces having two holes, we would expect each to be located between points 3 and 4; that is, at locations which would divide the length of the block into three equal sections. In twenty observed cases, nineteen were located at points 3, 3-4 or 4. Only one hole occurred at the edge (point 1) and this may have seated a clamp. Thus, both single and double holes tend to occur in "expected" positions.

Only ten possible beams were documented (see Tables 4, 5 and 25). The average width and height of observed beams is only slightly greater than those of capital blocks. Some of the shorter examples might be long capitals blocks or have had some other structural purpose.[13] However, one beam that is 165 cm long has a socket and channel for a clamp. Perhaps such shorter examples are broken. Nine had anchor holes in at least one face. Of five that could be observed fully, three had two holes in both upper and lower surfaces, one had only one hole in each surface, and one had a single hole in only one surface. One beam still held a basalt peg that projected 4 cm from the surface; three beams had channels for clamps; and a seating 64 cm long was deeply cut from the end of one example toward the centre.

The distribution of the locations of anchor holes differs from those of capital blocks. We would expect that holes over the central pillar would occur closer to the inner end of the beam (around position 2), while those over the outer pillars would be inset from the cantilevered end (around position 3). Table 5 indicates that observed values are consistent with the expected pattern: of 24 holes documented, fifteen occur near one end (positions 2 and 2-3) while nine occur from positions 3 to 4.

Based on the distance between the outer faces of the outer pillars of every fifth pylon (see Table 20), the length of the supporting structure (layer A) averages 533.1 cm (N = 24, SD = 43.55, range 493-680 cm). However, the length of the superstructure on these supports was probably greater. We have noted that the full superstructure preserved only in one case (Pylon 1). Here the combined length of the uppermost beams is 670 cm while the length of the supporting pillars is 493 cm; that is, the beams are 130 per cent longer than the supports.

The inter-pylon distance is also variable. We measured the distance between the north faces of upstream pillars for most examples (see Table 20). The average is 361.2 (N = 98, range 222–520 cm, SD = 56.06). While their alignment has not been mapped, pylons do not always appear to be parallel. Slightly differing orientations may have taken account of stream flow or, simply, the varying local conditions in the river bed. Thus, a particular inter-pylon distance downstream cannot be expected to be identical to that upstream. Nevertheless, the average and range of values downstream would probably be similar to the measured upstream values. If so, the latter are representative of the minimum and maximum spans that wooden beams supporting a road bed would have had to cover.

The Foundations and Bracing
(Figures 4-7, Plates 12-15)

Because the flow of the river in flood would have put great stress on the supporting elements of the bridge, it was particularly necessary to provide strong foundations for the pillars. A combination of at least five different means were used to support the base of the pillars; namely, sockets, stone boxes, basal braces, diagonal braces and a pavement held in place by a downstream wall.

Rectilinear sockets were excavated into the sheet-rock to hold the bases of pillars. (In one case a natural pothole in the rock was used.) Their sides slope very slightly inward, their bottoms are flat and there is a lip at the juncture of the sides and the surface. Rubble and sediments were packed between the side of the socket and the pillar. However, there are signs of greater wear on the downstream lips of some sockets, which indicates that the pressure of the moving water caused pillars to rub against this side. These sockets were measured whenever they were visible – chiefly on the sheet-rock rise where elements of the pylons have been swept clear; that is, between Pylons 15 and 44. Table 6 summarizes these metrical attributes (see also Table 20). We see that the average lengths of the sides are nearly equal, a slight exception being the lesser transverse length of downstream sockets. While average depths are also similar, they decrease slightly from upstream, through central to downstream examples. The same tendency is seen in the minimum and maximum depths. The builders of the bridge may have understood that the upstream pillars received more stress and should be more deeply seated. The spatial distribution of sockets exposed may also indicate the direction of moving water: the tops of 31 upstream sockets are exposed compared to 27 central and 28 downstream locations. At the same time, fallen elements that were shifted downstream probably gave some protection to the base of pillars there.

We can compare the size of sockets to the pillars they contained (see Tables 3 and 6). For upstream features, the difference between the average longitudinal dimensions of sockets and pillars is 7.4 cm and between their transverse dimensions is 10 cm. For central sockets, the differences are both 8 cm, while downstream they are 7.1 and 6.5 cm. This indicates, for example, that on the average a space only 3.25 to 5 cm was left between the top of the socket and the pillar. Because the walls of the former slope inward, the gap at the bottom would have been even smaller. Only sand, small rocks and other debris could have been used to pack this space to prevent movement of the pillar. While in different locations the average gap between pillars and socket walls is quite similar, somewhat less space was left for seating downstream pillars.

We noted the second type of support; that is, simple boxes of granite slabs surrounding pillar bases (F) in cases where the surface had not been swept clean by the river or not entirely covered by alluvium or fallen pylon elements (see Tables 19 and 26). We then recognized, in less stable contexts, parts of boxes that had been partly or entirely torn apart by the river. For boxes buried in sediment it was only possible to document their horizontal dimensions; the form and articulation of their constituents could not be seen. However, the long sides of several disarticulated elements had a distinctive "denticulated" form created by removing two broad notches from one long side. We observed that these were arranged around pillars so as to interlock; that is, slabs placed on opposite sides of a pillar with the notches facing down (almost always on upstream and downstream sides of pillars) interlocked with slabs with notches facing upward (almost always on the north and south sides). It was not possible to document all possible instances of such boxes or to determine if this interlocking system was used even in those examples exposed by erosion. However, it seems probable that this system was used in most, if not all, cases.

We measured 29 examples of the slabs that formed the boxes (see Tables 7 and 26). Their dimensions are quite variable; for example, maximum length and height are each more than two times greater than minimum figures. In one case (Pylon 71), dressed basement mouldings, one having an angled bevel and corner quarter-medallions, were used to form three sides of a box. However, most slabs were undressed. Notches could be seen in twelve of these but were measured in only four cases. The average depth of these notches is 33 per cent of the average height of the slabs. While these figures are based on small samples, they may indicate that two-thirds of each interlocking slab was articulated with the overlapping slab and one-third was exposed. If not protected, the exposed parts of each box could easily be de-coupled by the rapidly flowing river.

While these slabs do not form a statistically representative sample, they give an approximate idea of the dimensions and proportions of box sides. We note that the area formed by the inner faces of the boxes are considerably larger than the dimensions of pillars and pillar sockets.[14] This gap is filled with cobbles, smaller rubble and sediments.

Basal bracing (G) was observed in several instances. This consists of horizontal granite slabs laid between and abutting the slabs that formed stone boxes; that is, between upstream and central, and central and downstream pillars. We recorded whether it was present, absent or not observable. The number of cases between upstream and central pillars was 6 present, 97 absent and 14 not observable, while between central and downstream pillars the figures were 5 present, 99 absent and 13 not observable. Only two of these were measured: one was 169 x 51 x 23 cm and the second 159 x 46.5 x 23 cm (length x width x height). The second was broken and an additional small slab filled the gap between the boxes.

Evidence for diagonal bracing (H) was observed only in the north third of the bridge (see Tables 8, 19 and 21). The bracing system consists of several elements: a notch in the downstream face of the downstream pillar, a granite brace, and a socket cut into the sheet-rock. The notch has a triangular cross section, is about twice as wide as high, and is shallow. In cross-section the brace is slightly wider than high. The socket or footing cut into the sheet-rock is square or slightly rectangular in plan; its north and south sides and back are vertical and its front (i.e. facing the pillar) slopes down to the back or slopes down to a roughly levelled floor. Notches were observed in six pillars; 57 downstream pillars lacked notches. Braces were *in situ* in six cases (Pylons 9-11, 14, 15 and 16).[15] Sockets were observed in sixteen cases including thirteen cases where no pillars were preserved (Pylons 17-22 and 37-43); they were absent in 34 cases and could not be observed in 67 cases.

Six notches in downstream pillars were measured (see Tables 8 and 21). Their average dimensions are 32.3 x 15.5 x 4.1 cm (width x height x depth). The brace was measured in three cases. Average length of the brace outside of the notches is 230.3 cm. Height above the stone box encircling the pillar was measured in four cases: average 115.8 cm. (Note that the height above sheet-rock including that of the box would be several 10s of cm higher.) The distance between the pillar and brace sockets could be observed where the surface had been swept clean. Here the average is 149.3 cm (N=15). Because the average height of the notch in the pillar is probably greater than the average length between the pillar and the socket in the sheet-rock, the angle of the brace would be more than 45 degrees.[16]

One or two square large holes are located below the downstream pillar in eighteen cases, all in the northern third of the bridge (Pylons 19-32 and 39-42, and see Tables 9, 19 and 21). Of these, three have only one hole, fifteen have two holes, and in one case the presence or absence of a second hole could not be observed. When two holes are present the average distance between the pillar socket and each hole is very close (40.7 and 40.2 cm). The average plan dimensions of each are also virtually identical (18.2 x 18.2 cm and 18.1 x 18.3 cm) as are the depths (11.1 and 11.0 cm). These holes are absolutely larger and proportionately shallower than anchor holes. They may have seated a large peg: the base of a basalt object was found in each of seven holes. These objects have a square base but the rest of their form of is unknown, as is their precise function. However, it is probable that they formed part of the downstream bracing system.

Assuming that stone boxes surrounded the pillars associated with these large holes, we can imagine at least two possibilities. The basalt objects abutted the outer (downstream) face of the box and braced it, or they were immediately inside the box and perhaps supported one end of a short basal brace. Our analysis based on the average dimensions of the concerned elements indicates that the holes would have partly underlain the box's downstream side. However, it would have been possible to shorten the lateral sides of the box so that the basalt object was outside or to lengthen it so that it was inside. In the first case (assuming average values and that the stone box was symmetrical about the pillar) the side of the box would have been 140 cm long, and in the second case, 232 cm long. Either value fits within the observed range of box side length (126 to 290 cm). Given the stresses applied to the downstream side of stone boxes, the first arrangement seems more probable to us; that is, that these holes seated basalt plugs that braced the outside of the stone box.

We may examine the relationship between diagonal bracing, as indicated by notches on pillars or sockets in sheet-rock, and the large holes just described (see Tables 10 and 19). Between Pylons 9 and 43 there are 21 "sockets" and nineteen instances when at least one hole is present. Only in nine cases are both a socket and a hole present. In ten cases holes are present but sockets are absent, while in four cases holes are absent but sockets are present. In ten cases both are absent. One or the other feature cannot be observed in 34 per cent of the cases. Of the 35 cases where one of these features is observable, the nine cases where both are present constitute only 26 per cent of the total. These figures suggest that the two techniques of support are only weakly associated.

Where the bed of the river had not been swept clean of bridge elements – i.e. where sheet rock was not exposed, but also where it was not covered with fine alluvial sediments – we noted a kind of pavement between the exposed stone boxes. We did not systematically record the contents of this pavement, but it seemed to contain cobbles and pebbles, basalt fragments, and fine sediments. It is likely that the foundations of the bridge were stabilized by a thick and tightly packed layer of rubble that extended from the bed of the river to (at least) the top of the stone boxes. If the average height of such boxes was around 43.3 cm (only twelve instances were measured), then this layer could have averaged at least 50 cm deep and would have extended the length of the bridge and to an uncertain distance to either side.

If, indeed, a thick pavement extended the length and breadth of the bridge, then it would have formed a kind of weir or low dam that would have raised the level of the riverbed somewhat and thus slowed the flow of the river. However, the force of the current would then have been even greater where it dropped over the downstream edge of the weir and here the edge of the pavement would have been subject to erosion. There is evidence that the builders of the bridge tried to counter this attrition by creating a wall along at least part of the downstream edge of the pavement. The wall was held in place by rows of basalt pegs. Such a wall is indicated by three groups of anchor holes that occur below Pylons 10–22 (see Tables 11 and 27). Group I consists of thirteen holes and is located below Pylons 10–12; Group II, nine holes below Pylons 18 and 19; and Group III, eight holes below Pylons 21 and 22. The gap between the first two groups occurs between Pylons 12 and 18 and is covered with fallen architectural elements; the surface

cannot be seen. The gap between the second and third group, below Pylon 20 occurs where the level of the sheet-rock is low. The downstream lips of all holes in Group II were very smooth, indicating wear by the anchor peg as it transmitted the force of the moving stream to the sheet-rock. The bases of basalt-pegs were observed in three holes.

The size of the anchor holes falls within the range of those few documented on top of pillars (see above). The distance of the holes from the pylons ranges from 447 to 623 cm; this may indicate the downstream width of the weir at this point.[17] The average distance between holes, ranging between 25.5 and 92.9, indicates the minimum length of blocks that would have been set against the upstream faces of the anchor pegs. Probably they were much longer. No such blocks are seen now. The overall length of the Group I feature is 10.24 m; the other groups are shorter. Thus, this represents a very small fraction of the length of the bridge. We have not observed systems to prevent downstream erosion of the possible weir elsewhere amid the ruins of the bridge.

Other Features
(Plates 16-17)

The ruins of the bridge also contain evidence of other features, of possible structural and symbolic importance. Sockets for intermediate pillars were observed in addition to the standard set for each pylon (see Tables 12 and 23). They occur in a cluster at the south end of the north expanse of sheet-rock and intermittently further to the south. However, *in situ* examples of intermediate pillars are seen projecting from the alluvium and fallen architectural elements nearer the centre of the bridge (between Pylons 46-64). We did not record these sockets but described six pillars. They are all located between pylons, and equally distributed near upstream, central and downstream pillars. For example, three pillars occur near Pylon 53, all in the zone between the central and downstream pillar. They appear to be arranged in an approximate equilateral triangle and are not aligned.[18] Intermediate pillars differ from those in pylons in size and the presence of a top channel and

618

side groove. The shafts are shorter and thicker than the pillars in pylons (compare Tables 3 and 12). Thus, average height above the alluvium is greater than 104 cm compared to 412 cm for upstream pillars, while longitudinal dimension is 62.0 cm compared to 51.7 cm, and transverse dimension is 65.7 cm compared to 49.0 cm. In every case these pillars have a crudely worked channel on top parallel to the longitudinal axis of the bridge. This averages 62.8 cm long, 27.6 cm wide at top, 25 cm wide at bottom and 8.9 cm deep (N = 4-6). The sides of the channel slope down to a floor slightly convex in section. The band averages 49.0 cm below the top, 6.5 cm high (N = 4) and in one apparently typical case is 1 cm deep. We did not document the interval between these pillars.

Their purpose is problematic. They may have nothing at all to do with the bridge structure; for example, they may be remnants of an earlier construction;[19] or, they may have helped to brace the understructure of the bridge. However, they do not appear to add support to pillars and are too short to reach the road bed. Perhaps, they seated wooden bracing. Alternatively, they may have supported some construction that passed under the road bed. One possibility is that this construction was an aqueduct. However, arguing against this are the facts that the channels that would carry an aqueduct are not aligned and that the pillars are not closely spaced. For example, they are not spaced close enough to support trough-shaped stone elements of aqueducts found in the Royal Centre (see Fritz, Michell and Nagaraja Rao 1984: 53). And no such blocks have been observed in the rubble. While some longer bamboo or wooden channels could have been supported, the absence of alignment in potential supports makes this less likely. In short, the function of these pillars is uncertain. Future research locating all preserved examples and mapping their exact positions would clarify their interpretation.

Short inscriptions were observed on nine pillars. Their discovery was serendipitous and it is entirely possible that more exist. However, certain patterns emerge (see Table 13). Eight inscriptions are located on downstream and one on an upstream pillar. More cases are found on the upstream and south faces of these pillars (three each) and fewer on the north and downstream faces (two and one respectively). However, all face *into* the bridge structure where, presumably, the masons who carved the figures stood. Thus, the single example that faces downstream occurs on the single example on an upstream pillar; no examples on downstream pillars face downstream. These features have only been observed in the southern half of the remaining structure. But the dearth of fully standing pillars further to the north may account for this apparent pattern.

Six inscriptions consist of a single character, four corresponding to the Kannada sound "ra" and two to the Kannada number "2". One contains two letters arranged vertically on the pillar, which can be expressed as "ba sa". Another contains approximately four characters that are of uncertain significance. A further example contains five to six characters in what may be sixteenth-century Telugu script that may correspond to "kukkr barla".[20] No clear pattern emerges when we look at the spatial occurrence of these inscrip-tions. There is no constant interval between the pylons on which they appear; however, it may be significant that the three longer inscriptions are on adjacent pylons and that they are bracketed by pillars with the character for "ra". Other occurrences of "ra" are further afield; the two occurrences of "2" further to the south are separated by several pylons.

The purpose of these inscriptions is uncertain. It is clear that they are not dedicatory in character nor do they seem to provide labels naming a particular place. As well, they do not seem to designate parts of the structure in any way that would be useful for assembling or using it.[21] Rather, they may be marks by masons indicating that they had made or assembled bridge elements at these places.[22] Again, documentation of additional inscriptions might clarify these questions.

The "Flow" of the Bridge
(Plates 10, 11 and 18)

While we have not mapped the bridge, some further observation of substrate, plan and condition can be made (see Tables 14 and 19). One short and one long segment of standing pillars are preserved in the river bed. The former, consisting of twelve pylons, begins at the face of the lower embankment described above and ends at a channel that is intermittently active. Sheet-rock is exposed in the area from the embankment to Pylon 45, but it is partly covered with alluvium between Pylons 9 and 14. This is held in place by fallen architectural elements, which are abundant from Pylons 2 to 15. Sheet-rock rises on the other side of the channel, and here several sets of pillar sockets are exposed (Pylons 15-44) but few architectural elements, standing or fallen, survive. It is this area that receives the most direct water flow as the river leaves the gorge to the southwest. Further, the force of the water is accelerated by the curvature of the rock that acts as like an airfoil. These forces explain why the rock is swept clean of architectural elements (except where boulders caught them) that have been deposited several 10s of metres downstream.[23]

A second channel separates the sheet-rock from an elevated, heavily silted zone, held in place by grasses (Pylons 46-99). The long segment of standing elements begins here, extends through a lower channel (between Pylons 68 and 69),[24] and ends at the principal river channel, not far from the present south river bank. From Pylons 42 to 69, pillars are fragmentary, absent or stand intermittently; but almost all stand from Pylons 70 to 115. Sheet-rock is exposed from Pylons 100 to 116, but alluvium occurs again from Pylon 116 to the present main channel of the river. In this segment, the seating for pillars is apparently more secure, and some capital blocks and even a few examples of the blocks with intermediate beams are preserved *in situ* (Pylons 83, 93 and 98). Nevertheless, fallen architectural elements have accumulated between Pylons 79 and 89, and 96 and 117. By contrast, in the area of sheet-rock just referred to, pillars have mostly fallen, and they stand askew or, along with scattered capital blocks and beams, lie broken downstream.

No evidence of an embankment, standing pillars or sockets in bedrock indicate the position of the southern end of the bridge. While it is possible that part is preserved in the alluvium of the south bank of the river, it is more probable that it has been destroyed.

As the south bank is on the outside (convex side) of the river's main channel at this point, the shore, including any artificial embankment, appears to have suffered catastrophic erosion since the bridge was built.

During its course of at least 421 m to the south-southeast, the bridge curves several times.[25] At least in part, this change of course seems to take advantage of areas of sheet-rock elevated in the bed of the river. Pillars mid-stream are considerably taller than those at the north end (see Tables 14 and 20). This is to be expected as the river is naturally deeper mid-stream than near its banks. Nonetheless, the road bed probably descended from the north end to the centre by as much as 1 m.

The present south end of the bridge trends toward a fortified outcrop or hill west-southwest of the Vitthala temple. The fortification wall extends for several hundred metres both to the southwest and northeast of the hill (see map in Michell and Wagoner 2001: I, 44). After passing through a gateway (NGk/3) northeast of the hill, the pathway from Vitthala to Hampi runs along the southeast flank of the hill on top of the fort wall. Two passageways occur in the wall northeast of the hill; namely, a narrow entry that gives access to a lower area of sheet-rock below the wall via a stairway (NGk), and a wide opening, immediately northwest of the gateway, where the fort walls on either side turn to the east (NGk/6). There are no remains of a gateway here; the passage is partly obstructed by a temple on the main pathway (NGk/5). While no remains of a paved road are seen in the area, we may speculate on routes of movement from the bridge. Assuming that the bridge terminated in the vicinity of this hill, traffic could move in at least three directions. It could turn to the left (northeast) along the riverbank to the terrace between stone *ghats* along the river and the fort-cum-terrace wall of Vitthalapura; it could turn in the same direction and then enter Vitthalapura through the wide passageway; or, it could turn to the right (southwest) into a broad area below the walls. From here, traffic could continue to the west, between the riverbank and a fortified hill (with a gateway, NGn), or to the south-southwest up rock-cut staircases past Sugriva's Cave (NGo/1) to the right, or Sita-Sarovar (NGo/2) to the left.[26] These routes lead up to a gap in the fort wall to the Vitthala-Hampi pathway below the Narasimha temple complex (NGt/4). While the first two routes might have accommodated wheeled vehicles, it is unlikely that the third did so.

The Bridge: Northern Section (NBs)
(Plate 19)

On the north side of a large hill (sometimes identified as Rishyamukha) is a subsidiary channel of the Tungabhadra. While rarely entirely dry, it contains a substantial amount of water only when the river is high. The hill forms part of an island about 2 km long (east-west). The north segment of the bridge occurs north-northeast of the Chandramauleshvara temple at a point a short distance upstream from the point where the channel widens as it re-enters the main stream. No embankment is preserved at the north end, and it is not likely that one existed; but a high embankment occurs at the south end. As noted above, it consists of a sloping bank stabilized by rows of small boulders.

A modern pathway weaves through the remains of the bridge, continues northward beyond the bridge into a broad dirt road that then turns to the west and eventually leads to the village of Hanumanhalli. From this point a dirt track continues northward.

The Pylons

While the evidence for 30 pylons (numbered north to south) were documented, almost no pillars are standing, and fallen architectural elements have been pillaged (see Table 28). Only at Pylon 30, in the shelter of the embankment, are all three pillars *in situ* and here their bases are deeply buried in alluvium. In addition, in Pylons 12, 13 and 21 central pillars are preserved. Fragments are preserved in Pylons 13 and 14 (upstream only) and in Pylons 15, 16, 21, 23 and 24 (downstream only). Sheet-rock is exposed in the northern half of the riverbed (Pylons 1-12) and alluvium forms the surface further to the south. As in NBx, most of the architectural elements that fell onto the sheet-rock were swept downstream, while, in the centre of the stream bed, they lie approximately where they fell, and in the alluvium further the south they partly stand

or lie scattered. The low point of the north branch of the river occurs at Pylon 16 and architectural elements are scattered between Pylons 17-20 and 22-23 as well as at Pylon 27.

Anchor holes, but no basalt pegs or seatings for clamps were observed in pillars or elements of the superstructure.

If we compare pillar dimensions in the two bridges (see Tables 3 and 15), those in NBs are generally somewhat smaller. This may be due to the small number of observations that could be made of NBs or it may reflect the use of slightly shorter and smaller pillars. However, we have only an impression of pillar height in NBs.

We recorded a few superstructure elements on the sheet-rock: a capital with two anchor holes (the area around one was somewhat down cut), a capital, or, more likely, a broken beam with one socket at location 2, and two beams with two sockets each, one 311 x 43 x 39 cm (length x width x height), with anchor holes at position 1-2 and one at 3 (also in a down cut area), and one 298 x 50 x 40 cm, with anchor holes at the same positions (that at 1-2 is down cut 3.5 cm) with no holes on top.

Pylon length, based on exposed pillar sockets, averages 505.4 cm (N = 9, range 444 to 554 cm, SD 34.31). This again is somewhat smaller than in NBx, where average length is 533.1 cm. However, standing pillars were measured in the latter case; the only fully standing structure in NBs (Pylon 30), the base of which is buried by alluvium, is greater than 595 cm wide. This conforms to the values measured in NBx.

Inter-pylon distance could only be measured accurately in eleven cases, again using sockets rather than pillars. We estimated it in four cases were measurements were taken between pillar fragments from three to six pylons apart. If we exclude these cases, average distance is 348.6 cm (range 283 to 390 cm, SD 31.51). The average and maximum values are again somewhat smaller than NBx (358.6 and 520 cm respectively).

The Foundations and Bracing

Pillar sockets in sheet-rock were documented in the northern third of the bridge (see Table

16). Using average values, we see that in plan each socket is square or nearly so. They are similar in size in each location, the central sockets being only slightly larger. If we compare the values for NBx and NBs (Tables 6 and 16) we see that the former are much larger in plan dimensions. The upstream sockets are most extreme, where the values for NBs are 51.0 by 51.5 cm, and for NBx, 60.5 by 60.3 cm. This result supports the suggestion that the elements of NBs were somewhat smaller. Note however, that the one depth that could be measured (43 cm) is greater than any maximum value in NBx. If this value is not an anomaly, then the pillars in NBx may have been more deeply seated.

No evidence for stone boxes, basal or diagonal bracings, or downstream anchor holes were observed. However, at Pylons 10-12, pairs of rock-cut holes were documented (see Tables 17 and 30). In this small sample, the northern holes are somewhat closer to the pillar socket than are southern examples. The holes in NBs are closer to their pillars than are those in NBx where average distances are 5.2 and 8.7 cm longer (compare Tables 9 and 17). The dimensions in plan are similar to each other but are about 1.5 cm smaller than those in NBx. Depths could not be observed.

In the collapsed debris of this section of the bridge, no remains of intermediate pillars and no inscriptions were seen.

The "Flow" of the Bridge

This part of the bridge was about 108 m long.[27] While pillar sockets are not perfectly aligned, they change direction only slightly. From the north they bow to the west and then bow back to the east after the lowest point in the stream bed. As with NBx, areas of sheet-rock (to the north in both cases) are swept clean of superstructure remains while areas having alluvium have some standing remains and relatively more collapsed architectural elements. The abutment of the southern end of the bridge at a stone embankment is preserved and from here the road would have continued toward the Chandramauleshvara temple complex and then turned slightly eastward below the upper embankment. The north end of the bridge may simply have ended at the top of the sheet-rock. This rises steeply 50 to 100 cm just north of the north row of pillar sockets to the same elevation as the top of the pillar that still stands in one of these sockets. The route from the bridge continued northward along a road that may have followed the present dirt lanes. No seatings for horizontal elements were found at this end.

Interpretation

Construction

It is evident that the bridge was part of an elaborate and immense effort. The southern segment of the bridge required the construction of an embankment at its northern termination and almost certainly one at its southern end as well. The northern segment had a large embankment at its southern end. The elements of the bridge were monumental and were seated and joined carefully. A number of industries were involved, focused on granite and basalt, iron and wood. Thus, granite was quarried; pillars, beams and blocks were split to shape (probably at the quarry), transported and assembled. Masons roughly trimmed these portable elements and excavated sockets and holes of varying sizes. Basalt was quarried (possibly from a vein just north of the Vitthala bazaar street), transported and shaped. Iron bars for clamps were perhaps made nearby, were transported to the work site where they were beaten into place. Iron spikes, and brackets, and tools for masons and woodworkers may have been made at the site as well. For the roadway, timber was harvested, perhaps crudely shaped, transported, finely shaped and joined perhaps using iron spikes and brackets.[28] Finally, a thick bed of cobbles, pebbles and stone-working debris, perhaps 50 cm deep and from 11 to 19 m wide, was laid to consolidate the base.[29]

The scale of construction can be grasped when we consider the number of elements involved.[30] Each pylon consisted of thirteen granite elements (three pillars, six blocks and four beams), and fifteen stone pegs. Its foundation involved the use of twelve slabs to form the boxes (assuming that they were used for every pillar) and an unknown number of large pegs. The southern and northern bridges together included more than 147 pylons; thus, at least 441 pillars, 882 blocks, 588 beams, 2,205 pegs and 1,764 slabs for boxes were required. In addition, an unknown number of braces and large stone pegs were used to support pillars and boxes, and an equally unknown number of small anchor pegs and slabs or blocks were used to support the possible weir. A very crude estimate of the range of the volume of fill required for the weir is from *c*. 2,800 to 4,200 cubic metres.[31]

While we have no information on the construction of the road bed itself, it is likely that wooden beams that rested on the top of the superstructure of the stone pylons (layer E) supported the structure. Long beams could have extended between two or even three piers. Given the range of distances between adjacent pylons, these beams would have been between *c*. 220 and 520 cm in length; and, if they overlay three pylons, giving greater rigidity to the road bed, they would have been twice this length. Alternatively, a more elaborate corbelling system could have been employed in which short beams that overlay the pylons were in turn overlaid by one or more layers of longer beams until the gaps between pylons were bridged.[32] It is also possible that additional wooden elements were laid in the gaps between the upper set of capital blocks; that is, layer D. These could have supplied additional support in the horizontal plane or may have seated trusses bracing the top beams.

The road bed too was probably made of wooden planks laid transversely; that is, perpendicular to the wood beams.[33] Turning to the possible width of the roadway, we have already noted that the length of the super-structure of the first pylon is 130 per cent greater that that of the pillars that supported it. It is likely the uppermost beams of other pylons also projected outward from their base, but whether in the same proportion is uncertain. We cannot estimate the amount of wood required for the roadway, but an estimate of the surface area of the top of the superstructure of the two bridges gives a hint; that is, 3,600 sq m.[34]

The embankment at the north end of NBx, and possibly, that at its southern end, also required an enormous number of granite elements, although not so large or carefully quarried and fitted as those used in the bridge.

The bank stabilized by boulders at the south end of NBs also required the transport of a large number of these stones from nearby hillsides.

Dating (Plate 20)

We suggest that the bridge in its present form is a sixteenth-century construction. Other scholars have suggested dates from the beginning of the fourteenth to the early-mid sixteenth century. Thus, Devakunjari (1983: 62) asserts that it was built by Kampabhupa, said to be the brother of Harihara II (regnal period 1377-1404) (see also Settar n.d.: 87). However, she presents no evidence for this claim.[35] On the other hand, Sewell (1900: 259) notes that visitors such as Paes, who was at Vijayanagara in about 1520, make no reference to a bridge while describing the crossing of the river by coracles. Sewell concludes that the bridge must have been constructed after Paes' visit. Longhurst, writing later, makes the same point (1981: 120-21).[36] Alternatively, Verghese suggests that the bridge was built and subsequently fell into disuse, all before 1520. She bases her opinion on three inscriptions (two in the Vitthala temple) indicating the existence of active ferry services on the river date between 1535 and 1556 (Verghese 2000: 306-07). Previously, Verghese noted that the bridge would have rendered the capital more vulnerable to attack from the north (personal communication 1997). If so, construction during the early Tuluva dynasty is more probable, for this was a period of great wealth and apparent security.

An estimate of the date of the bridge can also be based on the context of the bridge. If our posited routes of movement from the south end of the bridge are correct, then it would have been built before or at about the same time as the fortification walls of Vitthalapura. The passageway, described above, would have allowed traffic from the bridge to enter into the temple precincts. However, the date of construction of the passage in the walls and the relation of this project to the building of the temple complex are uncertain. The dating of the temple itself is controversial. Verghese (1995: 59-63) reviews several claims and concludes that the main shrine was begun in the later fifteenth century. However, Michell (2001) argues for an early sixteenth-century date for the foundation of the temple.

The form of the bridge may also be consulted, specifically the types of construction and associated structures of the upper embankment, which retains the terrace that supports the Chandramauleshvara temple, and the lower embankment associated with the north end of NBx. If the two embankments were constructed at the same time, then the bridge would date at least to the mid-fifteenth century, when the temple was probably built (Michell and Wagoner 2001: I, xviii). However, there is reason to question the contemporaneity of the two embankments. The upper wall is a massive and intricate construction, based on the idea of a simple tripartite basement. But it involves the addition of a second basement set back above and perhaps behind it, an intermediate course and the use of soldier blocks. It seems plausible that this structure alone was intended to resist the river's flood with no intermediate wall buffering the force of the water. By contrast, the lower embankment, consists simply of courses of long blocks pegged into fill and piled one on top of the other.[37] This building technique is characteristic of other embankments in the region that arguably are of sixteenth-century date. These include the high embankment that supports the platform on which the Kadalekalu Ganesha temple (NLc/02) rests in part (Michell assigns it an early sixteenth-century date, personal communication 2002), and the wall of the embankment holding a mid-sized temple overlooking Achyutarayapura (NMd/03; see article by Marsh in this volume).

In short, in the absence of more specific historical information, we conclude that the bridge was built during the early Tuluva period. This, of course, was a period of massive public works in the area surrounding the city (Morrison 1995) and the building of the stone bridge would have been of commensurate scale.

Longevity

How long was the bridge used? Longhurst suggests that it may not have been finished,

or, if completed, could not have stood for very long (1981: 120-21). While we are not qualified to gauge the capacity of the bridge to withstand the force of the river in flood, there is a sense in which the construction could be described as "flimsy".[38] Like all post-and-beam constructions, its ability to resist the lateral forces, in this case, the considerable force generated by the moving river, depended on the aggregate weight of its elements as well as the structure which held individual elements together. Compared with later bridges (see following section and Table 18), the greater number of structural elements in each pylon, the lesser use of robust downstream diagonal bracing, the greater distance between pylons and the relatively lightweight structure of the road increased the vulnerability of the structure. Within each pylon, pegs, iron clamps and occasional shallow sockets cut into the beans resisted lateral movement. While the double layer of blocks and beams contributed to the weight on the pillars of each pylon, the wooden structure of the road would have been relatively light. This contrasts with later bridges where the road was made of stone slabs overlain with brick. The horizontal wooden beams supporting the road would add rigidity if they were tied to the superstructure of each pylon. No modifications of the surfaces of the upper beams of pylons have been observed that would indicate how longitudinal wooden beams were tied to these transverse members. In all probability, ropes bound the intersection of the beams; less likely, wooden or iron pegs could have extended through and below the wooden beams on either side of the stone elements or horizontal braces between pylons could have been suspended from wooden beams. Shearing strain between pylons could also be resisted by a system of wooden trusses; for example, diagonal braces that extended between pylons. But, again, no modifications of stone elements to seat such braces have been observed.[39]

In short, while the bridge can be considered an important experiment, it was one that obviously failed. The structure must have been strong enough to resist the river's current under average conditions. Did it then fail while Vijayanagara was occupied? Was the road bed taken up to prevent invaders from using it? Or, after the fall of the city, were the (remaining?) wooden elements disassembled and reused by local villagers? In any of these cases the integrity of the structure would have been compromised. These are all dramatic possibilities. Eventually, a flood large enough to sweep over the bridge occurred. The force of the water surging from the gorge to the south-southwest was directed at the northern third of the bridge and here, where pylons were seated in rising sheet-rock, the speed of the flow increased. If the water reached the beams of the roadway – or even if it piled debris around the pillars or stone superstructure – it would have exerted even greater force on the structure. Some element gave way: a pillar snapped, a stone peg was not adequate to hold a block and beam together, the binding of wooden beams to superstructure broke apart, the roadway was pushed off a pylon. Wherever the failure occurred, the bridge lost its rigidity and began to collapse. Stone components fell near the base of the pylons and those falling where the river was most swift were swept downstream. Wooden elements were eventually picked out and used for building or fuel. Subsequent floods continued to dismantle the structure and to push fallen elements on the sheet rock further down-stream.

Comparison to Other Bridges

A number of similar bridges exists in peninsular India and Sri Lanka. "Beam bridges on square stone pillars" are briefly described by Deloche (1984: 4-7, see Table 18.) His table (pp. 22 ff) and photographs provide further information on structures in Sri Lanka (three examples, p. 22), Tamil Nadu (ten examples, pp. 22-24), Karnataka (seven examples, including the one described here, pp. 24-26) and Maharashtra (one example, p. 27). These descriptions are based on Deloche's extensive study of travellers' accounts and Gazetteers descriptions as well as on direct observation. A drawing of what may be an additional case located near Mihintale in Sri Lanka was published in the nineteenth century (Anonymous 1890).[40]

The earliest bridges of this type are found in Sri Lanka where they were built with very substantial components in the first millennium. With the exception of a short, two-story bridge at Lakkundi, no bridges in peninsular India can be dated to before the fourteenth century. Some larger examples based on earlier techniques were constructed in the early nineteenth century during the period of British influence. Deloche does not describe the foundations of the structures he observed. However, it is apparent from photographs and reproduced plans (his Figure 2) that substantial basal and downstream diagonal bracing was employed in bridges built in the nineteenth century.

The arrangement of pillars to form pylons is noted in some cases or can be inferred from photographs and figures. In most cases each pylon includes two pillars. Exceptions are the unusual structure in a stepped tank at Lakkundi, the bridge on the Nallar river, where three pillars appear to be unequally spaced, the bridges at Sivasamudra where piers of two and three pillars are used, and the Tungabhadra River bridge described here. The spacing between pylons is not given, however approximate values can be determined for the Nallar River bridge (2.05 m), the Raliayankalvary River bridge (2.45 m) and the Lushington bridge (range 1.6-3.3 m, average 2.2 m). These dimensions compare with the Vijayanagara bridge's average of 5.3 m (range 4.9-6.8 m) where the span to be covered by elements supporting the road bed is twice as long.

The bridge superstructures can also be inferred from photographs. The simplest variety consists of beams laid transversely on pillar tops; slabs on beams provide a surface on which a road bed can be laid (Malvatu Oya River, Sri Lanka and Kannadiya canal, Tamil Nadu). Other examples have capital blocks (sometimes in two superimposed layers, perhaps to adjust the height and level the structure) and transverse beams. Slabs laid on these beams are covered with brickwork in the best-preserved cases (Nalar River and Ramasetua and Srirangapattana bridges). In no case is the superstructure as elaborate as that at Vijayanagara. In all cases where the underpinnings of the road bed are preserved, they are of slabs laid parallel to the long axis of the structure, rather like ceiling slabs in

John M. Fritz

colonnades and halls in temple complexes.
However, in these cases the inter-pylon
distance is generally less than 3 m, which is
similar to the inter-beam distance in temples.
As suggested previously, the much greater
inter-pylon distance in the Tungabhadra
bridge, as well as the absence of such slabs
argues for the use of wood here.[41]

Finally, the Tungabhadra bridge is by far
the longest built before the late eighteenth
century. The length of the southern section
(>424 m) is exceeded only by two early
nineteenth-century bridges – the Wellesley at
Srirangapattana (474 m) and the Lushington
at Sivasamudra (481 m). It is of interest that
these bridges, as well as several lesser examples,
were built in Karnataka. Among the reasons
for their concentration in this region may be
the abundance of granite, a raw material easy
to quarry and capable of being shaped into
long pillars. The nature of rivers here also may
be of importance. The river beds are broad,
relatively shallow and are underlain by granite
bedrock. As well, the flow of water is seasonal;
rivers are swollen only during and immediately
after the few months of the monsoon and are
low thereafter.

Epilogue: A Significant Part of Hampi's Heritage

Those of us conducting research at the Vijayanagara site sometimes hear suggestions that the
bridge at Vitthalapura should be "rebuilt".
There are important reasons to resist such
notions. Suppose a damaged sixteenth-century
manuscript from Vijayanagara was discovered.
Should we obliterate the remaining text and
images and superimpose new text and imagery
to make it "clear" or *pukka*? We believe that
scholars and other concerned people would
strongly oppose what the more contentious
might call "an act of cultural vandalism".
Scholars would see the original object as a
unique product of the Vijayanagara court and
of its artisans, and would know that new
techniques of investigation carefully applied
are capable of eliciting a great deal of information about the document. We suggest that
the same reasoning applies to the bridge and,
thus, suggestions to alter it should not be
considered.

First and most importantly, the ruins of the
bridge are a source of invaluable information
about the engineering skills of planners and
builders who worked in the city. As the author
of this article is acutely aware, a great deal more
should be done to ascertain details about the
structure and about its probable construction.
In several instances statistical descriptions here
are based on inadequate data; for example,
the form of boxes around pillars or the prop-
erties of beams used in superstructure. Further
investigation of inter-pylon pillars including
their careful mapping, might shed light on
their use. In addition, more inscriptions might
be discovered. In short, any physical disturbance of the present ruins would destroy evidence on which future interpretations could
be based.

Second, construction of the same form of
bridge is likely to be destroyed by future floods.
While the flow of the river is now controlled
by the Tungabhadra River dam in Hospet, as
the flood in November 1992 demonstrated,
massive floods in the future cannot be ruled
out.

The third reason is aesthetic: the ruins of
the bridge are beautiful in themselves. They
are an object of wonder and a subject for artists
in all media that speak in particular to the
engineering proficiency of Vijayanagara
builders and more generally to the struggle of
men and women to create a cultured society
in an untamed environment. And fourth, these
beautiful and informative ruins together
with the age-old coracles that continue to be
used to cross the river perpetuate the historic
landscape for which Hampi was listed among
UNESCO World Heritage sites.

No doubt, the builders anticipated that the
structure would survive for a long time – and
in a sense, it has. Today, a romantic and
beautiful ruin, the stone bridge on the Tungabhadra is a monument to the skill of its masons
and carpenters and the wealth and daring of
its patrons.

Acknowledgements

The author extends his grateful thanks to
Basavaraja Gujjal who helped him carry out
statistical observations over three seasons and
rescued him more than once when he fell off

the more slippery architectural remains in midstream. Nagaraja Shetty and Ravi Valmiki also have kindly assisted in this and other documentary projects. Shama Pawar Shapiro provided gracious local hospitality and stimulating conversation after long hot mornings of fieldwork. David Freed and George Arnold began this project when they prepared elegant architectural drawings of the Chandramauleshvara temple complex and its surroundings. Graham Reed has contributed superb analytical drawings of the structure of the bridge and has asked penetrating questions that have stimulated further interpretation.

Notes

1. Longhurst 1981: 120-21, Devakunjari 1983: 62 and Michell and Wagoner 2001: I, 11; see also Deloche 1984.

2. That the interior ends of these blocks have slumped downward is indicated by the slight upward tilt of their outer faces. This movement may also have caused the blocks to move forward of the plane of abutting parallel blocks a few centimetres.

3. In the north face of the wall at the northeast corner of the embankment only the top intermediate course is inset and courses below and above are aligned.

4. This was observed only at one place, north of the centre of the remaining east wall, where the top of the lower embankment had slumped appreciably.

5. The fact that the top blocks of the lower basement are generally horizontal, but the tops of the intermediate basement angle downward from front to back, support these relationships. The weight of the top basement has pushed down the back of the top of the intermediate structure.

6. Examples aligned near the centre of the remaining east wall measure 84 x 60 cm, 109 x 48 cm, 69 x 72 cm, 56 x 73 cm and 99 x 48 cm (length x height). The back of the blocks is buried by garden trash from the *ashram* located on the upper terrace, north of the Chandramauleshvara temple.

7. The embankments have not been precisely mapped; on the ground the east faces of the two walls appear to be parallel. Hence our drawing may be misleading.

8. In the late 1990s local people destroyed the beautifully worn surface of the sheet-rock leading from the base of this stairway to a coracle landing several 10s of metres to the south. They quarried sheets of granite by burning fires on the surface causing it to exfoliate.

9. Width x height x depth.

10. Examples of boulder-faced retaining walls behind fortifications include those to east and west of the Talarighat gate (NJs, Michell 1990: I, 16-17), to the north and south of a gate in the Urban Core (NQh, Michell 1990: I, 90) and sections preserved in the southeast walls of the Urban Core. An eroded example behind a *bund* occurs in the irrigated valley (NMm and NMs, Michell and Wagoner 2001, but not described there), while a section of the walls of the nearby Hiriya canal that is partly concealed by a large and enigmatic structure (NMs/3, Michell 1990: 27; see also Fritz 1991) is also supported by terraced rows of boulders.

11. When observed the bottoms of the retaining wall and pillars were buried; the top of the highest pillar stood 220 cm above the silt. The successive layers of capital blocks and beams were 36, 36, 38 and 29 cm high respectively.

12. Similar seatings, several still containing metal clamps, have been observed by the author on the great platform (IVb/1, see Fritz, Nagaraja Rao and Michell 1984), and on temples built on the edge of the river (NGm/1, NGm/2, see Michell and Wagoner 2001: I, 46-47). They were probably used in most large structures and in buildings subject to flooding.

13. The average length of the upper beams in Pylon 1 is 335 cm; as noted above, this pylon had the shortest length, and may possibly have had a short superstructure as well.

14. A thought experiment: The inner face of the box is *c.* 134 cm square; that is 190 cm (average length of slabs, rounded), minus two times 28 cm (average width of interlocked slabs). The average socket is 60 cm square and the average pillar about 52 cm square. Thus, a gap of 41 cm would exist between a box and the pillar it contained, and a gap of 34 cm would exist between the box and the pillar socket.

15. The downstream pillar of Pylon 16 has fallen but the diagonal brace still stands, party supported by fallen architectural elements.

16. This assumes that the pillars are perpendicular to the surface.

17. It is also possible that a paved weir could have served as a roadway when the water level was low. Such roadways are seen today in Karnataka adjacent to bridges. However, the northern entry to the road would have had to enter the river bed before the lower embankment and to run along its base. But there are large boulders here now, and such a roadway is unlikely.

18. If the bridge here is assumed to be oriented north-south, then the three intermediate pillars are 106 cm northwest, 296 cm west-northwest and 175 cm southwest of the central pillar of Pylon 53. The downstream pillar may have been approximately 170 cm to the west.

19. Some support for this possibility is given by the

observation that the north side of the box around the upstream pillar of Pylon 97 is made from part of a pillar with a groove like those found on intermediate pillars. This may indicate that a pre-existing structure was partly cannibalized.

20. T.M. Manjunathaiah (Karnatak Department of Archaeology and Museums) and Balasubramanya (Kannada University, Kamalapura) who offered possible translations kindly examined photographs and sketches of these inscriptions (personal communications, 2003).

21. Compare the systematic use symbols and letters used in assembly of the stepped tank in the Royal Centre (article by Jagdish, this volume).

22. Inscriptions by builders do occur at Vijayanagara. Short texts found on the walls of the Zenana (Enclosure XIV) in the Royal Centre of Vijayanagara state that named masons built particular sections (Nagaraja Rao and Patil 1985: 38-39, Nos. 23-27, see also Patil and Patil 1995: 93, Nos. 321-23). However, the inscriptions on the bridge are too short to deduce either a name or associated act.

23. Ben Marsh (personal communication, Vijayanagara, January 2000).

24. During a period of especially low water (January 2003) it was observed that a wide basalt dike cuts through the granite at this point, parallel to the flow of the river. Perhaps, the channel is low here because the basalt has been more susceptible to erosion than the surrounding granite into which it was intruded.

25. The length of the bridge can be estimated using average inter-pylon distance 3.59 m (N = 99) times the number of intervals between pylons plus an estimated distance between the last observed pylon and the next (117) plus the gap between the last pylon and the bridge end (1) or 1.18 m = 421.21 m.

26. If the fort wall with the aforementioned gateway continued to the northeast, this latter route would have been blocked. However, the past course of this wall is now uncertain.

27. Average inter-pylon distance (348.6 m, N = 11) x the number of intervals between pylons and between pylons and the embankments at each end (31) = 108.07 m.

28. No iron elements have been observed in the bridge debris. However, spikes, nails and brackets have been recovered from structures cleared by the ASI and KDAM in the Royal Centre (see Devaraj 1991).

29. This estimate is based on the following: the anchor holes that may have stabilized the downstream wall of the weir are from 447 to 623 cm (average 531 cm) from the pylons, the pylons are from 493 to 680 cm (average 533 cm) wide. If the weir began at the upstream pylon, and using average values, then it would have averaged 10.6 m in width; but if it were as wide on the upstream side as on the downstream,

then it would have averaged 15.9 m. If the maximum values are used, then it could have been as wide as 19.3 m.

30. The scale of the construction can be compared with that of the aqueduct that crosses the northern branch of the Tungabhadra River at Hanumantahalli, some 2 km to the west.

31. This estimate is based on the following calculations: combined length of two bridges (532 m) x depth of fill (0.5 m, based on average height of side of slab box), x range of width of weir (10.6 using averages, and assuming the weir extended only under the bridge and to the downstream side and 15.9, assuming that the weir extended equally on both sides). The actual figures, rounded off in the text, are 2,819.6 and 4,229.4 cu m.

32. This system would require more but shorter wooden elements, and would have the advantage of putting more weight on the pylons but the disadvantage of having more parts, which could be moved by shearing forces.

33. No stone beams or slabs are seen in the riverbed. Longhurst (1925: 10), who suggests that the bridge consisted of "two rows of monolithic uprights carrying cross beams supporting flat roof slabs," cannot have carefully inspected its ruins.

34. The actual figure is 3,564.4 sq m. This is based on the following calculation: combined length of two bridges (532 m) x the width of the superstructure (6.70 m). The latter is based on the width at the first pylon, and as the width of the base of this pylon is the shortest of all, we can take the width of its superstructure as close to a minimum value.

35. This suggestion appears to be based on an inscription on a boulder on the north side of the river near the coracle crossing between Talarighat and Anegondi (*The Quarterly Journal of the Mythic Society*, VII, Inscription No. IV and *Annual Report on Indian Epigraphy 1958-59*, No. B 682). A summary states, "that Kampabhupa (son of Harihara [*sic*]) had a path made to the Tungabhadra" (Patil and Patil 1995: No. 33). It is more likely that an access to the river some 2.5 km downstream from the site of the bridge is referred to; this is the crossing point for one of the major routes into the city (Fritz, Michell and Nagaraja Rao 1984: 13).

36. Longhurst (1981) shows the ruined bridge at high water (Figure 55, p. 122).

37. It is of some interest that the lower embankment has resisted the river more effectively than the upper embankment. This in itself may indicate that the lower embankment was built later; that is, when builders had more experience.

38. A qualified engineer might estimate its durability, given its construction, siting and the dynamics of the river.

39. While a survey of the structure of wooden architecture of the Deccan and Southern India has yet to be written, cursory observation by the author has not revealed the use of such bracing.

40. Graham Reed has brought this article to my attention. Deloche notes three bridges on the Malvatu Owa River east of Anuradhapura in Sri Lanka. Mihintale is 11 km east of this site. It is possible that the bridge illustrated in 1890 is one of these.

41. Deloche reproduces plans of the Ramasetua and Lushington bridges in 1830 (1984: 5, Figure 2) that show that the inter-pylon distance in sections having only two pillars per pylon is greater than those with three pillars per pylon. It is possible using map legends to calculate an average figure for the central section of the latter bridge; that is, 3.3 m (based on 100 "chesmas" or pylons extending over 330 m). It is possible that here wood was used as well.

Works Cited

ARSIE, Annual Report on South Indian Epigraphy.

Anonymous, 1890, Stone Bridge Probably of the Sixth Century A.D. Recently Discovered in a Ceylon Forest. *The Daily Graphic,* 1st May: 13.

Deloche, J., 1984, *The Ancient Bridges of India,* Sitraram Bhartia Institute of Scientific Research, New Delhi.

Devakunjari, D., 1983, *Hampi,* reprint, Archaeological Survey of India, New Delhi.

Devaraj, D.V., 1991, I. Excavations. In, *Vijayanagara: Progress of Research, 1984- 1987,* edited by D.V. Devaraj and C.S. Patil, pp. 3-15, Directorate of Archaeology and Museums, Mysore.

Fritz, J.M., 1991, Documentation of the 'Irrigated Valley'. In, *Vijayanagara: Progress of Research, 1987-88,* edited by D.V. Devaraj and C.S. Patil, pp. 95-104, Directorate of Archaeology and Museums, Mysore.

Fritz, J.M., G. Michell and M.S. Nagaraja Rao, 1984, *Where Kings and Gods Meet: The Royal Centre at Vijayanagara, India,* University of Arizona Press, Tucson.

Longhurst, A.H., 1981, *Hampi Ruins Described and Illustrated,* reprint, Asian Educational Services, New Delhi.

Michell, G., 1990, *Vijayanagara: Architectural Inventory of the Urban Core,* 2 volumes, Directorate of Archaeology and Museums, Mysore.

——, 2001, Foundation Date of the Vitthala Temple at Vijayanagara. In, *Hemakuta: Recent Research in Archaeology and Museology,* edited by A.V. Narasimha Murthy, K.M. Suresh, K.P. Poonacha and K.R. Basavaraj, II, pp. 324-28, Bharatiya Kala Prakashan, Delhi.

Michell, G. and P.B. Wagoner, 2001, *Vijayanagara: Architectural Inventory of the Sacred Centre,* 3 volumes, Manohar and American Institute of Indian Studies, New Delhi.

Morrison, K.D., 1995, *Fields of Victory: Vijayanagara and the Course of Intensification,* Contributions of the Archaeological Research Facility No. 53, University of California Press, Berkeley.

Nagaraja Rao, M.S. and C.S. Patil, 1985, Epigraphical Studies. In, *Vijayanagara: Progress of Research, 1983-84,* edited by M.S. Nagaraja Rao, pp. 21-53, Directorate of Archaeology and Museums, Mysore.

Patil, C.S. and V.C. Patil, editors, 1995, *Inscriptions at Vijayanagara (Hampi),* Directorate of Archaeology and Museums, Mysore.

Settar, S., n.d., *Hampi, a Medieval Metropolis,* Kala Yatra, Bangalore.

Sewell, R., 1900, *A Forgotten Empire (Vijayanagara),* Sohhenschien, London.

Verghese, A. 1995, *Religious Traditions at Vijayanagara: As Revealed Through Its Monuments,* Manohar and American Institute of Indian Studies, New Delhi.

——, 2000, Crossing the Tungabhadra. In, *Archaeology, Art and Religion: New Perspectives on Vijayanagara,* pp. 303-10, Oxford University Press, New Delhi.

Table 1. Upper Embankment:
Metric Attributes of Selected Constituent Elements of Each Basement (in cm)

	Height	Length	Depth	Alignment
Upper Basement Elements				
Upper course, Example 1	36	179	64	Parallel
Example 2	32	311	>46	Parallel
Intermediate course	31	396	29	Parallel
	41	199	43	Parallel
Lowest course	45	410	>05	Parallel
	31	123	57	Parallel
Foundation course	>15	N.O.	N.O.	Parallel
Intermediate Basement Elements				
Upper course	38	180	48	Parallel
	36	144	42	Parallel
	34	38	>199	Perpendicular
	34	54	>35	Perpendicular
Second Intermediate course	38	202	42	Parallel
	38	36	>50	Parallel ?
First Intermediate course	42	158	>10	Parallel
	44	54	>35	Perpendicular
Lowest course	N.O.	N.O.		Parallel
Lowest Basement Elements				
Upper course	26	138	61	Parallel
	31	163	57	Parallel
Second Intermediate course				
First Intermediate course	40	172	36	Parallel
	40	42	135	Perpendicular
Lowest course	>20	172	63	Parallel
	>21	48	>21	Perpendicular

Notes: Offset between lowest and intermediate basements is 85-117 cm with average close to latter; offset between intermediate and upper basement is 100-125 cm; the range of measurements given here is intended to be "representative" of smaller and larger stone blocks within each course, but it is not based on a statistical sample; N.O. = not observable; Parallel = in all stages, designated elements are parallel to the face of the wall; Perpendicular = in the lowest and intermediate basements, designated elements are perpendicular to the face of the wall; when blocks are laid perpendicularly, their length is less than "depth"; i.e. the dimension parallel to the face of the embankment is less than the perpendicular distance; N.O. = not observable.

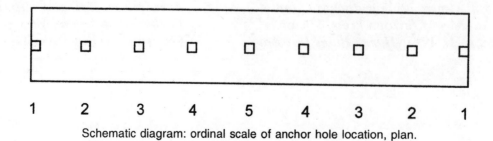

Schematic diagram: ordinal scale of anchor hole location, plan.

Table 2. NBx, Clamp Seating in Beams:
Metrical Attributes of Selected Examples (in cm)

Location	Length	Width	Depth	Distance to Edge
Py2, CP>DSP	3.5	4.0	6.0	6.5?
Py3>Py4	4.0	4.0	5.0	12.5
Py3>Py4	3.0	5.0	5.0	27.0
Py4>Py5, CP>DSP	3.5	3.5	5.0	27.0

Notes: Py = pylon; USP = upstream pillar; CP = central pillar; DSP = downstream pillar; ">" = between, as Py3>Py4, between Pylons 3 and 4.

Table 3. NBx, Pillar Dimensions, by Location (in cm)

	Upstream			Central			Downstream		
	Height	Long	Trans	Height	Long	Trans	Height	Long	Trans
Count (N)	15	21	21	N.O.	18	18	19	21	21
Minimum	226	45	35	N.O.	31	42	215	40	36
Maximum	582	60	60		62	67	648	62	66
Average	438.3	53.1	50.3		52.1	52.5	464.4	53.0	51.8
St Dev	138.87	3.90	6.84		7.95	6.46	141.01	5.39	6.93

Notes: Pillars in every 5th pylon measured whenever possible; Long = longitudinal dimension; i.e. parallel to the long (north south) axis of the bridge; N.O. = not observed; St Dev = standard deviation; Trans = transverse dimension; i.e. perpendicular to the long axis.

John M. Fritz

Table 4. NBx, Dimensions of Fallen Capital Blocks and Beams (in cm)

	Capital Blocks			Beams		
	Length	Width	Height	Length	Width	Height
Count (N)	17	17	17	10	10	10
Minimum	91	37	36	165	41.5	31
Maximum	140	54	46	334	50.5	47.5
Average	115.6	45.0	40.5	271.7	46.2	41.2
St Dev	15.92	4.58	2.68	62.21	2.62	4.93

Note: St Dev = standard deviation. (See Table 31 for revised data.)

Table 5. NBx, Predicted and Observed Locations of Anchor Holes
in Face of Capital Blocks and Beams

Ordinal Scale	1	1-2	2	2-3	3	3-4	4	4-5	5
Capital Blocks: 1 Hole									
Predicted									P
Observed Cases	1				2			6	9
Capital Blocks: 2 Holes									
Predicted						P			
Observed Cases					14	4	1		
Beams									
Predicted			P		P				
Observed Cases			13	2	4	1	4		

Note: P = predicted location of anchor hole. (See Table 32 for revised data.)

Table 6. NBx, Dimensions of Pillar Sockets (in cm)

	Upstream			Central			Downstream		
	Long	Trans	Depth	Long	Trans	Depth	Long	Trans	Depth
Count (N)	31	31	19	27	27	20	28	27	18
Minimum	48	51	31	54	55	30	53	52	20
Maximum	68	68	40	67	68	40	82	64	37
Average	60.5	60.3	34.4	60.1	60.4	33.7	60.1	58.3	32.5
St Dev	4.34	4.40	2.54	3.13	3.41	2.56	5.52	3.34	3.6

Notes: Long = longitudinal dimension; i.e. parallel to the long (north-south) axis of the bridge; St Dev = standard deviation; Trans = transverse dimension; i.e. perpendicular to the long axis; these measurements were taken at the top of the socket.

Table 7. NBx, Dimensions of Slabs Forming Boxes and of Associated Notches (in cm)

	Slabs			Notches	
	Length	Width	Height	Length	Depth
Count (N)	26	29	12	4	4
Minimum	126	18	23	28	11
Maximum	290	58	63	43	18
Average	189.5	27.7	43.3	35.8	14.5
St Dev	34.89	7.61	11.14	6.18	3.11

Note: Length of notch measured at top; St Dev = standard deviation.

Table 8. NBx, Dimensions of Components Diagonal Bracing (in cm)

| | Pillar Notch | | | Brace | | | | Pillar to Sheet-Rock Socket | Sheet-Rock Socket | | |
	Width	Height	Depth	Height above box	Length	Width	Height		Long	Trans	Depth
Count (N)	6	6	6	4	3	3	3	15	16	16	13
Minimum	26	12	4	93	202	30	25	98	**33**	20	9
Maximum	38	21	4.5	139	245	34	30	193	42	44	15
Average	32.3	15.5	4.1	115.8	230.3	32.3	27.3	149.3	37.1	32.8	12.1
St Dev	5.24	3.39	0.20	20.65	24.54	2.08	2.52	25.34	2.78	2.78	1.89

Notes: Height of pillar notch measured from top of stone box to its base; length of brace measured along bottom from point where it enters each socket; distance between pillar and socket in sheet-rock measured to upstream (west) side of latter; Long = longitudinal; Trans = transverse; St Dev = standard deviation.

Table 9. NBx, Dimensions of Large Holes (in cm)

| | Hole 1 | | | | Hole 2 | | | |
	Pillar Base to Hole	Long	Trans	Depth	Pillar Base to Hole	Long	Trans	Depth
Count (N)	17	18	18	14	17	18	18	8
Minimum	34	14	14	8	33	15	15	10
Maximum	46	21	21	14.5	45	21	22	13
Average	40.7	18.2	18.2	11.1	40.2	18.1	18.3	11.0
St Dev	3.65	1.82	1.79	1.71	3.50	1.51	1.61	1.07

Notes: Hole 1 is the more northerly when two are present; distance between hole and pillar base could not be observed in one case; Long = longitudinal; Trans = transverse; St Dev = standard deviation.

Table 10. NBx, Association of Large Holes and Sockets
for Diagonal Braces; Pylons 9-43

		Large Holes			
		Present	Absent	N.O.	Totals
Socket or Notch for Brace	Present	9	4	8	21
	Absent	10	0	0	10
	N.O.	0	4	0	4
	Totals	19	8	8	35

Note: N.O. = not observable.

Table 11. NBx, Dimensions of Downstream Anchor Holes (in cm)

	Group I				Group II				Group III			
	P > AH	Long	Trans	Depth	P > AH	Long	Trans	Depth	P > AH	Long	Trans	Depth
Count (N)	3	6	6	N.O.	2	5	5	2	2	4	4	4
Minimum	447	8.5	8.5		599	7.5	7	7	533	8	8.5	5
Maximum	494	9.5	9.5		623	8.5	9.5	7	554	10	11	8.5
Average	469.7	9.0	8.8		611.0	8.5	8.4	7.0	543.5	8.9	9.3	7.3
St Dev	23.54	0.45	0.41			0.94	0.96			0.85	1.19	1.66

Notes: AH = anchor hole; Long = longitudinal; i.e. parallel to the long axis; N.O. = not observed; P = downstream pillar; Trans = transverse; i.e. perpendicular to the long axis.

Table 12. NBx, Dimensions of Inter-Pylon Pillars (in cm)

Location	Shaft			Channel				Band		
	Height	Long	Trans	Length	Top Width	Bottom Width	Depth	Below Top	Height
Count (N)	6	6	6	5	5	4	6	4	4
Minimum	55	48	61	55	23	21	6	45	6
Maximum	225	94	72	80	32	28	11	51	7
Average	104.2	62.0	65.7	62.8	27.6	25	8.9	49.0	6.5
St Dev	62.44	16.24	3.67	9.83	4.04	3.16	2.33	2.71	0.58

Note: Long = longitudinal; Trans = transverse; St Dev = standard deviation.

Table 13. NBx, Kannada Inscriptions: Location, Characters

Pylon	Pillar	Face	Number of Characters	Kannada	Notes
68	DSP	SF?	1	Ra	Pillar fallen
74	DSP	NF	1	Ra	Pillar turned 45[0]
75	DSP	USF	2	Ba Sa	Arranged vertically
76	USP	DSF	5-6	Kukkr barla?	16C? Telugu?
77	DSP	USF	ca 4	?	
78	DSP	SF	1	Ra	Pillar turned 45[0]
81	DSP	USF	1	Ra	
84	DSP	SF	1	"2"	
93	DSP	NF	1	"2"	

Notes: DSF = downstream face; DSP = downstream pillar; NF = north face; SF = south face; USF = upstream face; USP = upstream pillar; Kannada terms read by T.M. Manjunathaiah and Balasubramanya.

Table 14. NBx, Height, Condition, Architectural Elements and Substrate Associated with Piers (in cm)

Height	226		313		506		530*													
USP	P	P	P	P	P	P	A	A	A	A	A	A	F	A	A	A	A	A	A	A
AE		AE	AE	AE	AE	AE	AE	AE												
Sub	SR	SR	SR	SR	AL	AL	AL	SR	SR	SR	SR	SR	SR	SR	SR	SR	SR	SR	SR	SR
Pylon	1	3	5	7	9	11	13	15	17	19	21	23	25	27	29	31	33	35	37	39

Height									544*			567			582*				497	567*
USP	A	F	F	F	F	F	F	A	F	F	A	A	F	P	F	P	P	P	P	P
AE				AE	AE	AE								AE		AE				AE
Sub	SR	SR	SR	AL	AL	AL	AL	AL	AL	AL	AL	AL	AL	AL	AL	AL	AL	AL	AL	AL
Pylon	41	43	45	47	49	51	53	55	57	59	61	63	65	67	69	71	73	75	77	79

Height	546		568		>553*			>274					290		267*	315	257*		
USP	P	P	P	P	P	P	P	F	P	P	P	P	P	P	P	P	A	P	A
AE	AE	AE	AE	AE	AE				AE	AE	AE	AE	AE	AE	AE	AE	AE	AE	AE
Sub	AL	AL	AL	AL	AL	AL	AL	AL	AL	AL	SR	SR	SR	SR	SR	SR	SR	AL	AL
Pylon	81	83	85	87	89	91	93	95	97	99	101	103	105	107	109	111	113	115	117

Notes: ">" = greater than; A = absent; AE = fallen architectural elements present; AL = Alluvium; F = fragment present; Height = height of pylon above sheet-rock or top of slab box ("*" = height of USP of preceding Pylon); P = present to full height; Pylon = number of pylon as numbered approximately from north to south; SR = sheet-rock; Sub = substrate; USP = upstream pillar.

Table 15. NBs, Pillar Dimensions, by location (in cm)

	Upstream			Central			Downstream		
	Height	Long	Trans	Height	Long	Trans	Height	Long	Trans
Count (N)	N.O.	3	3	1	3	3	N.O.	4	4
Minimum		34	44	150	36	48		42	49
Maximum		51	52	150	48	55		56	53
Average		44.0	48.0		42.0	52.0		47.75	51.3
St Dev		8.89	4.00		6.00	3.61		6.24	2.06

Notes: Pillars in every pylon measured whenever possible; Long = longitudinal dimension; i.e. parallel to the long (north-south) axis of the bridge; N.O. = not observable; St Dev = standard deviation; Trans = transverse dimension; i.e. perpendicular to the long axis.

Table 16. NBs, Dimensions of Pillar Sockets (in cm)

	Upstream			Central			Downstream		
	Long	Trans	Depth	Long	Trans	Depth	Long	Trans	Depth
Count (N)	11	11	N.O.	12	10	N.O.	8	8	1
Minimum	38	38		50	50		45	46	43
Maximum	56	56	>15	58	56	>20	55	55	43
Average	51.0	51.5		53.5	53.3		50.4	51.4	
St Dev	4.96	1.97		2.41	2.21		3.05	3.20	

Notes: Long = longitudinal dimension; i.e. parallel to the long (north-south) axis of the bridge; N.O. = not observed; St Dev = standard deviation; Trans = transverse dimension; i.e. perpendicular to the long axis; the measurements were taken at the top of the socket.

Table 17. NBs, Dimensions of Large Holes (in cm)

	Hole 1				Hole 2			
	Pillar Socket to Hole	Long	Trans	Depth	Pillar Socket to Hole	Long	Trans	Depth
Count (N)	3	3	3	N.O.	3	3	3	N.O.
Minimum	30	16	16		31	15	15	
Maximum	34	17	17		38	17	19	
Average	32	16.7	16.7		35.0	16.0	16.7	
St Dev	2.00	0.58	0.58		3.61	1.00	2.08	

Notes: Hole 1 is the more northerly; N.O. = not observed; Long = longitudinal; Trans = transverse; St Dev = standard deviation.

Table 18. Comparison of Beam Bridges

Location	Date	Sections	Dimensions
Kala Oya River, Sri Lanka	4C ?	1	
Natur River, near Batticoala, Sri Lanka		1	
Malvatu Oya River, Anuradhapura, Sri Lanka	5C-9C	1	
Nallar river, Coimbatore District, Avinasi taluk, Tamil Nadu	16C	1	24.65 m long, 5.85 m broad
Kannadiyan canal, Kallidaikkurichchi, Tirunelveli District, Cheranmahadevi Taluk, Tamil Nadu	14C-16C	1	27 m long, 4.5 m broad
Kannadiyan canal, Cheranmahadevi, Tirunelveli District, Cheranmahadevi Taluk, Tamil Nadu	14C-16C	1	
Moat, Dharmapuri District, Hosur Taluk, Tamil Nadu	18C	1	
Ralaiyankalvay River, Melpalaiyankurichchi, Tirunelveli District & Taluk, Tamil Nadu		1	27 m long, 1.4 m broad
Rivulet, Pillaikulam, Tirunelveli District, Ambasamudram Taluk, Tamil Nadu		1	10 m long, 5 m broad
Rivulet, Puliyangudi, Tirunelveli District, Sankaranainarkovil Taluk, Tamil Nadū		1	
Ralaiyaru River, Suchindram, Kanniyakumari District, Agastisvaram Taluk, Tamil Nadu			
Kaveri River, Srirangam, Tiruchirapalli District, Tamil Nadu	14C?		
Uppary River, Valukkumparai, Kanniyakumari District, Agastisvaram Taluk, Tamil Nadu			
Creek; Bhatkal, Uttara Kannada District, Honavur Taluk, Karnataka	*c.* 1450?	2	North: 13.2 m long. 1.2 m broad; south: 25 m long, 2.1 m broad

in Sri Lanka, Tamil Nadu and Karnataka

Pylons	Foundation	Superstructure	Remarks	References (Deloche 1984)
Pillars			2nd of same plan, down river of first	p. 22
Pillars		Beams		p. 22
2? P/Py, >5 Py		1 layer B, 1 layer SS surface	4 bridges on same river	pp. 22, 54; photo 5
3 P/Py, 11 Py		1 layer large CB, 1 layer small CB, 1 trans layer B, 1 layer SS surface, brickwork		pp. 22, 54; photo 6
		1 layer B, 1 layer SS ? surface, brickwork	pp. 23, 54; photo 7	
2 P/Py, 6 Py		1 layer B, 1 layer SS ? surface, brickwork	pp. 23, 54; photo 8	
2 P/Py			Leads to fort built by Tipu Sultan	p. 23
2 P/Py, 10 Py				p. 23
2 P/Py				p. 23
"8 pillars"				p. 23
			3 ruined bridges on this river	p. 23
			Referred to by inscription; physical remains not discovered	p. 23
"2 rows of pillars remain"			Pillars used to build new	pp. 23-24
N: 2 P/Py, 6 y Py; S: 2 P/Py, 8 P				p. 24

Table 18.

Location	Date	Sections	Dimensions
Step-well, Lakkundi, Dharwar District, Gadag Taluk, Karnataka	1123 or 1241?	1	
Small river, Dakshina Kannada District, Mangalore Taluk, Karnataka			"probably on pillars"
Mdabidri, Dakshina Kannada District, Mangalore Taluk, Karnataka			
Kaveri River, Sivasamudra, Mandya District, Malavalli Taluk, Karnataka		2: rebuilt bridges named Ramasetua & Lushington	Ramasetua: 300 m long, 3.9 m broad, 6.9 m high; Lushington: 481 m long (excluding approaches)
Kaveri River, Srirangapattana, Mandya District, Srirangapattana Taluk, Karnataka	Late 18 C, early 19 C	2: South & North, or Wellesley bridge	North: 474 m long
Tungabhadra River, Vijayanagara	16 C?	2: NBs (north) & NBx (south)	NBs: *c.* 100 m long, >6 mbroad; NBx >424 m long, *c.* 6.7 m broad, P: >6 m high

Notes: B = beam; CB = capital block; Long = longitudinal; P = pillar.

Continued

Pylons	Foundation	Superstructure	Remarks	References
4 P/Py, 4 Py 1st story, 6 Py 2nd story		1st story: CB, B, 2nd story: CB, B x 3 (long, trans, long), SS surface	2 story structure	pp. 24, 87; photo 15
			"... not traced; but it may refer to the next one"	p. 24
				p. 24
Ramasetua: 2 & 3 P/Py, includes reused temple pillars; Lushington: 2 & 3 P/Py (3 only at ends of structure)	Ramasetua & Lushington: lateral? & diagonal bracing	1 or 2 CB, trans B, SS surface?, brickwork	Ruinous early 19 C; rebuilt in 1821 & 1832; Lushington destroyed in 1924	pp. 5 (Fig. 2), 24-25, 85 (photo 11), 86 (photo 14)
North: 2 P/Py	Basal & diagonal bracing	CB, trans B, long B, SS surface?, brickwork	South: built by Tipu Sultan, North: built by a divan of Mysore	pp. 25-26, 85 (photo 10), 86 (photo 13)
3 P/Py; NBx: ca 30 Py, NBs: >117 Py	P socket, basal & diagonal bracing, slab box, large pegs?, weir?	CB, B, CB, B; wood beams & surface?		pp. 25-26, 85 (photo 9), 86 (photo 12)

Py = pylon; P/Py = pillar per pylon; SS = stone slab; Trans = transverse.

Table 19. NBx, Qualitative

Pylon	Context	Upstream Pillar				Central Pillar			
Number		Footing	Pillar	Super-structure	Basal Bracing	Footing	Pillar	Super-structure	Basal Bracing
1	SR	RC	P B, L	B, L,	A	RC	P B, L	B, L,	A
2	SR, AE	N.O.	P	A	A	RC	P	A	A
3	SR, AE	N.O.	P	B, L	A	RC	P	A	A
4	SR, AE	RC	P	A	A	RC	P	B, L?	A
5	SR, AE	RC	P	A	A	RC	P	A	A
6	SR, AE	RC	P	A	A	RC	P*	A	A
7	SR, AE	RC	P	A	A	RC	P	A	A
8	SR, F, AE	RC	50%	A		Box	30%	A	A
9	AL, F, AE	Box	P	A	S	Box	P	A	S
10	AL, F, AE	Box	20%	A	S	Box	P	A	S
11	AL, F, AE	N.O.	P	A	S	N.O.	P	A	S
12	AL, F, AE	N.O.	P*	A	S	Box?	20%	A	A
13	AL, F, AE	Box	P	A	S	Box	P	A	S
14	AL, F, AE	RC, IB	P	A	A	Box	A	A	S
15	SR, AE	RC	A	A	A	RC	30%	A	A
16	SR	RC	A	A	A	RC	1%	A	A
17	SR	RC	A	A	A	RC	BF	A	A
18	SR	RC	A	A	A	RC	BF	A	A
19	SR	RC	A	A	A	RC	BF	A	A
20	SR	RC	A	A	A	RC	BF	A	A
21	SR	RC	A	A	A	RC	BF	A	A
22	SR	RC	A	A	A	RC	A	A	A
23	SR	RC	A	A	A	RC	A	A	A
24	SR	RC	A	A	A	RC	A	A	A
25	SR	RC	BF	A	A	RC	A	A	A
26	SR	RC	A	A	A	RC	A	A	A
27	SR	RC	A	A	A	RC	A	A	A
28	SR	RC	A	A	A	RC	A	A	A
29	SR	RC	A	A	A	RC	A	A	A
30	SR	RC	A	A	A	RC	A	A	A
31	SR	RC	A	A	A	RC	A	A	A
32	SR	RC	A	A	A	RC	A	A	A
33	SR	RC	A	A	A	RC	A	A	A
34	SR	RC	A	A	A	RC	A	A	A
35	SR	RC	A	A	A	RC	A	A	A
36	SR	RC	A	A	A	RC	A	A	A
37	SR	RC	A	A	A	RC	A	A	A
38	SR	RC	A	A	A	RC	A	A	A
39	SR	RC	A	A	A	RC	A	A	A
40	SR	RC	A	A	A	RC	A	A	A

Attributes of Pylons

Downstream Pillar			Diagonal Bracing			Large Holes	Pillar	Inscription	Notes
Footing	Pillar	Super-structure	Pillar Notch	Brace	Socket for Brace		Turned ~45%		
RC	P B, L	B, L,	A	A	A	A			
N.O.	P	A	A	A	A	A			
RC	A	A	N.O.	A	A	A			
RC	A	A	A	A	A	A			
RC	P	A	A	A	A	A			
RC	P	A	A	A	A	A			*Leaning
RC	P*	A	N.O.	A	N.O.	N.O.			*Fallen in place
Box	P	A	A	A	A	A			
IB	P	A	P	P	P	A? (N.O.?)			
IB	P	A	P	P	P	N.O.			
Box	P	A	P	P	P	N.O.			
Box	1%	A	P	A	N.O.	N.O.			*Peg on top?
Box	P	A	P	A	N.O.	N.O.			
N.O.	P	A	P	P	N.O.	N.O.			
N.O.	A	A	N.O.	P	N.O.	N.O.			
RC	20%	A	N.O.	P	P	N.O.			
RC	A	A	N.O.	A	P	A		N.O.	
RC	A	A	N.O.	A	P	A		N.O.	
RC	A	A	N.O.	A	P	P=1		N.O.	
RC	A	A	N.O.	A	P	P=1		N.O.	
RC	A	A	N.O.	A	P	P=1		N.O.	
RC	A	A	N.O.	A	P	P=2		N.O.	
RC	A	A	N.O.	A	A	P=2		N.O.	
RC	P*	A	A	A	A	P=2			*Leaning
RC	A	A	N.O.	A	A	P=2		N.O.	
RC	A	A	N.O.	A	A	P=2		N.O.	
RC	A	A	N.O.	A	A	P=2		N.O.	
RC	A	A	N.O.	A	A	P=2		N.O.	
RC	A	A	N.O.	A	A	P=2		N.O.	
RC	A	A	N.O.	A	A	P=2		N.O.	
RC	BF	A	N.O.	A	A	P=2		N.O.	
RC	A	A	N.O.	A	A	P=2*		N.O.	*1 BBF
RC	A	A	N.O.	A	A	A		N.O.	
RC	P	A	A	A	A (N.O.)	A		N.O.	
RC	P	A	A	A	A	A			
RC	A	A	N.O.	A	A	A		N.O.	
RC	A	A	N.O.	A	P	A		N.O.	
RC	A	A	N.O.	A	P	A		N.O.	
RC	A	A	N.O.	A	P	P=2*		N.O.	*2 BBFs
RC	A	A	N.O.	A	P	P=2*		N.O.	*2 BBFs

Table 19.

Pylon	Context	Upstream Pillar				Central Pillar			
Number		Footing	Pillar	Super-structure	Basal Bracing	Footing	Pillar	Super-structure	Basal Bracing
41	SR	RC	A	A	A	RC	A	A	A
42	SR	RC	BF	A	A	RC	BF	A	A
43	SR	RC	20%	A	A	RC	A	A	A
44	SR	RC	BF	A	A	RC	A	A·	A
45	SR	RC-.5	5%	A	A	B	5%	A	A
46	AL	RC	BF	A	A	IB	5%	A	A
47	AL	IB	1%	A	A	IB	1%	A	N.O.
48	AL	IB	A	A	A	IB	10%	A	N.O.
49	AL	IB	1%	A	A	IB	1%	A	A
50	AL	IB	A	A	A	IB	1%	A	A
51	AL	IB	1%	A	A	IB	15%	A	A
52	AL	IB	10%	A	A	N.O.	1%	A	N.O.?
53	AL	IB	10%	A	A	IB	30%	A	A
54	AL	IB	25%	A	A	N.O.	A?	A	A
55	AL	N.O.	A?	A	N.O.	IB	10%	A	A
56	AL	IB	10%	A	A	N.O.	5%	A	N.O.
57	AL	IB	10%	A	A	N.O.	15%	A	N.O.
58	AL	N.O.	A? (N.O.)	A	N.O.	B	20%	A	N.O.
59	AL	IB	10%	A	A	B	BF	A	N.O.
60	AL	IB?	A	A	A	I?B	P	A	A
61	AL	N.O.	N.O.	A	N.O.	I?B	30%	A	A
62	AL	N.O.	A? (N.O.)	A	N.O.	IB	P	A	A
63	AL	I?B	A	A	A	I?B	P	A	A
64	AL	IB	A	A	A	IB	A	A	A
65	AL	IB	25%	A	A	IB	P	A	A
66	AL	N.O.	N.O.	A	N.O.	N.O.	N.O.	A	N.O.
67	AL	N.O.	P	A	N.O.	I?B	P	A	A
68	AL	B?	P	A	A	I?B	P	A	A
69	AL	IB	1%	A	A	IB	P	A	A
70	AL	IB	P	A	A	I?B	P	A	A
71	AL	IB	P	A	A	IB	P	A	A
72	AL	IB	P	A	A	IB	P	A	A
73	AL	IB	P	A	A	N.O.	P	A	A
74	AL	IB	P	A	A	IB	P	A	A
75	AL	IB	P	A	A	IB	P	A	A
76	AL	IB	P	A	A	IB	P	A	A
77	AL	N.O.	P	A	A	N.O.	P	A	A

Continued

Downstream Pillar			Diagonal Bracing			Large Holes	Pillar	Inscription	Notes
Footing	Pillar	Super-structure	Pillar Notch	Brace	Socket for Brace		Turned ~ 45%		
RC	A	A	N.O.	A	P	P=2*		N.O.	*1 BBF
RC	A	A	N.O.	A	P	P=2*		N.O.	*1 BBF
RC	A	A	N.O.	A	P	P (1&N.O.)*		N.O.	*1 BBF
N.O.	A?	A	N.O.	A	N.O.	N.O.		N.O.	
B	10%	A	N.O.	A	N.O.	N.O.		N.O.	
B	5%	A	N.O.	A	N.O.	N.O.		N.O.	
N.O.	35%	A	A	A	N.O.	N.O.			
N.O.	A?	A	N.O.	A	N.O.	N.O.		N.O.	
IB	1%	A	N.O.	A	N.O.	N.O.		N.O.	
A?	A	A	N.O.	A	N.O.	N.O.		N.O.	
IB	15%	A	N.O.	A	N.O.	N.O.	USP		
N.O.	N.O.	A	N.O.	A	N.O.	N.O.	USP	N.O.	
N.O.	15%	A	N.O.	A	N.O.	N.O.	USP		3 IPs near CP, to N & S
N.O.	N.O.	A	N.O.	A	N.O.	N.O.			
IB	10%	A	N.O.	A	N.O.	N.O.		N.O.	
N.O.	N.O.	A	N.O.	A	N.O.	N.O.		N.O.	
N.O.	N.O.	A	N.O.	A	N.O.	N.O.			
IB	25%	A	A	A	N.O.	N.O.			
N.O.	N.O.	A	N.O.	A	N.O.	N.O.			
B	10%	A	N.O.	A	N.O.	N.O.			
I?B	A	A	N.O.	A	N.O.	N.O.	USP &?		
N.O.	N.O.	A	N.O.	A	N.O.	N.O.	USP &?		
I?B	P	A	A	A	N.O.	N.O.			
I?B	A	A	N.O.	A	N.O.	N.O.		N.O.	
I?B	A	A	N.O.	A	N.O.	N.O.			
IB	P	A	A	A	N.O.	N.O.			
B?	A	A	N.O.	A	N.O.	N.O.	USP & ?		
N.O.	N.O.	A	N.O.	A	N.O.	N.O.		SF?, DSP (fallen, 1 char)	{Stream lowest
IB	P	A	A	A	N.O.	N.O.			{between 68 & 69
IB	P	A	A	A	N.O.	N.O.			
IB	P	A	A	A	N.O.	N.O.			
IB	P	A	A	A	N.O.	N.O.			
IB	P	A	A	A	N.O.	N.O.			
IB	P	A	A	A	N.O.	N.O.	DSP	NF, DSP (1 char)	
IB	P	A	A	A	N.O.	N.O.		* USF, DSP	Seen 26ii03
IB	P	A	A	A	N.O.	N.O.		DSF, USP (5-6 char)	
IB	P	A	A	A	N.O.	N.O.		USF, DSP (4 char)	

Table 19.

Pylon Number	Context	Upstream Pillar				Central Pillar			
		Footing	Pillar	Super-structure	Basal Bracing	Footing	Pillar	Super-structure	Basal Bracing
78	AL	N.O.	P	A	A	N.O.	P	A	A
79	AL, AE	I?B	P	A	A	B?	P	A	A
80	AL, AE	IB	P	A	A	N.O.	P	A	A
81	AL, AE	IB	P	A	A	IB	P	A	A
82	AL, AE	IB	P	A	A	I?B	10%	A	A
83	AL, AE	IB	P	B, L	A	I?B	P	B, L	A
84	AL, AE	I?B	P	A	A	IB	P	A	A
85	AL, AE	N.O.	P	A	N.O.	I?B	50%	A	A
86	AL, AE	I?B	P	A	A	IB	P	A	A
87	AL, AE	N.O.	P	B	A	N.O.	P	A	A
88	AL, AE	N.O.	P	B	A	I?B	P	A	A
89	AL, AE	N.O.	P	A	N.O.	N.O.	P	B	N.O.
90	AL	N.O.	P	A	A	N.O.	P	A	A
91	AL	N.O.	P	A	N.O.	N.O.	P	B, L	A
92	AL	N.O.	5%	A	N.O.	N.O.	A?	A	N.O.
93	AL	IB	P	A	A	IB	P	A	A
94	AL, AE	I?B*	P	A	A	N.O.	P	A	A
95	AL	N.O.	60%	A	N.O.	N.O.	P	A	A
96	AL, AE	N.O.	N.O.	A	N.O.	IB	P	A	A
97	AL, AE	I?B*	P	A	A	IB	P	A	A
98	AL, AE	I?B	P	B, L, B	A	IB	P	B, L	A
99	AL, AE	N.O.	P	B	P	RC	P	A	N.O.
100	SR, AE	RC	1%	A	A	RC	P*	A	A
101	SR, AE	RC	1%	A	A	RC	P	A	A
102	SR, AE	RC	P	A	A	RC	P	A	A
103	SR, AE	RC	P	A	A	RC	P	B	A
104	SR, AE	RC	P	A	A	RC	P	A	A
105	SR, AE	RC	P	A	A	RC	P	A	A
106	SR, AE	RC	P	A	A	RC	P	A	A
107	SR, AE	RC	P	A	A	RC	P	A	A
108	SR, AE	RC	P	A	A	RC	P	A	A
109	SR, AE	RC	P	B	A	RC	P	A	A
110	SR, AE	RC	P	A	A	RC	P	A	A
111	SR, AE	RC	P	B	A	RC	P	A	A
112	SR, AE	RC	P	A	A	RC	P	A	A

Continued

Downstream Pillar			Diagonal Bracing			Large Holes	Pillar	Inscription	Notes
Footing	Pillar	Super-structure	Pillar Notch	Brace	Socket for Brace		Turned ~45%		
IB	30%	A	A	A	N.O.	N.O.	DSP	*SF, DSP (1 char); USF, USP(?)	Insc on USP not seen iii03
I?B?	10%	A	N.O.	A	N.O.	N.O.			
IB	P	A	A	A	N.O.	N.O.			
IB	P	A	A	A	N.O.	N.O.		USF, DSP (1 char)	
IB	P	A	A	A	N.O.	N.O.			
IB	5%	A	N.O.	A	N.O.	N.O.			
IB	P	A	A	A	N.O.	N.O.		SF, DSP (1 char)	
IB	P	A	A	A	N.O.	N.O.			
IB	P	A	A	A	N.O.	N.O.			
I?B	P	A	A	A	N.O.	N.O.			
IB	P	A	A	A	N.O.	N.O.			
I?B	P	A	A	A	N.O.	N.O.			Cx: S on G
N.O.	P	A	A	A	N.O.	N.O.	USP		Do
N.O.	P	B, L	A	A	N.O.	N.O.			Do
N.O.	40%	A	A	A	N.O.	N.O.			Do
N.O.	P	A	A	A	N.O.	N.O.	USP & ?	NF, DSP (1 char)	Cx: S & G; low spot
I?B	P	A	A	A	N.O.	N.O.			Do
N.O.	P	A	A	A	N.O.	N.O.			Cx: S on G
N.O.	P	A	A	A	N.O.	N.O.			Do
N.O.	P	A	A	A	N.O.	N.O.			Do; *NS box side = split IP
N.O.	P	A	A	A	N.O.	N.O.			Cx: Do
N.O.	P	A	A	A	N.O.	N.O.			Cx: S & G on SR
RC	P	A	A	A	N.O.	N.O.			*Broken & leaning
RC	P	A	A	A	A	A			2 sockets between CP & DSP
RC	P	A	A	A	A	A			
RC	P	A	A	A	N.O.	N.O.			
N.O.	P*	A	A	A	N.O.	N.O.			* Paired w 2nd pillar?
RC	P	A	A	A	A	A			
RC	P	A	A	A	A	A			
RC	P	A	A	A	A	A			
RC	P	A	A	A	A	A			
RC	P	A	A	A	A	A			
RC	P	A	A	A	A	A			
RC	P	A	A	A	A	A			
RC	P	A	A	A	A	A			

Table 19.

Pylon	Context	Upstream Pillar				Central Pillar			
Number		Footing	Pillar	Super-structure	Basal Bracing	Footing	Pillar	Super-structure	Basal Bracing
113	SR, AE	RC	A	A	A	RC	P	A	A
114	SR	RC	P	A	A	RC	1%	A	A
115	SR, AE	RC	P*	A	A	RC	P	B	A
116	SR, AL, AE	RC	N.O.	A	N.O.	N.O.	N.O.	A	N.O.
117	AL, AE	N.O.	N.O.	A	N.O.	N.O.	20%	A	N.O.

Notes: % = % standing if not 100; "*" = see note in far right column; A = absent; AE = architectural elements; CP = central pillar; Cx = context; DSF = downstream face; DSP = downstream pillar; G = gravel; IB = box formed by pillar; L = beam present; NF = north face; N.O. = not observable; P = present; RC = rock cut, into sheet-rock; pillar.

Continued

Downstream Pillar			Diagonal Bracing			Large Holes	Pillar	Inscription	Notes
Footing	Pillar	Super-structure	Pillar Notch	Brace	Socket for Brace		Turned ~45%		
RC	A*	A	A	A	A	A			* Lies adjacent
RC	P	A	A	A	A	A			
RC	A	A	N.O.	A	A	A			* Leaning
N.O.	N.O.	A	N.O.	A	N.O.	N.O.	N.O.		Cx: S on SR
N.O.	N.O.	A	N.O.	A	N.O.	N.O.			Cx: S

AL = alluvium; B = column block present; BBF = basalt basal fragment; Box = formed by slab surround; Char = character; interlocking notched slabs; I?B = box present but interlocking not observable; Insc = inscription; IP = intermediate S = slab present between this and next pillar; SF = south face; SR = sheet-rock; Insc = USF = upstream face; USP = upstream

Table 20. NBx, Quantitative

Pylon			Upstream Pillar					
			Socket			Pillar		
Number	Length	Inter-Pylon	Long	Trans	Depth	Long	Trans	Height
Wall		76sf2f						
1	493	283				53	44	226
2		312						
3		362						
4		387						
5	532	357	63	65	>10	54	57	313
6		392						
7		386						
8		353						
9		359						506
10	501	397				56	55	
11		370						
12		352						
13		437						
14	516	345				54	57	530
15		420	58	56	45??			
16		398	65	65				
17		393	68	66	37			
18		355	67	67	>37			
19		393	66	68	>20			
20	528	380	65	64	37			
21		327	68	68	>/= 37			
22		473	62	65	36			
23		386	62	60	31			
24		394	61	59	34			
25	505	347	57	58	33			
26		341	61	61	34			
27		343	58	57	31			
28		337	61	62	31			
29		338	63	62	40			
30	519	339	61	61	33			
31		349	51	55	32.5			
32		330	62	62	35.5			
33		256	59	56	36.5			
34		349	48	51	34.5			
35	511	343	59	61	33			
36		406	57	56	>36			
37		380	59	56	37.5			
38		407	59	57	37.5			
39		380	59	53	>5			
40	521	397	59	59	>26			
41		355	58	58	34			

Attributes of Pylons and Pillars (in cm)

Central Pillar						Downstream Pillar						Notes
Socket			Pillar			Socket			Pillar			
Long	Trans	Depth	Long	Trans	Height	Long	Trans	Depth	Long	Trans	Height	
			58	51					54	54	215 387(USP), 378(DSP)	face to face H top SS:
						66	64	20				
			57	52					60	52	284	
			62	62					53	62	445	USP: H to box top DSP, IB = 75 cm deep
									54	50	510	H USP: to SR, DSP: to rubble
58	58	>22				54	54	>17				
64	64	>16				66	61	>30				
62	60	>26				63	62	>38				
62	62	>22				62	58	37				
60	59	>21				62	63	?				
56	58	32				63	60	34				
60	61	34				62	62	31				
58	57	30				82						
54	59	32				58	58	33.5				
61	60	36				58	57	34				
61	61	35				61	60	32				
60	59	33				60	61	34				
56	56	30				53	53	31				
58	59	30				58	60	34.5				
60	68	31				55	54	>27				
62	58	33.5				58	58	35.5				
59	59	33				61	57	>28				
57	57	34				56	54		49	56	332	
58	55	37				56	52		60	55		
67	67	33.5				58	59	32				
65	67	36				59	57	30				
64	64	>39				55	56	34.5				
60	61	33				59	59	32.5				
63	60	34				54	63	33.5				
59	63	36				60	57	35				

Pylon			Upstream Pillar					
Number	Length	Inter-Pylon	Socket			Pillar		
			Long	Trans	Depth	Long	Trans	Height
42		222	57	57	>13			
43		506	62	62	>10	59	59	
44		496	62	62	>29			
45	680					49	50	
46								
47								
48								
49								
50	*266					56	46	
51								
52								
53	493					46	54	
54								
55								
56								
57	504					60	35	
58								
59		380						
60		430						544
61		280						
62		344						
63	540	455				54	44	567
64		455						
65		402.5						
66		402.5						
67	629	430				45	60	
68		402						
69		327						
70	581	520				53	59	582
71		300						
72		399						
73		311						
74		300						
75	548	258				58	44	497
76		289						
77		356						
78		252						
79		373						
80	518	321				57	52	567
81		263						546

Continued

Central Pillar						Downstream Pillar						Notes
Socket			Pillar			Socket			Pillar			
Long	Trans	Depth	Long	Trans	Height	Long	Trans	Depth	Long	Trans	Height	
64	62	40				60	54	>27				
56	56	>55				63	54	31.5				
			52	56					56	62		
			53	50								*W sides USP & CP only
			59	52					49	50		
									40	66		
			31	67					62	50	586	Py>Py at CP Py>Py at CP Py>Py at CP H USP: to box top
											568	Pylon not certain
			51	46					54	48		
			48	56					60	56	592	H USP & DSP: to box top
			62	49					44	45	503	H IB *c.* 40 cm more
			58	52					53	36	582	H USP & DSP: to box top
											552	H IB USP +74, DSP +67; N side of channel

Pylon			Upstream Pillar					
Number	Length	Inter-Pylon	Socket			Pillar		
			Long	Trans	Depth	Long	Trans	Height
82		289						
83		367						
84		391						
85	559	252				51	43	568
86		344						
87		300						
88		387						
89		350						
90	508	370				54	45	>553
91		393						
92		290						
93		383						
94		391						
95	530	335				54	52	>274
96		348						
97		374						
98		471						
99		355						
100	515	374				50	48	
101		339						
102		407						
103		269						
104		331						
105	544	335				51	59	290
106		341						
107		333						
108		304						
109		335						
110	500	439				52	46	267
111		368						315
112								
113								
114	520	355				50	48	257
115								
116								
117								

Continued

Central Pillar						Downstream Pillar						Notes
Socket			Pillar			Socket			Pillar			
Long	Trans	Depth	Long	Trans	Height	Long	Trans	Depth	Long	Trans	Height	
			54	52					49	55	648	DSP: base exposed below box
											537	H DS IB = 38 cm
			48	45					48	53	>547	P Bases covered w sand
			54	57					56	52	607	USP in sand hill, DSP base covered by sand; Py>Py at CP Py>Py at CP
			37	54					53	40	508	Py>Py at CP Py>Py at CP Py>Py at CP
			54	59					55	49	387	
			51	43					51	49	229	
			48	42					54	48	275	

Table 20.

Pylon			Upstream Pillar					
Number	Length	Inter-Pylon	Socket			Pillar		
			Long	Trans	Depth	Long	Trans	Height
Count (N)	4	98	31	31	19	21	21	15
Minimum	493	222	48	51	31	45	35	226
Maximum	680	520	68	68	40	60	60	582
Average	533.1	361.2	60.5	60.3	34.6	53.1	50.3	438.3
St Dev	43.55	56.06	4.34	4.40	2.54	3.90	6.84	138.87

Notes: ">" = greater than; in the notes = between; empty cell = not observed or not observable; CP = central pillar; upstream pillar to north face of next pillar to the south, except where noted; IP = intermediate pillar; upstream to downstream faces, except as noted; SS = superstructure; St Dev = standard deviation;

Continued

Central Pillar						Downstream Pillar						Notes
Socket			Pillar			Socket			Pillar			
Long	Trans	Depth	Long	Trans	Height	Long	Trans	Depth	Long	Trans	Height	
27	27	20	18	18		28	27	18	21	21	18	
54	55	30	31	42		53	52	20	40	36	215	
67	68	40	62	67		82	64	37	62	66	648	
60.1	60.4	33.7	52.1	52.5		60.1	58.3	32.5	53.0	51.8	464.4	
3.13	3.41	2.56	7.95	6.46		5.52	3.34	3.60	5.39	6.93	141.01	

DSP = downstream pillar; H = height; IB = Interlocking Box; Inter-Pylon Distance = measured from north face of Long = longitudinal, parallel to long axis of bridge; PF = pillar face; Py = pylon; Pylon Length = measured between Trans = transverse, perpendicular to long axis of bridge; USP = upstream pillar.

Table 21. NBx, Quantitative

Pylon	Diagonal Bracing	Socket in Sheet-Rock			Large Holes
No.	Pillar to Socket	Long	Trans	Depth	PF to Hole 1
8					
9	175	38	30	N.O.	N.O.
10	193	37	33	N.O.	N.O.
11	>18.0	37	33	N.O.	N.O.
12	N.O.	N.O.	N.O.	N.O.	N.O.
13	N.O.	N.O.	N.O.	N.O.	N.O.
14	>125	N.O.	N.O.	N.O.	N.O.
15	>65	N.O.	N.O.	N.O.	N.O.
16	147	33	30	11	N.O.
17	135	38	34	11	A
18	133	33	34	11	A
19	166	34	25	11	38
20	135	38	41	14	38
21	141	42	44	13	43
22	98	33	34	10	37
23					41
24					N.O.
25					39
26					34
27					40
28					43
29					41
30					35
31					44
32					39
33					A
34		N.O.			A
35					A
36					A
37	116	40	22	9	A
38	133	36	20	10	A
39	159	39	33	14	45
40	168	37	32	15	46
41	166	38	35	14	46
42	175	41	44	14	43
43					
44					A
Count (N)	15	16	16	13	17
Minimum	98	33	20	9	34
Maximum	193	42	44	15	46
Average	1493	37.1	32.8	12.1	40.7
St Dev	25.34	2.78	6.76	1.98	3.65

Notes: ">" = greater than; empty cell = not observed or not observable; A = absent; Long = longitudinal; i.e. parallel to
St Dev = standard deviation; Trans = transverse; i.e. perpendicular to long axis of bridge.

Attributes of Bracing (in cm)

Long	Trans	Depth	PF to Hole 2	Long	Trans	Depth	Notes
							PN = A
							PN = P
							PN = P
							PN = P
							PN = P
							PN = P
							PN = P
							PN = N.O.
							PN = N.O.
							PN = N.O.
							PN = N.O.
20	19	8					PN = N.O., 1 hole
17	17	?	36	17	19		PN = N.O.,? holes
18	17	9	43	17	19		PN = N.O.,? holes
17	19	11	38	20	21	11	PN = N.O.
19	19	11	41	18	19	10	PN = N.O.
21	21	12	N.O.	21	19	>6	PN = A
19	19	11	36	17	18	13	PN = N.O.
18	18	13	39	17	18	11	PN = N.O.
19	19	12	40	19	19	10	PN = N.O.
18	19	11	43	18	18	11	PN = N.O.
18	18	10	40	18	19	>5	PN = N.O.
18	18	10	37	19	18	10	PN = N.O.
17	19	10	44	16	16	>7	PN = N.O.
21	20	13	38	19	18	12	PN = N.O.
							PN = N.O.
							PN = A
							PN = A
							PN = N.O.
							PN = N.O.
							PN = N.O.
14	14	>10	42	15	15	>5	PN = N.O.
15	15	>2	43	17	17	>6	PN = N.O.
18	16	14.5	45	19	17	>10	PN = N.O.
20	20	>11	45	18	18	>11	PN = N.O.
			33	20	22	> 8	PN = N.O.
							PN = N.O.
18	18	14	17	18	18	8	
14	14	8	33	15	15	10	
21	21	14.5	45	21	22	13	
18.2	18.2	11.1	40.2	18.1	18.3	11.0	
1.82	1.79	1.71	3.50	1.51	1.61	1.07	

long axis of bridge; N = number; N.O. = not observable; P = present; PF = pillar face; PN = pillar notch;

Table 22. NBx, Fallen Pillars;

Location	Architectural Element		At Base		At Top	
	Type	Height	Length	Width	Length	Width
Py 7, DSP	P	449	52	50	48	47
Py 60>Py 61, DSP	P	>568	62	49	48	41
~Py 64, USP	P	>610	44	39	52	51
~Py 36, ~CP	P	342	55	53	59	51
Count (N)		2	4	4	4	4
Minimum		342	44	39	48	41
Maximum		449	62	53	59	51
Average		395.5	53.3	47.8	51.8	47.5
St Dev		75.66	7.46	6.08	5.19	4.73

Notes: ">" under location = between; elsewhere = greater than; "~" = adjacent to; BBF = basalt basal fragment; BF = basal PB = peg base; Py = Pylon; St Dev = standard deviation; USP = upstream pillar.

Table 23. Attributes of

Inter Pylon	Architectural Elements	Dimensions	At Base		At Top	
	Type	Height (greater than)	Length	Width	Length (Long Axis)	Width
Py 46, ~ CP	IP	55	59	72	59	72
Py 52>Py 53, USP	IP	99	58	67		
Py 52>Py 53, DSP	IP	59	59	65		
Py 53>Py 54, USP	IP	84	48	65		
Py 57>Py 58, ~ CP	IP	103	94	64	94	64
Py 63>Py 64, DSP	IP	225	54	61		
Count (N)		6	6	6	2	2
Minimum		55	48	61	59	64
Maximum		225	94	72	94	72
Average		104.2	62	65.7	76.5	68
St Dev		62.44	16.24	3.67	24.75	5.66

Notes: ">" = between; "~" = adjacent to; BBF = basalt basal fragment; CP = central pillar; DSP = downstream pillar; USP = upstream pillar.

Dimensions of Anchor Holes (in cm)

Socket: Location		Socket: Dimensions			Notes
In Top of Pillar	In Base of Pillar	Length	Width	Depth	
Centred	None	8	7.5	7.5	Dim of pillar above base: 63 x 58
Centred	None	8	7	N.O.	PB in socket; BF remains in IB
Centred	N.O.	8.5	8	6.5	Top of pillar 5 sided; BF remains in IB
Centred	None	6	5	7	Dim above base: 64 x 58
		4	4	3	
		6	5	6.5	
		8.5	8	7.5	
		7.6	6.9	7	
		1.11	1.31	0.5	

fragment; CP = central pillar; DSP = downstream pillar; IB = interlocking box; N.O. = not observable; P = pillar;

Inter-Pylon Pillars (in cm)

Channel				Horizontal Band		Notes
Length	Width at Top	Width at Bottom	Depth Below Top	Distance	Height	
59	23		6			
60	24		11	50	6	Part of top broken off, polished
60	28	21	7.5	45	7	Top polished
55	31	24	11	50	7	Top polished, NW corner broken off
		28	7			
80	32	27	11	51	6	Not polished; band 1 cm deep
5	5	4	6	4	4	
55	23	21	6	45	6	
80	32	28	11	51	7	
62.8	27.6	25	8.9	49	6.5	
9.83	4.04	3.16	2.33	2.71	0.58	

IP = inter-pylon pillar; N.O. = not observable; P = pillar; PB = peg base; Py = Pylon; St Dev = standard deviation;

Location	Architectural Element	Dimensions			Anchor Holes	
	Type	Length	Width	Height	No. UF	No. LF
Py 1>Py 2	BC	106	42	46	2	2
Py 1>Py 2	BC	92	37	43	1	1 (+?)
Py 1>Py 2	BC	132	49	40	1	N.O.
Py 2>Py 3	BC	116	51	41	1	N.O.
Py 2>Py 3	BC	140	46.5	37.5	1	1
Py 2>Py 3	BC	121	46	40.5	2	2
Py 3>Py 4	BC	115	46.5	40	1	1
Py 4>Py 5, CP>DSP	BC	127	40	39.5	2	2
Py 4>Py 5, USP>CP	BC	130	54	44.5	1	0
Py 4>Py 5, USP>CP	BC	140	41	36	1	0
Py 5>Py 6, USP>CP	BC	123	43	37	1	1
Py 5>Py 6, ~ CP	BC	119	44	39.5	2	2
Py 6>Py 7, USP>CP	BC	103	42	38.5	1	1
Py 7>Py 8, CP>DSP	BC	118	47.75	38.5	1	N.O.
Py 8>Py 9, CP>DSP	BC	94	39.5	42.5	2	N.O.
Py 8>Py 9, CP>DSP	BC	99	50.5	43	1	2
Py 8>Py 9, at Py 9 CP	BC	91	46	41	1	1
Count (N)		17	17	17		
Minimum		91	37	36		
Maximum		140	54	46		
Average		115.6	45.0	40.5		
St Dev		15.92	4.58	2.68		

Notes: ">" = between; "~" = adjacent to; AH = anchor hole; BC = block capital; CP = central pillar; DS = downstream; St Dev = standard deviation; UF = present upper face; USP = upstream pillar.

Fallen Block Capitals (in cm)

Location		Dimensions			Notes
UF	LF	Length	Width	Depth	
1 at 3, 1 at 1	2 at 3	7.5	7.5	7	AH: both have same dimensions; Half cubical quarry holes occur at one end
1 at 3					
1 at 5	N.O.	8	8.5	8	
1 at 5	N.O.	9	9.5	8	Lies on side
1 at 3	1 at 4				
1 at 3, 1 at 3	1 at 3, 1 at 4	7.5	7	6	2nd AH: 6.5 x 7 x 6; half of "UF" deeply cut & has 1st AH
1 at 4-5	1 at 4	6.5	6.5	7	"Top" slightly concave in transverse section
1 at 3, 1 at 3	1 at 3, 1 at 3	7	7	6	Half of "UF" deeply cut
1 at 5		10	9.5	9	
1 at 5		9	8	7	
1 at 5	1 at 4-5				One end angular = fractured?
2 at 3-4	2 at 3				"Top" cut convex transversely at DS end
1 at 4-5	1 at 4-5	9.5	9	6.5	Basalt peg projects from LF 5 cm
1 at 5	N.O.	8	8	7.5	
1 at 3, 1 at 3-	N.O.				
1 at 5	1 at 3, 1 at 3+				This and next entry lie adjacent
1 at 5	1 at 5				
		10	10	10	
		6.5	6.5	6	
		10	9.5	9	
		8.2	8.05	7.2	
		1.14	1.07	0.95	

DSP = downstream pillar; LF = present lower face; N.O. = not observed; P = pillar; PB = peg base; Py = Pylon;

Location	Architectural Element				Anchor Holes		Location	
	Type	Length	Width	Height	No. UF	No. LF	UF	LF
Py 2, CP> DSP	B	304	50.5	46.5	2	2	1 at 2, 1 at 3	1 at 2, 1 at 4
Py 1>Py 2	B?	190	46	31	0	1	N.O.	1 at 2
Py 3>Py 4	B?	165	44	38.5	1+	0 ?	1 at 4	N.O.?
Py 3>Py 4	B	312	45.5	42	2	2	1 at 2, 1 at 3	
Same Beam								1 at 2, 1 at 3
Py 4>Py 5, CP>DSP	B	246	45	39.5	2	2	1 at 2, 1 at 2-3	1 at 2, 1 at 2-3
Py 4>Py 5, USP>CP	B	217	41.5	39.5	1	1 (DS)	1 at 2	1 at 2
Py 5>Py 6, USP>CP	B?	334	45	42	0	0		
Py 6>Py 7, USP>CP	B	319	48	39	2	3	1 at 3, 1 at 4	1 at 2+, 1 at 2
Same Beam Py 7>Py 8, CP>DSP	B	332	47.5	46.5	0	2	N.O.	1 at 3-4(US), 1 at 2 (DS)
Py 8>Py 9, CP>DSP	B	298	49	47.5	0	2	N.O.	1 at 2(US), 1 at 4(DS)
Count (N)		10	10	10				
Minimum		165	41.5	31				
Maximum		334	50.5	47.5				
Average		271.7	46.2	41.2				
St Dev		65.25	2.57	4.68				

Notes: ">" = between; AH = anchor hole; B = beam; CP = central pillar; DS = downstream extremity; DSP = downstream
US = upstream extremity; USP = upstream pillar.

Fallen Beams (in cm)

Dimensions			Clamp Seating		Clamp Seating				Notes
Length	Width	Depth	Number of Holes	Distance Apart	Length	Width	Depth	Channel Length	
7.5	8	7	2		3.5	4	6.5		
7.5	7	6							Upside down
7.5	7.5	6.5		12.5	4	4	5		
7	7.5	6.5	2		3	5	5	27	
10.5	7	5.5							
7	7	7.5		13	3.5	3.5	5	27	
8	7.5	6							
									LF, DS seating cut deeply, 64 cm long; no sockets?
9	9	7			P: (DS)				AH: DS, UF; Basalt peg 3 projects 4 cm from US, LF AH: US, UF
8	7.5	7.5							
8	8.5	9							AH: DS
10	10	10	2	2	5	4	4	2	
7	7	5.5	2	12.5	3	3.5	5	27	
10.5	9	9	2	13	4	5	6.5	27	
8	7.7	6.9			3.5	4.1	5.4		
1.05	0.67	1.00			0.41	0.63	0.75		

pillar; LF = lower face; N.O. = not observable; P = pillar; Py = Pylon; St Dev = standard deviation; UF=upper face;

Location Side	Architectural Elements				Notches	
	Type	Length	Width	Height	UF	LF
Py 9, CP, USS	BS	147	24.5	N.O.	N.O.	N.O.
Py 9, DSP, USS	BS	N.O.	31	N.O.	N.O.	N.O.
Py 9, DSP, DSS	IBS	126	21.5	34	0	2
Py 10, DSP, DSS	IBS	177	39	60	0	2
Py 10, DSP, USS	IBS	194	25	>50	0	N.O.
Py 11, DSP, DSS	BS	197	26	>38	0	N.O.
Py 13, DSP, DSS	BS	>135	28	>15	0	N.O.
Py 13, DSP, USS	BS	>75	28.5	>8	0	N.O.
Py 14, USP, NS	IBS	230	30	63	2	0
Py 59, USP, USS	IBS	207	30	41	0	2
Py 59, USP, DSS	IBS	235	24.5	>31	0	2
Py 59, USP, NS	IBS	215	25	>10	2	0
Py 59, USP, SS	IBS	222	26	>27	2	0
Py 60, CP, DSS	BS	186	34	>51	N.O.	N.O.
Py 61, CP, DSS	BS	290	28	>34	N.O.	N.O.
Py 63, USP, USS	IBS	193	25.5	>21	0	?
Py 63, USP, DSS	IBS	222	30	>53	0	?
Py 67, CP, DSS	BS	183	21	48	N.O.	N.O.
Py 67, DSP, DSS	BS	127	23	>30	N.O.	N.O.
Py 68, CP, SS	IBS	170	34	>42	2	0
Py 69, DSP, NS	BS	171	58	23		
Py 69, DSP, USS	IBS	168	32	45	2	0
Py 70, DSP, DSS	BS	210	29	37	N.O.	N.O.
Py 71, USP, USS	BS	180	21.5	50	N.O.	N.O.
Py 71, USP, DSS	BS	181	26	45	N.O.	N.O.
Py 71, USP, NS	IBS	191	18.5	38	2	N.O.
Py 71, USP, SS	IBS	154	18	>32	2	N.O.
Py 71, CP, SS	IBS	169	19	36	2	N.O.
Py 72, CP, DSS	IBS	182	26	>/= 51	N.O.	N.O.
Count (N)		26	29	12		
Minimum		126	18	23		
Maximum		290	58	63		
Average		189.5	27.7	43.3		
St Dev		34.89	7.61	11.14		

Notes: ">" = greater than; ">/=" = greater or equal to; "∧" = facing up; "∨" = facing down; AE = architectural element; LF = lower face; N.O. = not observed; NS = north side; Py = pylon; SS = south side; St Dev = standard deviation;

Select Slab Boxes (in cm)

Dimensions of Selected Notch				Notes
Base	Top	Depth	Facing	
			∧	AE: Length approximate
			v	AE: Width approximate
			v	Length approximate
			v	Length approximate
				Part covered by AE's
				Part covered by AE's
35, 26			∧	
			v	
			v	
			∧	Width approximate
			∧	
			v	
			v	
			v	
			v	
	35	11	∧	Lies on side; eroded by stream action
	43	18	v	Lies on side, eroded; note type
	37	16	∧	Lies on side, eroded; note type
				CP has same arrangement
			v	
			v	Slab is dressed basement course
			v	Slab is dressed basement course
			∧	Slab is dressed basement course
			∧	Slab not dressed
	28	13	∧	
			v	
	4	4		
	28	11		
	43	18		
	35.8	14.5		
	6.18	3.11		

BS =slab box; CP = central pillar; DSP = downstream pillar; DSS = downstream side; IBS = interlocking box slab; UF = upper face; USP = upstream pillar; USS = upstream side.

Table 27. NBx, Attributes of

Group I	Long	Trans	Depth	Distance to Pylon	
1					
2	9	9	>5	447	Py 10
3	9.5	9	>6		
4					
5					
6					
7	9	9	>17	494	Py 11
8					
9	8.5	8.5	>3		
10	9	8.5	>5		
11					
12	8.5	8.5	>3	468	Py 12
13					
Average	9.0	8.5		469.7	
St Dev	0.45	0.41		23.54	
Gap					Py 13-17
Group II					
1	10	9.5	>6.5		
2				623	Py 18
3	8.5	9	>3.5		
4					
5	8	8.5	>6		
6				599	Py 19
7	7.5	8	7		
8					
9	8.5	7	7		
Average	8.5	8.4	7	611	
St Dev	0.94	0.96			
Gap					Py 20
Group III					
1					
2	8	9	7		
3					
4	9	8.5	8.5	554	Py 21
5					
6	8.5	8.5	8.5		
7				533	Py 22
8	10	11	5		
Average	8.9	9.3	7.3	543.5	
St Dev	0.85	1.19	1.66		

Notes: ">" between; elsewhere = greater than; AH = anchor hole; Distance to Pylon = distance from downside

Downstream Anchor Holes, by Group (in cm)

Inter-AH Distance		Notes
1>2	83	
2>3	82	
3>4	82	
4>5	78	
5>6	89	
6>7	83	
7>8	87	
8>9	93	
9>10	94	
10>11	81	
11>12	82	
12>13	90	
	85.3	
	5.12	Cumulative Length = 1024
		No holes visible; covered by fallen architectural elements
		Worn downstream lip; base of basalt peg
1>2	95.5	
2>3	94	Worn downstream lip; base of basalt peg
3>4	91.5	
4>5	81	Worn downstream lip; base of basalt peg
5>6	79.5	
6>7	86	Worn downstream lip
7>8	81.5	
8>9	89	Worn downstream lip
	87.3	Cumulative Length = 689
	6.19	
		Low area, no anchor holes
1>2	82.5	
2>3	95	
3>4	98	
4>5	88	
5>6	96	
6>7	95.5	
7>8	95	
	92.9	Cumulative Length = 531
	5.53	

to downside of pillars; Py = pylon; St Dev = standard deviation.

Table 28. NBs, Qualitative

Pylon	Context	Upstream Pillar				Central Pillar			
Number		Footing	Pillar	Super-structure	Basal Bracing	Footing	Pillar	Super-structure	Basal Bracing
1	SR	RC	A	A	A	N.O.	P	A	A
2	SR	RC	A	A	A	RC	A	A	A
3	SR	RC	A	A	A	RC	A	A	A
4	SR	RC	A	A	A	RC	A	A	A
5	SR	RC	A	A	A	RC	A	A	A
6	SR	RC	A	A	A	RC	A	A	A
7	SR	RC	A	A	A	RC	A	A	A
8	SR	RC	A	A	A	RC	A	A	A
9	SR, AE	RC	A	A	A	RC	A	A	A
10	SR	RC	A	A	A	RC	A	A	A
11	SR	RC	A	A	A	RC	A	A	A
12	SR	RC	A	A	A	RC	P	A	A
13	AL, AE	N.O.	1%	A	N.O.	N.O.	P?	A	N.O.
14	AL	N.O.	2%	A	N.O.	N.O.	A	A	N.O.
15	AL	N.O.	N.O.	A	N.O.	N.O.	N.O.	A	N.O.
16	AL, Stream	N.O.	N.O.	A	N.O.	N.O.	N.O.	A	N.O.
17	AL, AE	N.O.	N.O.	A	N.O.	N.O.	N.O.	A	N.O.
18	AL, AE	N.O.	N.O.	A	N.O.	N.O.	N.O.	A	N.O.
19	AL, AE	N.O.	N.O.	A	N.O.	N.O.	N.O.	A	N.O.
20	AL, AE	N.O.	N.O.	A	N.O.	N.O.	N.O.	A	N.O.
21	AL	N.O.	N.O.	A	N.O.	N.O.	P	A	N.O.
22	AL, AE			A				A	
23	AL, AE	N.O.	30%	A	N.O.	N.O.	N.O.	A	N.O.
24	AL	N.O.	40%	A	N.O.	N.O.	N.O.	A	N.O.
25	AL	N.O.	N.O.	A	N.O.	N.O.	N.O.	A	N.O.
26									
27	AL, AE	RC*	N.O.	A	N.O.	RC	N.O. ?	A	N.O. ?
28									
29									
30	AL	N.O.	P	A	N.O.	N.O.	P	A	N.O.

Notes: % standing if not 100%; A = absent; AE = architectural elements; AL = alluvium; CP = central pillar; USP = upstream pillar.

Attributes of Pylons

Downstream Pillar			Diagonal Bracing				Pillar	Notes
Footing	Pillar	Super-structure	Pillar Notch	Brace	Socket	Footing	Turned ~45%	
N.O.	A	A	N.O.	A	N.O.	N.O.		Surf quarried
N.O.	A	A	N.O.	A	N.O.	N.O.	DS of CP	Surf quarried
N.O.	A	A	N.O.	A	N.O.	N.O.	DS of CP	Surf quarried
RC	A	A	N.O.	A	N.O.	N.O.	DS of CP	Surf part quarried
RC	A	A	N.O.	A	A	A	DS of CP	Surf part quarried
RC	A	A	N.O.	A	A	A	DS of DSP	
RC	A	A	N.O.	A	A	A	DSP	
RC	A	A	N.O.	A	A	A		
N.O.	A	A	N.O.	A	A	A		DSP footing under AE
RC	A	A	N.O.	A	P=2	·P		
RC	A	A	N.O.	A	P=2	P		
RC	A	A	N.O.	A	P=2	P		
N.O.	N.O.	A	N.O.	N.O.	N.O.	N.O.		
N.O.	N.O.	A	N.O.	N.O.	N.O.	N.O.		
N.O.	4%	A	N.O.	N.O.	N.O.	N.O.		
N.O.	·5%	A	N.O.	N.O.	N.O.	N.O.		Stream begins here
N.O.	N.O.	A	N.O.	N.O.	N.O.	N.O.		Gap of 4 pylons (17-20)?
N.O.	N.O.	A	N.O.	N.O.	N.O.	N.O.		
N.O.	N.O.	A	N.O.	N.O.	N.O.	N.O.		
N.O.	20%	A	N.O.	N.O.	N.O.	N.O.		
		A	N.O.	N.O.	N.O.	N.O.		= Gap of 1 pylon?
N.O.	70%	A	N.O.	N.O.	N.O.	N.O.		
	75%	A	?	N.O.	N.O.	N.O.		
N.O.	N.O.	A	?	N.O.	N.O.	N.O.		
		A						Gap of pylon
N.O.?	A?	A	N.O.	N.O.	N.O.	N.O.		*in fissure
		A						Gap of 2 pylons (28-29)?
		A						
N.O.	P	A	?	A	N.O.	N.O.		Set into embankment

DSP = downstream pillar; N.O. = not observable; P = present; RC = rock cut into sheet-rock; SR = sheet-rock; Surf = surface;

Table 29. NBs, Quantitative Attributes

| Pylon | | | Upstream Pillar | | | | | | Central Pillar | | |
| Number | Length | Inter-Pylon | Socket | | | Pillar | | | Socket | | |
			Long	Trans	Depth	Long	Trans	Height	Long	Trans	Depth
1		382	51	49							
2		331	50	50					54	>/=52	
3		352	49	52					54		
4	513	352	50	51	>10				51	55	
5	522	334	52	52					52	54	
6	520	358	51	50					50	52	
7	554	323							51	51	
8	444	343	38	53					54.5	50	
9		387	55	53					54	56	
10	492	283	53	50					57	51	>19
11	504	390	56	56					58	56	>5
12	524	323.25	56	51	>15				52	55	>20
13		323.25									
14		323.25						2%			
15		323.25									
16		356.7									
17		356.7									
18		356.7									
19		356.7									
20		356.7									
21		356.7									
22		338.3									
23		338.3				47	44				
24	458	338.3				51	52				
25		346.2									
26		346.2									
27		346.2	In crack in SR						54	53	
28		346.2									
29		346.2									
30	< 595					34	48	P			
Cum Length		10014									
Count (N)	9	29	11	11	2	3	3	4	12	10	3
Minimum	444	283	38	49		34	44		50	50	
Maximum	554	390	56	56		51	52		58	56	
Average	503.4	345.3	51	51.5		44	48		53.5	53.3	
St Dev	34.31	21.48	4.96	1.97		8.89	4		2.41	2.21	

Notes: % = percentage standing; Longitudinal = parallel to axis of bridge; P = present; Pylon Trans = length measured pillar to next to south, except where noted; SR = sheet-rock; Transverse = perpendicular to axis of bridge.

of Pylons and Pillars (in cm)

			Downstream Pillar						Notes
Pillar			Socket			Pillar			
Long	Trans	Height	Long	Trans	Depth	Long	Trans	Height	
48	48	150							Surface quarried DS of CP
									Surface quarried DS of CP
									Surface quarried DS of CP
			45	46	>9				Surface partly quarried DS of CP
			45	50	>15				
			50	50					
			52	49					
			55	55					
			54	55					DSP under AE's
			53	52	>10				
			49	54	43				P12 > P15? = 1293 cm
	5%								
									Py 15> est. Py 21=2140 cm
									No. of Pylons estimated
									No. of Pylons estimated
									No. of Pylons estimated
									No. of Pylons estimated
42	53					56	53		Inter-Pylon estimated
									Gap probably of 1 Pylon
									Est Py 21>est Py24=1015 cm
									USP23 > USP24 = 351 cm
									No. of Pylons estimated
									Py?27 > Py 30? = 993 cm
									= 331 x 3
									Gap probably of 1 Pylon
									Gap probably of 1 Pylon
36	55	P							Base buried in bank
	3	3		8	8				
36	48		45	46					
48	55		55	55					
42	52		50.4	51.4					
6	3.61		3.85	3.20					

from upstream to downstream faces, except as noted; Pylon to Pylon Distance = measured from north side of upstream

Table 30. NBs, Quantitative Attributes of Bracing and Large Holes (in cm)

Pylon Number	Diagonal Bracing	Hole 1				Hole 2				Notes
		PF to Hole	Long	Trans	Depth	PC to Hole	Long	Trans	Depth	
1										Surface quarried DS of CP
2										Surface quarried DS of CP
3										Surface quarried DS of CP
4										Surface partly quarried DS of CP
5	A	A	A	A	A	A	A	A	A	
6	A	A	A	A	A	A	A	A	A	
7	A	A	A	A	A	A	A	A	A	
8	A	A	A	A	A	A	A	A	A	
9	A	A	A	A	A	A	A	A	A	
10	A	30	17	17	>8	36	17	19	>8	
11	A	32	17	17	N.O.	31	15	15	9	
12	A	34	16	16	N.O.	38	16	16	N.O.	N.O.
Etc.										
Count (N)		3	3	3		3	3	3	3	
Minimum		30	16	16		31	15	15	9	
Maximum		34	17	17		38	17	19	9	
Average		32	16.7	16.7		35	16	16.7	9	
St Dev		2	0.58	0.58		3.61	1	2.08		

Notes: ">" = greater than; A = absent; CP = central pillar; DS = downstream; N.O. = not observable; PC = pillar socket; St Dev = standard deviation.

Addendum

We revisited NBx in January 2004 and carried out additional documentation of the embankments, structural elements of the bridge and downstream anchor holes. Measurements of a larger, albeit non-random, sample of examples increased statistical precision and are incorporated into Tables 31 and 32.

During further observation of diagonal braces we noted that an anchor hole was present at the top of each notch in the downstream face of the downstream pillar and further, that a channel, of a size to receive an anchor peg, was cut into the top of each surviving brace. This channel angles down towards the pillar. We conclude that the tendency for the brace to move away from the pillar was resisted by a peg the base of which was seated in the pillar and the shaft of which lay in the channel on top of the brace. This discovery is reflected in Figures 5-7 and Plates 14 and 15, but not in the text above.

Table 31. NBx, Dimensions of Capital Block and Beams

	Capital Block			Beams		
	Length	Width	Height	Length	Width	Height
Count (N)	34	34	34	27	27	27
Minimum	87	37	36	165	38	31
Maximum	190	67	61	342	57	50
Aver	111.7	46.9	43.5	303.4	46.4	41.7
St Dev	20.80	6.34	6.27	45.50	4.48	4.43

Table 32. NBx, Predicted and Observed Locations of Anchor Holes updated in Capital Blocks and Beams

Ordinal Scale	1	1-2	2	2-3	3	3-4	4	4-5	5
Capital Blocks: 1 Hole									
Predicted									P
Observed Cases					2		2	4	25
Capital Blocks: 2 Hole									
Predicted						P			
Observed Cases	1				28	5	7		5
Beams									
Predicted			P		P				
Observed Cases			43	7	9	15	3		

Note: P = predicted location of anchor hole; updating Table 5.

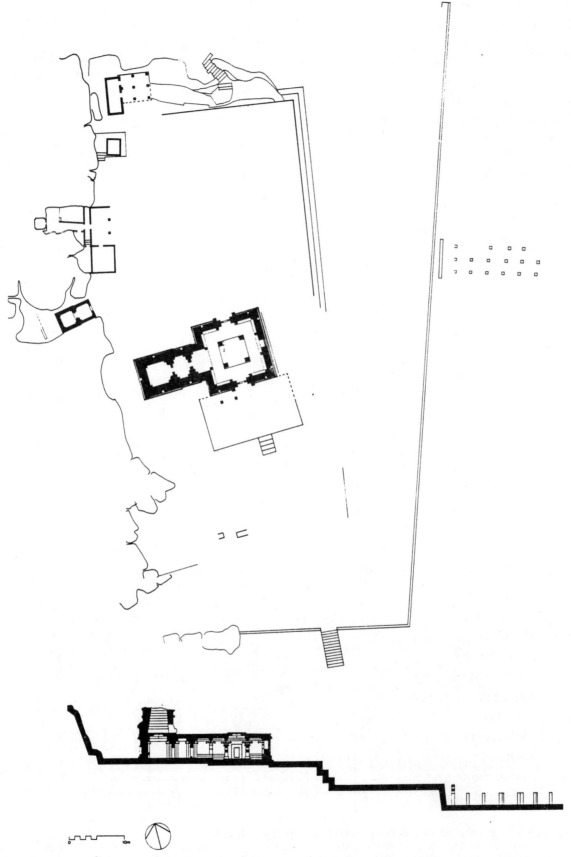

Figure 1. Chandramauleshvara temple complex with embankment and bridge, section and plan.

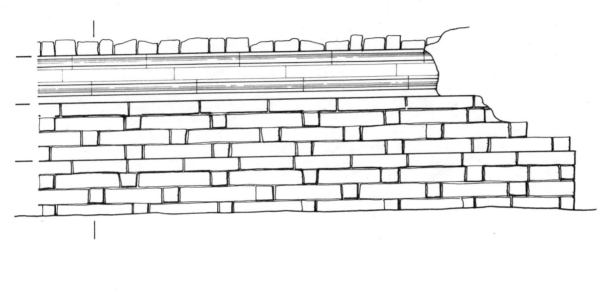

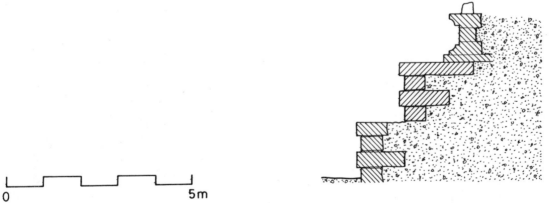

Figure 2. Upper embankment, section and elevation.

0   5m

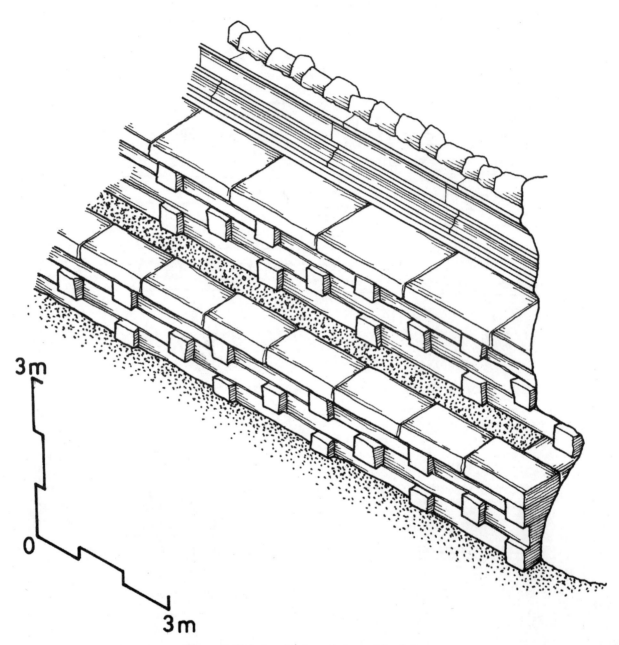

Figure 3. Upper embankment, isometric view.

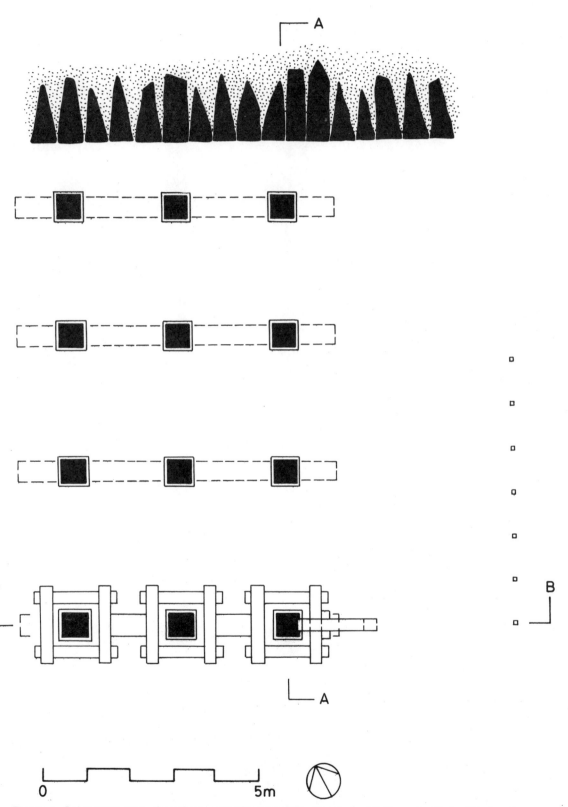

Figure 4. Schematic plan of northern end of bridge NBx showing sockets and pillars, slab boxes,
diagonal bracing and downstream anchor holes.

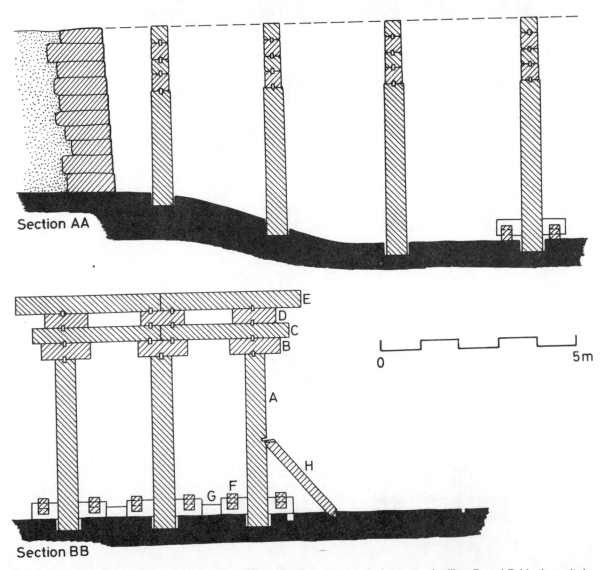

Figure 5. Sections of northern end of bridge NBx indicating structural elements: A pillar, B and D block capitals, C and E Beams, F interlocking slab box, G horizontal brace, H diagonal brace.

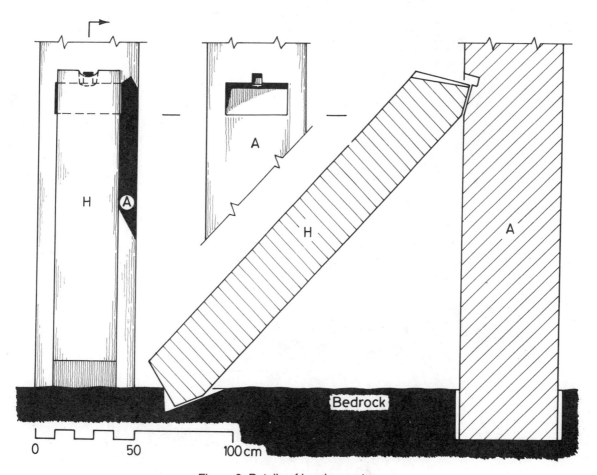

Figure 6. Details of bracing system.

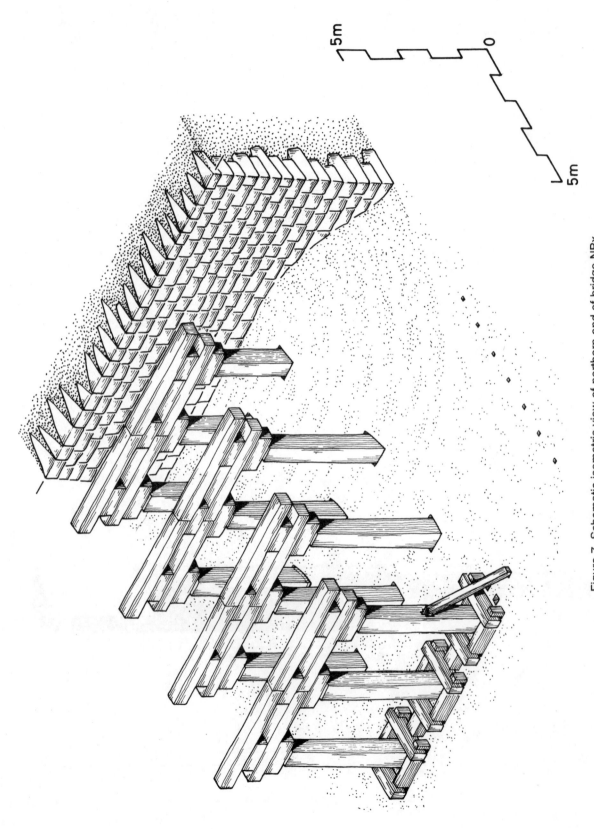

5m

0

5m

Figure 7. Schematic isometric view of northern end of bridge NBx.

Plate 1. Chandramauleshvara temple complex from the south showing lower embankment with staircase.

Plate 2. Upper embankment, east side, lower, intermediate and upper basements.

Plate 3. Upper embankment, south side, showing collapsing upper basement; upper bevelled course ends in a block, possibly indicating a passageway.

Plate 4. Lower embankment and staircase, south side.

Plate 5. Top of lower embankment, east side, with first pylon of bridge visible to left.

Plate 6. Lower embankment, detail at southeast corner showing slabs stacked in alternating directions, as seen from above.

Plate 7. First pylon at northern end of bridge NBx showing pillars and
complete supersructure; lower embankment visible behind.

Plate 8. Collapsing remains of pylons at the northern end of bridge NBx showing *in situ* and fallen pillars, capitals and beams; note anchor holes.

Plate 9. Fallen parts of bridge superstructure showing beam cut down to seat capitals.

Plate 10. View of bridge NBx from the north showing sinuous line of pillar either side of sheet-rock with pillar sockets exposed in the middle of the Tungabhadra.

Plate 11. South end of bridge NBx from the southwest showing fallen elements of the superstructure as they appeared in 1992; these elements have subsequently disappeared.

Plate 12. Bridge foundation exposed on sheet rock showing three aligned pillar sockets, a pair of large holes and a footing for a diagonal brace.

Plate 13. Two sides of an eroded box foundation at base of a pillar showing notches facing both up and down.

Plate 14. Diagonal braces set into notches on the downstream side of two downstream pillars.

Plate 15. Detail of a channel cut into the top of a diagonal brace, and an anchor hole at the top of a notch in the side of a pillar, both were intended to seat an anchor peg.

Plate 16. Kannada inscription on pillar; the two letters
(ba sa) are arranged vertically (chalked for emphasis).

Plate 17. Standing and fallen pylon elements; an intermediate pillar (left) has a
channel on top and a shallow horizontal band around the sides.

Plate 18. East entry into Vitthalapura (NGk/6), with bridge in the distance.

Plate 19. Collapsed remains of bridge NBs from north-northwest; the embankment here
is faced with small boulders.

Plate 20. Collapsing northeast corner of the embankment below the
Ganesha temple (NLc/2) above Hampi in 1993.